ODD
MAN
OUT

ODD MAN OUT

A Year on the Mound
with a Minor League Misfit

Matt McCarthy

Viking

VIKING
Published by the Penguin Group
Penguin Group (USA) Inc., 375 Hudson Street, New York, New York 10014, U.S.A.
Penguin Group (Canada), 90 Eglinton Avenue East, Suite 700, Toronto, Ontario, Canada M4P 2Y3
(a division of Pearson Penguin Canada Inc.) • Penguin Books Ltd, 80 Strand, London WC2R 0RL,
England • Penguin Ireland, 25 St Stephen's Green, Dublin 2, Ireland (a division of Penguin Books
Ltd) • Penguin Books Australia Ltd, 250 Camberwell Road, Camberwell, Victoria 3124, Australia
(a division of Pearson Australia Group Pty Ltd) • Penguin Books India Pvt Ltd, 11 Community
Centre, Panchsheel Park, New Delhi–110 017, India • Penguin Group (NZ), 67 Apollo Drive,
Rosedale, North Shore 0632, New Zealand (a division of Pearson New Zealand Ltd) • Penguin
Books (South Africa) (Pty) Ltd, 24 Sturdee Avenue, Rosebank, Johannesburg 2196, South Africa

Penguin Books Ltd, Registered Offices: 80 Strand, London WC2R 0RL, England

First published in 2009 by Viking Penguin, a member of Penguin Group (USA) Inc.

3 5 7 9 10 8 6 4 2

Copyright © Matthew McCarthy, 2009

Grateful acknowledgment is made for permission to reprint excerpts from the following copyright-
ed works:
"Doctoral Candidate" by Gordon Edes, *The Boston Globe*, February 26, 2006. Copyright ©
2006 Globe Newspaper Company, Inc. Reprinted with permission.
"Loaded Gun: Great Arm, but Jenks No Angel" by Tom Friend, *ESPN The Magazine*, June 9,
2003. By permission of *ESPN The Magazine*.
"Former Chowan Student/Pitcher, Randy Burden Passes Away" by Stephen Dunn, *Roanoke-
Chowan News-Herald*, December 9, 2002. By permission of the *Roanoke-Chowan News-Herald*,
Ahoskie, North Carolina.
"'97 World Series: A Rookie Who Knows About Pressure; After His Problems Adapting to the
U.S., Livan Hernandez Takes the World Series in Stride" by Buster Olney, *The New York Times*,
October 18, 1997. © 1997 The New York Times. All rights reserved. Used by permission and pro-
tected by the copyright laws of the United States. The printing, copying, redistribution, or retrans-
mission of the material without express written permission is prohibited.

LIBRARY OF CONGRESS CATALOGING-IN-PUBLICATION DATA
McCarthy, Matt.
Odd man out : a year on the mound with a minor league misfit / Matt McCarthy.
p. cm.
ISBN 978-0-670-02070-6
1. McCarthy, Matt. 2. Pitchers (Baseball)—United States—Biography.
3. Minor league baseball—United States. I. Title.
GV865.M218A3 2008
796.357092—dc22
[B]
2008029038

Printed in the United States of America   Set in Goudy Old Style

To my teammates

ODD MAN OUT

Chapter 1

||||||||||||||||||||||||||||||||||||||||||||||||

W HEN I WAS TWENTY-ONE, I could throw a baseball 92 miles an
hour. This led to a strange courtship between my left arm and a
series of pencil-mustached, overweight middle-aged men. I eventually
gave up the game and later found myself as far away from the baseball
diamond as one could possibly be—living in rural villages in Cameroon and later Malaysia, colorful places that still somehow paled in
comparison to the alien environment of my first home in professional
baseball: Provo, Utah. It was the height of the steroid era, and while
Barry Bonds and Mark McGwire were rewriting the record books,
those of us in the minors were trying like hell to break into the big
leagues. In our clubhouse, amphetamines were passed around like candy
and the allure of steroids was ever present.

It was the summer of 2002 and I was playing for the Provo Angels,
an affiliate of the Anaheim Angels, who would go on to win their first
World Series that year. Defeating the San Francisco Giants in an upset, the Angels attributed their success to the hard-nosed, unselfish
play of low-profile players like David Eckstein and Francisco Rodriguez.
But in Provo, we were a team divided.

"Separate but equal" was how Blake Allen, a right-handed pitcher
from Tuscaloosa, Alabama, first described the team dynamic to me.
Blake had been drafted in the thirty-fifth round of the 2001 draft and
had already played one season in Provo when I joined the team. With
his slack jaw, pot belly, and slow, deliberate manner of speaking, Blake

was the yokel out of central casting that many of my classmates at Yale would have ridiculed. But he was also a reflective man who enjoyed dissecting people. He would've fit better in a Faulkner novel than in a baseball uniform.

He'd been on the disabled list for the past year and confided in me that he thought he'd never be healthy enough to pitch again. "I've got a wife and kid at home and I need the paycheck," he said one afternoon in June while we were finishing our Grand Slams at Denny's. "They can't cut ya when you on the disabled list. It violates the collective bargaining agreement. So I just sit back and cash the checks."

It was then that I learned about the two-party system of minor league baseball. "You've got your Dominicans and you've got everybody else," he said in between bites of sausage. "You don't want nuthin' to do with the Dominicans. They're loud, they don't speak English, they don't have no respect for nobody, and for God's sake, don't ever go in the shower when they in there."

The team was, in fact, divided between the Dominicans (a catch-all term for Hispanic players) and those of us from the United States. There were a dozen Dominicans on our team, hailing from Venezuela, Mexico, Puerto Rico, Panama, and, yes, the Dominican Republic. And Blake was right—they were loud and didn't speak English. Just seventeen or eighteen years old, many had been snatched out of poverty within the last year and signed to lucrative six-figure contracts. Wearing large smiles, larger gold chains, and designer sunglasses, they seemed to be playing life with Monopoly money.

"The thing about the Dominicans," Blake told me, "is that they can play. Most of the ones on this team *could* play in the big leagues someday. But they won't." He stopped eating for a moment and looked out the window. "A typical rookie ball team will have fifteen Dominicans. Double-A will have half that. Triple-A even less. As you move up the ladder you'll see that they just wash out." The idea of "washing out," I would learn, was a recurrent theme among players. It implied that your career was cut short for no apparent reason—not an injury or a slump. One day you'd show up to the field and there'd be a pink slip in your locker and no one would tell you why.

He returned to his pancakes for a moment before adding, "But I tell ya what . . . in every goddamn town we go to this year, those Dominicans will have fat white girls waiting for them."

The Americans, in contrast, were from places like Marianna, Florida, and Tulsa, Oklahoma. Most had signed professional contracts directly out of high school and baseball was the only life they knew or wanted to know. They were fond of saying that Don Zimmer, the Yankees' bench coach, had lived a model life because at seventy-one, he had never drawn a paycheck outside of professional baseball. I was one of the few who had graduated from college, although several had attended briefly. In general these were quiet, pious men whose priorities were the Lord and the girl back home. Pregame rituals included chapel, chewing tobacco, and numerous phone calls to family members.

After road games, we would pile into the bus and head to dinner as a team. It was an endless, nauseating cycle of Applebee's, Chili's, and T.G.I. Friday's. In the restaurant, the Dominicans sat on one side, the Americans on the other. On the bus, the Dominicans all sat in the back. After games, the Dominicans showered first. During the five weeks of spring training, Dominican players would be assigned American roommates because the organization felt it was "good for them," but during the season, a Dominican would almost never be paired with an American for road trips. "That would be cruel," our strength and conditioning coach once said. "Six months of living with one of them? Shit." And it was the language barrier that was always used to defend the status quo. "I mean, what the hell am I gonna say to them?" Blake had asked me one day as we were walking to the ballpark, *"Ho-la, amigo?"*

It took five years of distance to be able to write this after I walked away from professional baseball, although shoved out is a more apt description. Some of my former teammates became stars in the big leagues while others washed out of the minors and returned home to install carpeting. Blake returned to Alabama to run the family farm and raise roosters for cockfights. I, of course, had no idea how it was all going to pan out, or that my stay in baseball would be a brief one. A year later I'd be on the other side of the country in Boston, preparing to enter medical school and begin a new life—a life after baseball, if that's ever possible.

BUT THIS STORY does not begin in Utah. It starts in New Haven, Connecticut, a place I first visited as a senior in high school. I was invited by the coach of the Yale baseball team to visit the campus on an all-expenses-paid trip, the kind that has become a ritual of the varsity athlete recruiting process. Yale was the first school to show any interest in me and I was ready to commit to them the moment I set foot on Old Campus. The other high schooler on the recruiting visit was not nearly as impressed. Chris Young hailed from Houston, Texas, and, at six feet ten inches and 230 pounds, was the largest person I had ever met. Chris and I spent the weekend meeting the coach, touring the campus, watching a football game, and spending time with players on the baseball team.

On Saturday night, the team held its semiannual Kangaroo Court, where players recounted sex acts with undergraduates in graphic detail while teammates howled and came up with nicknames for the girls, like "Donkey Punch" and "The Beating." Between stories, players chugged beers and accused one another of engaging in activities unbecoming of a Yale baseball player, like being seen in a French restaurant or meeting a professor for coffee.

The event took place off campus in the backyard of a house where the seniors lived and the alcohol flowed freely. When Chris Young refused the first beer offered to him, several players snickered and the captain halted court proceedings to announce that Chris was destined to become "a typical Yale nerd." A few moments after the proclamation, Chris lumbered over to me and in his slow drawl said, "I don't have time for this crap."

At the stroke of midnight, shouts of "Toad's!" began to ruffle through the crowd.

"What's Toad's?" I quietly asked one of the freshmen.

"It's the bar everyone goes to on Saturday night," he said. "Tons of people. Tons of girls. It's great. . . ."

Another player had been listening in and put his arm around me.

"Tons of *sluts* is what he meant to say. They get bused in from all over Connecticut. University of New Haven. Southern Connecticut State. Quinnipiac. They all come to Toad's!"

"All you have to do is drop the Y-bomb," another player offered before taking a swig of Jack Daniel's from a bottle that was being passed around. "Tell 'em you go to Yale and next thing you know you're in their pants."

I looked over at Chris and asked if he was interested.

"No, thanks. I, uh, have to get up early tomorrow," he mumbled.

I didn't want to ditch him, but as a seventeen-year-old, my interest in Toad's had been piqued.

"I'm in," I said to cheers from the drunken players, "but I don't have a fake ID."

"No problem," the captain said. "Let's just figure out who you look like." The next few moments were excruciating as the Yale players gathered around to examine me.

"Let's see . . . about six feet tall."

"Kinda big nose."

"Brown hair with a high forehead."

"Yeah, a high forehead. Is it a receding hairline?"

"Nah, probably not. But maybe."

"Decent build. Not really thin, not really fat."

"He kinda has a big neck."

"Definitely a big neck."

"You know who he looks like? The Pope!"

Everyone erupted in laughter and quickly agreed that I looked like the Pope, which came as a bit of a surprise to me. I was hoping for something along the lines of Matt Damon, but that night I learned an early lesson about baseball team dynamics: never look for affirmation from a group of baseball players. The Pope, it turned out, was Ben Johnstone, a center fielder on the team who was waiting until marriage to lose his virginity. Players found this act of religious observance so incredible that they'd dubbed him "The Pope."

He lent me a spare driver's license and with that we were off to the bar. My first night at Toad's was a blur, but I do remember being introduced to dozens of people as "Little Pope," "The Pope's Little Brother," and "Undersecretary to the Papacy." I would come to know Toad's much better as the years wore on.

The next day at the airport, Chris Young made his intentions clear.

"What'd you think of Yale?" I asked as we waited to check in for our flights.

"You really want to know?" he replied grimly. He was reaching for his wallet with one hand and tucking in his shirt with the other.

"Of course."

"Well, I can safely say that I never met so many arrogant, self-centered, spoiled assholes in my life."

"Things definitely got a little crazy last night."

"Crazy? You want to know what's crazy? Those jackasses aren't good enough to play baseball at a big-time program and they're not smart enough to get into Yale on their own. So what are they?"

I didn't have a response. I was still thinking about all the fun I'd had.

"What are they?" he insisted, becoming angrier.

I shook my head.

"There's no way in hell I'm going to Yale," he said finally.

Chris opted for Princeton and within three years had signed a contract for $1.7 million with the Pittsburgh Pirates. He made his first Major League Baseball All-Star team by the age of twenty-five and went on to become one of the best pitchers in professional baseball.

The Yale nine, it turns out, could have used his services. The university has a sterling reputation in many arenas; unfortunately, baseball is not one of them. I went on to suit up for the Elis and was a part of several record-breaking teams during my four years in New Haven. We eclipsed the mark for losses in a season with 29 in my freshman year, only to outdo ourselves the following year by losing 31. After those two seasons, our coach finally came upon a solution to stop all the losing: he scheduled fewer games. In my four years, the team's record was 53–109, the worst four-year span in the history of the university.

I took in the carnage from atop the pitcher's mound. As a left-handed pitcher, my teammates expected me to be irreverent and eccentric, and it was a reputation that suited me. It's unclear exactly how southpaws gained the distinction as oddballs—undoubtedly the "Spaceman," Bill Lee, had something to do with it—but I'd embraced it for as long as I could remember.

Conventional wisdom says that every baseball team needs a left-handed reliever in the bullpen, and I spent my senior season trying to convince major league teams that I was the guy they were looking for. Professional scouts will tell you that as a lefty, you need to throw 90 miles per hour at least once to have a shot at being selected on the first Tuesday in June at the Major League Baseball draft. Since I'd reached 92 in my first game of my senior season, a handful of scouts were showing up when I pitched to chart my progress, despite my team's dismal play.

I knew from the beginning that the scout/player relationship was a tenuous one. Conscious that they could turn their backs on me at any moment, I was willing to say or do just about anything to please these khaki-clad men. And since they held such sway over my professional aspirations, I of course felt the need to mock them, too. At Yale we used to say that you could spot a scout from a mile away—emerging from a Chrysler LeBaron convertible, invariably flipping through a team-issued notepad while talking on a team-issued cell phone to one of the higher-ups at the organization about some new prospect. The outfit was always the same: hat and tucked-in polo shirt with the logo of the team they represented, dark sunglasses, the slick haircut of a graying politician, and, of course, a radar gun. And they shared a common vernacular, casually using phrases like "live arm-action," "plus secondary pitches," "clean repetition of delivery," and "excellent makeup."

Their appearance and affect was somewhere between golf professional and used-car salesman—they never told you exactly what you wanted to hear but it seemed like they'd be good with a sand wedge. They were the head cheerleader and the varsity quarterback; you detested them, but deep down you'd give anything for a sign of their approval.

In dealing with scouts, I quickly learned that being a Yalie was not going to work in my favor. When I spoke to a scout after a game or before a workout, the first question was typically some variation of "You're a biophysics major at Yale—how serious are you about baseball as a career?" Over the course of the season, my answer had evolved from "I'm very serious" to "I can't imagine doing anything else in my life other than playing baseball, sir. I eat, breathe, and sleep baseball," followed by a few made-up stories about skipping class and watching baseball instead of studying.

In mid-May, a day after my collegiate career ended and another disastrous Yale season had mercifully been put to rest, I received a call from a scout for the New York Yankees named Cesar Presbott. He began the conversation by announcing, "It is I, Cesar Presbott, scout for the New York Yankees." His self-importance oozed through the phone. I'd seen him at several of my games, but never spoken to him. He had a booming voice and an impeccably manicured goatee, but what made him stand out was that Yankees hat and the radar gun. He was calling to invite me to a predraft workout that the Yankees were holding in Staten Island on June 1, three days before the draft.

As I hung up the phone, I started for the kitchen and a celebratory beer. A number of thoughts swirled through my head as I glided across the living room, but before I reached the refrigerator, I remembered that I had two phone calls to make.

THE FIRST CALL was to Florida to speak to my parents. As the child of two professors, I'd grown up in the suburbs outside of Orlando in a house where baseball was discussed along with philosophy, literature, and politics. My parents were fond of bringing their work home with them, so the typical dinner conversation revolved around the irrationality of capital punishment or what Raskolnikov could tell us about the Unabomber.

My father, Bernie, grew up in a large, working-class Irish-Catholic family in Salem, New Hampshire. He was the eldest of five children and always assumed he'd grow up to be a fireman or a police officer. After college, he took a job at a prison in upstate New York and the experience caused him to change course and pursue academia; eventually he became an expert on terrorism. In graduate school at SUNY Albany he met my mother, Belinda. They'd spent the last twenty-five years teaching at various universities around the southeastern United States. I was born in Charlotte, while they were both teaching at UNC, but we soon moved to Alabama. Shortly after my tenth birthday we moved again, this time to Florida, when my parents took jobs at the University of Central Florida. It was there—in sunny, baseball-crazed Florida—that I would spend the remainder of my childhood.

But growing up in the South was a mixed blessing. On the one hand, I was able to play baseball year-round with some of the country's finest athletes. Six of the nine starters on my Little League team were drafted to play professionally, and two—Tim Raines Jr. and Corey Patterson—made it all the way to the big leagues, with the Baltimore Orioles and the Chicago Cubs, respectively.

But my time in the South also exposed me to Jim Crow–like race relations. At my middle school, Jackson Heights, a public school in Oviedo, Florida, we spent every recess in the fall playing "Blacks Versus Whites Football." In the winter, the game switched to "Blacks Versus Whites Basketball," and one year, when our homeroom teacher tried to teach us math through card games, we played "Blacks Versus Whites Gin Rummy." No one ever questioned the logic of divvying up by race, so when I heard Blake's description of the minor league team dynamic, it sounded all too familiar.

Eventually I left Jackson Heights and went to Oviedo High School, a public school just down the road. Like it is for most people, my freshman year was painful. Aside from harboring an unrequited love and fighting a losing battle with acne, I was the victim of two random acts of violence: I was shoved down a flight of stairs when a fight in the cafeteria spilled over into a hallway, and I was given the nickname "Birdman" by the freshman baseball coach, Ed Norton, who thought I looked like Larry Bird.

By the end of my freshman year I was miserable. I felt lost among the eleven hundred freshman in my class, and Coach Norton, a short man with a bloated face and a voice one octave too high for a baseball coach, kept me on the bench for almost the entire season. At the end of the school year he pulled me aside to tell me I had no hope of ever making the varsity squad and indulged me with a song he had written called "Birdman, You're a Nerd, Man."

So I decided to transfer to Bishop Moore High School, a private Catholic school in downtown Orlando. Students at Bishop Moore wore uniforms and were required to say a group prayer before every class, but the only thing I knew about the school was that it had a great baseball team that needed a left-handed pitcher. Though I had been raised Catholic, I never paid much attention in church and knew virtually nothing about my own religion, but I figured I could just wing it at Bishop Moore. The baseball coach, Dave Wheeler, was eager for me to transfer, but to be accepted to the school I had to pass the entrance interview with the principal, Dr. Connie Halscott.

"Everything looks great," Dr. Halscott said as I sat with my parents in her office on a muggy July afternoon. I fidgeted with my tie as she reviewed my application. "Just a few more questions and then we'll get to the paperwork."

"Okay," I said nervously.

"So, Matt, I haven't asked . . . are you Christian?"

The sad truth was that I had no idea. I had heard the words *Catholic* and *Christian* used at home, but I didn't know if they were mutually exclusive. I looked at my father, who was nodding.

"Yes," I said halfheartedly.

The principal looked at my father and then back at me.

"Are you Catholic?"

I again turned to my father, who was now sitting with his arms folded. I was going to get only one free pass.

"I . . . uh . . . I don't know. I could be."

"You . . . could be?"

"I know I'm Irish."

"Well," she said, adjusting her glasses, "that's a start. Do you realize this is a Catholic school?"

"I do."

"We take religion very seriously here, Matt. I hope you can appreciate that."

"Oh, I appreciate it," I said enthusiastically.

"So let's try a different line of questioning," she said as she put my file down. "Why do you want to come to Bishop Moore?"

"Well, I know it's a great school, the facility is nice . . . it's on a lake, I like that . . . and the baseball team . . ."

"And he got beat up," my mom blurted out. "He got beat up at his other school."

I glared at my mother.

"No, I didn't!" I said defiantly.

"Oh, yes, honey, yes, you did. Remember?"

"Jesus Christ! No, I didn't."

"Excuse me?" said the principal, taking off her glasses.

"I'm sorry, but I don't know what she's talking about," I said. "I didn't get beat up."

"He did," my mom whispered across the desk to the principal, "but he's not a wimp."

A few more awkward moments and the interview drew to a close.

"Well," my dad said as we walked to the parking lot, "I think that went pretty well."

The next day the baseball coach, who also served as the dean of students, made a phone call on my behalf and I was accepted to Bishop Moore.

It was the right move to leave Oviedo High School, but in truth, the three years I spent in Catholic school did me no demonstrable good. I was a conscientious objector as my classmates prayed in one class after another and I faked my way through three years of theology. But on the baseball field it was a different story. With a new team came a new nickname. On the field and around campus I was known as "The General"—as in General Douglas MacArthur—after one of my new teammates mistakenly called me Matt MacArthur. It was quite an upgrade from Birdman.

I hit a growth spurt during my sophomore year, and when the spring rolled around I stepped in as a starter on one of the top baseball teams in Florida. At times we were ranked among the top ten high school teams in the country and we sent numerous players to top collegiate programs like Florida State, Florida, and Auburn. In my senior year we rode a thirteen-game winning streak to the state finals, where we lost to our archrival, Key West High School, which was led by a flashy shortstop named Khalil Greene, who went on to play with Chris Young for the San Diego Padres.

I was a good player in high school—good enough to make All-State, good enough to get some attention from professional scouts—but not someone whom major league teams seriously considered drafting. I wasn't particularly big and I didn't throw all that hard, and those were the two most important qualities a scout was looking for in a high school left-handed pitcher. I went to college with the hope that I could increase my velocity a bit—from 85 to 90—and that maybe, just maybe, someone would give me a shot at playing professionally. But it was a gamble, and not one that my parents were betting heavily on.

So getting this invitation from the Yankees four years later was a big deal for me. In college, when I called home to talk about baseball, my father would invariably change the subject to my studies, and I was never sure if he did so simply because it interested him more or if it was his way of sending me a message. I wasn't sure how he was going to react when I called to tell him about the conversation I'd just had with Cesar Presbott, scout for the New York Yankees.

"Dad."

"Hey, boy."

"I just got off the phone with a Yankees scout. They just invited me to a predraft workout."

Silence.

"Workout for the Yankees," I repeated. "Invitation only."

"What? Really?"

"This Saturday in New York."

More silence. Then, finally:

"Holy shit!"

"This Saturday at their minor league park in Staten Island," I said with increasing excitement.

"I'll be there!" he said. "Holy shit! Let me get your mother."

THE OTHER PHONE CALL I had to make was to my best friend, Craig Breslow. I met Craig on the first day of college—a sun-soaked day in late August 1998. I had arrived at Tweed airport in New Haven around noon that day with two large duffel bags, a baseball mitt, and the na-ïveté of a typical college freshman away from home for the first time. Since I didn't know where my dorm was, I had the taxi driver drop me off in the center of campus. I wandered up and down Chapel Street before finding Broadway and the eventual route to my dorm room in Timothy Dwight College—known by Yale administrators as "the dorm closest to Paris" and to students simply as "the worst dorm."

The first order of business after dropping off my bags was not to track down my new roommates but to find a ride out to the baseball field. The team was having its first unofficial practice of the year and I did not want to be late. I quickly flagged down a taxi and instructed him to "take me to the Yale baseball field." The driver said he had never heard of it. After a few detours, we found our way to the stadium.

While most Ivy League teams play at modest baseball parks, Yale plays at a twelve-thousand-seat stadium that was built in 1928 and has hosted several major league teams before and during World War II. But the stadium might be best known for hosting Babe Ruth when he came to New Haven during one of his last public appearances. Weakened by age, he arrived to present the Yale captain, George H. W. Bush, with a copy of his autobiography for the Yale Library.

I paid the cabbie and entered the stadium through a door by the left-field wall, emerging to find a mass of men in blue shorts and gray T-shirts playing catch on an immaculately manicured field. I started jogging toward the group, and before I got there, the captain, Mike Finnegan—a six-foot-six pitcher from Minnesota—called the team together. Standing before me were twenty-five returning players and six freshmen. My initial impression was that these guys were all very tall and very white. All but one were Caucasian (the other was Indian) and six of the players were six feet four or taller.

We all said our names and where we were from. Craig Breslow was the only other freshman left-handed pitcher and we became fast friends. He had short dark hair, brown eyes, and a respect for authority that could come only from having a coach as a father. At five feet ten, he was one of the shortest players on the team. Craig had grown up a few miles away in Trumbull, Connecticut, and had just led his high school team to the state baseball championship when I met him. But it was clear from the beginning that he didn't like talking about himself, and that has always held true.

What initially drew me to Craig was his quiet confidence and even-keeled nature. He was a calming presence amid the flurry of activity at Yale and he always knew what to say when disaster struck. When I failed my first calculus exam as a freshman, he was there to pick up the pieces. When my high school girlfriend dumped me, he was there to point out her flaws. And within a week he had me set up on a blind date that ultimately failed, because, as Craig put it, "You can't kiss a girl on the forehead on the first date. It just makes you look like an impotent creep."

He called me Woody Allen for the better part of the semester after that mishap, until I kissed another girl—this time on the mouth—at which point he said I had earned my old name back. His way of finding the humor in my mistakes and misfortunes particularly came in handy on the baseball field, where we struggled through one abominable season after another.

By the time graduation rolled around, people started to notice that Craig and I had more than a few things in common. Gordon Edes wrote in *The Boston Globe*:

> Clones? These guys came out of the same laboratory, literally. Both were left-handed pitchers. They entered Yale the same year, as members of the Class of '02. They shared not only the same mind-stretching major, molecular biophysics and biochemistry, studying under the renowned Dr. Joan Steitz, they were lab partners for four years.

The big difference between us, I liked to say, was that Craig looked exactly like motivational speaker and author Joel Osteen and I did not.

As the two players on our Yale squad who had any hope of getting drafted our senior year and because we played the same position, Craig and I were invariably competing for the same scouts' attention. We always rooted for each other, but when a scout would approach me after a game, Craig was always the first to come over afterward and ask, "So what did *he* have to say?" And vice versa. So I felt obliged to tell him about the Yankees tryout.

"Guess who I just got a call from?" I said eagerly.

"Who?"

"Cesar Presbott," I said, trying to imitate his voice.

"Scout for the New York Yankees?" he snickered.

"You know him?" I asked.

"Yeah, he just called me. Said something about an invitation-only workout for the Yankees," Craig said, a little too nonchalantly.

A kick to the solar plexus.

"You got the invite?" I asked.

"Yeah, but I don't think I'm gonna go."

"Craig, are you crazy? This is a big deal. I think it's a big mistake for you to . . ."

"It's just that the Red Sox invited me to a workout on the same day," he said, "and their workout is at Fenway Park. The Yankees are holding theirs at some minor league field."

"Oh, okay, that makes sense," I offered.

"Yeah I just spoke to Theo Epstein from the Sox—he's a Yale guy, you know—and he said they're really interested in me."

"Wow, great. Good luck," I said and quietly hung up the phone.

I was left shaking my head. Were the Yankees really inviting a select few to a pre-draft workout or was this going to be a run-of-the-mill open tryout? And why weren't the Red Sox interested in me? Little did we know that four years later Craig would actually be pitching for the Red Sox and I'd be in the stands watching him with my physician friends.

IN LATE MAY, with the hangover of graduation festivities behind me and three days to kill before the Yankees tryout, I decided to pay my coach a visit in his office. It was an opportunity to thank him for four memorable years at Yale and, more important, to see if he could use any of his connections to get me selected in the draft, which was now just one week away.

Before taking over the head coaching job at Yale nine years earlier, John Stuper had pitched for the St. Louis Cardinals and the Montreal Expos. He had been drafted out of Butler Junior College, and, following a meteoric rise to the big leagues, found himself pitching in game 6 of the 1982 World Series. He won that game and the Cardinals went on to win the Series that year. Over the years, his game 6 win would frequently be referred to as one of the ten best performances by a rookie in the history of postseason play. But after that chilly October night in St. Louis, his career sputtered. He pitched a few more forgettable seasons before taking the helm at Yale.

Stuper was a "players' manager," meaning he frequently kidded around with players like he was just another twenty-year-old. A team meeting would often begin with him calling everyone together to ask something like, "Does anyone have a class with Claire Danes? What's she like?"

He also liked to draw a distinction between himself and his Yale players. "I'm just a regular guy from Butler, Pennsylvania," he would say to any of us who would listen. "As meat-and-potatoes as they come. I don't read poetry and I don't drink lattes. I'm not fancy like some of you." And he was fond of proclaiming, "I never could've gotten into Yale, but I'm smarter than just about all of you."

But he also knew when to be serious, like during recruiting season, which he referred to as "the lifeblood of the program." He knew exactly what to tell parents who weren't sure if they should shell out forty thousand dollars a year for their kid to go to Yale. Prep school parents would hear, "There's nothing better than to receive a liberal arts education while being immersed in a liberal student body," while parents from the Deep South would hear, "Bill O'Reilly is one of my personal heroes."

The reason Stuper was such a popular coach was that he could take a ribbing just as well as he could dish it out. We took delight in asking him outlandish questions just to see how he'd respond. Despite his imposing presence—six feet two inches and 220 pounds with tightly cropped red hair—he was really just a big kid. He was the younger brother who just happened to be twenty-five years older than you and also your head coach. One day I suggested to Stuper, who was recently divorced, that he should go introduce himself to Jordana Brewster, the actress, who was an undergraduate at Yale at the time.

"She's hot," he said as we watched her on the treadmill at the Yale gym. "Damn."

"I know, that's why you should go talk to her," I said with a smile.

"Mac, she's twenty-five years younger than me."

"So? You pitched in the big leagues. She's an actress. You're both celebrities."

"What am I going to say to her?" he asked while fighting back a smile. "I won game six, you wanna have sex?"

I was fond of Stuper, but I also considered him a tragic figure. He was the only person I knew who could pinpoint the exact day that his life had peaked. But instead of living like the rest of life was a letdown, he just kept living like it was 1982. "Now, that's a Bo Derek fastball!" he would often say while watching one of us pitch. "It's got a nice tail on it." He also enjoyed describing to us his romantic conquests as a result of the World Series victory. "After game six, I scored the trifecta," he once announced during a bus ride to Princeton. "Flight attendant, an NFL cheerleader, and a Playboy Playmate. A Playboy Playmate! May she rest in peace."

At a diner, he once interrupted me to say, "You know, I played with the best there ever was," and then pointed to a bottle of ketchup, a young boy eating an omelet, and a chair behind him. An older player had to tell me that he was pointing to an imaginary first base, pitcher's mound, and shortstop and that he was referring to Keith Hernandez, Jim Kaat, and Ozzie Smith—his teammates on the 1982 Cardinals team.

But for all his foibles, for all of his silly sayings and references to 1982, Stuper had our respect. He'd endured a difficult separation and divorce in the mid-1990s, and during the separation, his sister-in-law and brother-in-law were tragically killed in a car accident. Without batting an eye, Stuper had adopted their children, a boy and a girl, and raised them as his own. Though he had spent the last decade concocting speeches designed to motivate his players and teach them right from wrong, it was the way he lived his own life that had the most profound effect on us.

Whenever I saw Coach Stuper, his adopted son, Robbie, was by his side. He brought him to our practices, on our road trips, and to nearly all of our team dinners. He even let him sit in the dugout during games. When Robbie reached adolescence and players started teasing Stuper that his son was more interested in Pokémon than pitching, Stuper smiled and said it was fine with him.

A year later, when Robbie showed up to one of our practices and announced that he didn't want to play baseball anymore, Stuper put his arm around him and said, "Do what makes you happy, son."

And Stuper relished having a daughter. He was fond of calling the team together to remind us that no matter what we accomplished on the baseball field or in life, we would never be good enough to date his daughter. He did his best to keep her away from ballplayers, he said, because he knew what they were really like. And for the most part, he was successful.

As a sophomore, I threw a shutout against Harvard, and as I walked off the field, Stuper shook my hand, gave me a hug, and whispered, "She's still off-limits."

When I walked into Stuper's office that day in late May he immediately got up from behind his desk and gave me a firm handshake.

"Can you believe it's been four years?" he said.

"I can't."

"Time flies."

"It sure does."

"Even when you're losing," he said plaintively.

The poor man had tried everything to right the ship, but he just couldn't find a way to put a winning team on the field. In my freshman year he decided to be more hands-on, pushing his assistant coaches aside to teach the team hitting, fielding, base running, and pitching all by himself. When that didn't work, he announced in the fall of my sophomore year that he was going to "take a page out of Freud and become a laissez-faire coach."

My teammates and I exchanged a few confused glances before one of our starting pitchers took Stuper to task.

"Hey, Stupe," he said as he put down a ninety-five-pound barbell, "I think you just made what has to be called a 'Freudian slip.'"

"I don't think so," Stuper said confidently. "A player is not allowed to psychoanalyze his coach. Not gonna happen. No way."

When those two strategies failed, Stuper fired both of his assistant coaches—but it didn't stop the losing. So the next fall he hired a sports psychiatrist, an old man in a tweed coat who was laughed out of the room in the middle of our first session.

But for all of Stuper's schemes, for all of his grand plans to turn the program around, one idea towers above the rest. During my freshman year, he announced that we were all going to become volunteers in the New Haven chapter of the Big Brother/Big Sister Program.

"What I've realized," he said as we circled around him in the weight room, "is that to be a winner on the field, you must be a winner off the field. So we're going to start working with some underprivileged youths. Children are the future, fellas. You can't argue with that."

So the next day, instead of going to practice, we met in the conference room of the Ray Tompkins House, an old brick building next to the gymnasium. The room was large and had hardwood floors and a fireplace. The walls were covered with old team photos and there were three trophy cases filled to capacity. We spread out on four green leather couches in the center of the room as we waited to be interviewed by a representative from the Big Brother Program.

The interviewer's name was Ruth and she was wearing a black pantsuit and dark wire-rimmed glasses. "So why do you want to be in the Big Brother Program?" she asked our third baseman.

"I don't," he said flatly. "I'm only here because my coach is making me."

"Oh," she said, "well, we don't want to force you to volunteer."

"No, no, it's fine," he said, looking over at the rest of his teammates.

"Would you like for me to continue with the interview?"

"Sure," he said as we giggled on the couch, "I suppose I have to."

"We do a background check on all of our volunteers, so I have to ask these questions. Do you have a criminal record?"

"What do you mean by 'criminal'?"

"Well . . . have you ever been arrested?"

He sat back in the chair and pulled up his right sleeve, exposing a large New York Yankees tattoo. "Arrested? No."

"Excellent."

"Detained? . . . Yes."

"Oh, okay, that's fine I think, but I'll have to check," she said as she scribbled on her notepad. "And do you drink alcohol?"

"Oh, sure."

"How many drinks would you say you have . . . in a given week?"

"Well, let's see . . ." he said. He took a deep breath and looked at the ceiling as he started to count. "Oh . . . I'd say between twenty and thirty drinks . . . give or take."

"A week?" the woman exclaimed.

"Yeah. If it's a good week maybe a few more."

"Are you . . ."

"But I'm usually in no state to count. You may have to ask one of the guys on the couch over there," he said, pointing to us.

Yale baseball's venture into volunteering turned out to be an unmitigated disaster. Several of my teammates simply stopped showing up to meet with their Little Brothers. As a team we were expelled from the program, I was told, because one of our players had become romantically involved with the mother of the child he was mentoring.

Needless to say, Stuper and I had been through a tumultuous four years together.

We chatted for a few minutes in his office on that cloudy day in May before I got down to business.

"Coach," I said, "I need some help. You know I'm a guy on the fringe when it comes to the draft next week. Do you have any advice for me?"

"Control that which you can control," he said reflexively. It had been one of his favorite sayings since I'd known him and one that I still use in medicine.

"I know, I know, but is there any part *you* can control? Do you have any connections? Anything? I've got a workout with the Yankees but that's only one team."

He leaned back in his chair, put his hands behind his head, and let out a deep breath.

"Well, you know, I did pitch for the Cardinals . . ."

We both smiled.

"I think you've mentioned it once or twice."

"I'll tell you what I'm gonna do," he said while flipping through his Rolodex. "I'm gonna call Chuck Fick. He's a big-time scout with the Cards and a close personal friend of mine."

"Great."

I stared at a picture of my coach with Ozzie Smith from 1982 that he had framed on his wall while he dialed the phone. In the eighties Stuper had big bushy red hair that resembled Ronald McDonald's, and over the years many of us had used his image as inspiration for Halloween costumes.

"Chuck Fick, this is John Stuper. How ya doing?"

They exchanged pleasantries and small talk for a few minutes before Stuper mentioned me. I had my hands clasped and my teeth were clenched.

"I'm calling about one of my players, Matt McCarthy. He's a left-handed pitcher who . . ."

He stopped in midsentence and a scowl began to appear.

"Wait, wait, what?"

Silence. Stuper looked down at his desk and began shaking his head.

"You do what now?"

Silence.

"You're an actor?"

A pause.

"You do commercials?"

"Well, never mind what I was calling about. Say hi to the wife and kids for me."

Stuper hung up the phone and looked at me. He let out a deep breath and again put his hands behind his head. He looked away and then down at his desk. A minute elapsed without either of us saying a word. This wouldn't have happened in '82, he was probably thinking.

"That really couldn't have gone any worse, could it?" Stuper finally said to me.

"No, it really couldn't."

I later learned that Chuck Fick was indeed an actor—he'd appeared in *Mr. Baseball* and *The Naked Gun*—but if the conversation had lasted a little longer, Stuper would've learned that Fick was also still the St. Louis Cardinals' national cross-checker, one of the top scouts in the organization, and one of the men who'd be calling the shots on draft day.

JOHN STUPER COULDN'T do much to help my draft day prospects but I still had something else working in my favor. It was a strange circumstance, but despite fielding perennial cellar-dwellers, Yale still ended up having more players drafted than any other Ivy League team. Stuper knew how to recruit; he just had trouble getting his players to put the team before their own aspirations. Still, for all the credit he got for his recruiting acumen, his biggest prize fell into his lap.

Jon Steitz was born and raised in New Haven and attended high school less than a mile from Yale Field. Physically he was a modern-day Billy Budd—tall and muscular with bright blue eyes, a strong nose, and an all-American look ripped straight from the pages of a Ralph Lauren catalog.

His parents were both world-renowned Yale professors. His mother, Joan, was the first female graduate student to work for James Watson (of Watson and Crick fame) at Harvard. She did her postdoctoral work under Crick before taking a biochemistry professorship at Yale, where she's been teaching and doing RNA research for more than three decades. It was in graduate school that she met her husband, Tom, a biophysicist who has solved some of life's most intricate molecular mysteries using X-rays and nuclear magnetic resonance. Somehow these two scientists produced a son with a model's good looks and a 94-mile-per-hour fastball. Those of us who knew him suspected he'd been genetically engineered.

Jon Steitz always knew he was going to attend Yale. His parents' connections alone probably could've gotten him in, but it didn't hurt that he recorded a perfect score on his SAT IIs, was the quarterback of his high school football team, and was drafted in the forty-fourth round by the Anaheim Angels while he was still in high school. So when he arrived on Yale's campus for his recruiting visit one week after me, it was more as a formality.

Steitz joined the freshman baseball class of 2002 with Breslow and me, and from the moment I met him, I was engulfed by jealousy. He was smarter than me, could throw harder, and had his pick of the ladies at Toad's. He was everything Breslow wasn't and he didn't seem particularly interested in acquainting himself with me.

But toward the end of freshman year, Stuper paired the two of us as roommates for our annual spring break baseball trip, where for a fortnight we served as punching bags for various teams around the Southeast in return for sunshine and Southern hospitality. The daily humiliation helped forge a friendship, and as the years progressed and my jealousy gradually waned, I found Steitz to be one of the most loyal friends I had at Yale.

While playing baseball in the Cape Cod league after his sophomore year, Jon made a phone call to his father—the country's leading biophysicist—and got me a job in his lab. His father spent most of that summer traveling to conferences and we got to speak only once while I worked for him, when he pulled me aside in the hallway outside of his laboratory to say, "Matt, would you like to know why I like gardening? Because it's the only hobby that's commensurate with the time frame of human emotions."

Exactly.

Jon played for the Orleans Cardinals in the Cape that summer and wowed the scouts. He threw a no-hitter and dominated players from all of the top college programs. He was considered a shoo-in to be a first-round draft pick, and the following spring—our junior year—dozens of scouts flocked to see Jon pitch. And every once in a while they'd stick around long enough to notice Craig or me.

A few weeks after junior year drew to a close, Breslow, Steitz, and I gathered together to follow the draft. Jon was the only one of us who had a realistic shot at being chosen that day, but Breslow and I both privately held out hope that we would be selected as well. We each carried our copy of *Baseball America* into Jon's living room, where we read and reread the article that rated him the twenty-sixth best player in the country, which meant he could expect to be selected in the first round and offered a seven-figure signing bonus.

But after two rounds and sixty draft picks, Steitz's name had not been called. Our previously upbeat conversation gradually stalled and I sat on my magazine. Eventually Jon left the room. Craig and I spent the next ten minutes exchanging glances until Steitz returned, phone in hand, to announce with a touch of disappointment that he'd been selected in the third round by the Milwaukee Brewers. As I leaned in to give him a hug, I was once again reminded that nothing could be taken for granted on draft day.

AT THE CRACK OF DAWN on the day of the Yankees workout, my father and I stuffed my baseball equipment into the back of his green Toyota

Camry rental car and we headed south for Staten Island. In addition to my glove, I'd packed white baseball pants, a blue T-shirt, and my high school baseball hat. There would be no trace of Yale on me today. I tried to sleep as he drove down I-95, but I found it impossible to relax. Part of it was nerves, the other part was my father—every few minutes he would prod me with another question about the Yankees.

"So what do you think you'll do for the tryout?" he asked as he sipped his coffee.

"I don't know. The hitters will hit and the pitchers will pitch," I said as I stretched out in the passenger's seat. "I'm going to try to sleep a bit before we get there."

"Okay, but before you do, tell me exactly what the Yankees scout said to you."

"I've told you, what, ten times now?"

"One more time."

He was just as nervous as I was. Eventually I decided to forget sleep and started listening to the radio.

"So what's your plan today?" he asked. The one thing he was always interested in was "my plan," whether it was taking a new class, learning a new pitch, or driving to a new destination. Every new adventure required a plan of attack. He'd spent his career trying to get into the minds of some of the most hardened criminals and I liked to think that their penchant for intricate plots had rubbed off on him. How was I going to pull this off, he was probably wondering—how was I going to get the Yankees to draft me. I'm sure he had a detailed plan of his own, but I was trying to keep things as simple as possible.

"I'm going to throw every pitch as hard as I possibly can," I said.

"Make sure you throw strikes," he added.

"They don't really care about that," I said, leaning forward to turn down the radio.

"Sure they do."

"No, they don't," I countered. "Today is about seeing who has the potential to get major league hitters out. Scouts are convinced that someone who throws eighty or eighty-five can't be a big league pitcher. Derek Jeter is going to hit an eighty-mile-per-hour fastball no matter where it crosses the plate. They'd much rather see me throw ninety and be wild than eighty-three with pinpoint control." There was nothing I was more sure of.

"Seems like you've got it figured out," he said.

"These guys think they can teach you to throw strikes . . ."

"But they can't teach velocity," he said, repeating a statement I'd made to him dozens of times.

"I've just gotta hit ninety today," I said.

"Well, you've done that before."

At eight-thirty New York Harbor came into view and a few minutes later we were pulling into the parking lot of Richmond County Bank Ballpark, the minor league stadium for the Staten Island Yankees. It was a warm day, probably about 90 degrees, and the lot was mostly empty, save for the occasional Chrysler LeBaron convertible. At the entrance to the stadium, I met a man in his early forties wearing shorts and a Staten Island Yankees T-shirt.

"Name?" he said, staring at his clipboard.

"McCarthy," I said curtly. I was always trying to be stoic around scouts. I couldn't say why for sure, but I got it into my head that they liked that.

"Welcome. Go take a seat in the third-base dugout. We'll be starting soon."

My father took a seat in the stands and I headed down to the dugout, where I found fifteen guys doing what baseball players do—stretching, chewing tobacco, lacing up spikes, and generally just shooting the shit. I didn't recognize anyone so I sat down and laced up my shoes. And unlaced them. And repeated this several more times before five portly, white-haired men in full Yankee uniforms came into the dugout to address us.

The man in the middle, the one with the largest belly hanging out over his pinstripes, stepped forward. "Thank you all for coming today. We're excited to have you here. Obviously someone from our organization saw you this spring and thinks you can play. Today we'll see if they were right. Here's how the day is gonna work. You'll stretch from nine to nine-thirty A.M. Then we'll do the sixty-yard dash. Pitchers, you're excused from this. Next up we'll hit you some ground balls and see if you can field. Pitchers, you're also excused from this. Then some batting practice, and at the end, the pitchers can finally get off their asses and throw to hitters. And we'll gun ya. The whole thing should take about four hours.

"Before we get started," the old man continued, "we're gonna take roll." And he proceeded to read the names and schools of all in attendance. There were eighteen in all, a mix of high school and college players, from as far away as California and as close as Rutgers. It clearly was the invitation-only workout that I'd hoped for, but I hadn't heard of any of the other players, which was a bit surprising since I'd been reading *Baseball America* almost every day for the past two months. *Baseball America* was the most comprehensive resource for predraft information and had been my bible as the draft had drawn near. For what it was worth, it had listed me as one of the top ten professional prospects in "Lower New England," but it had spelled my name wrong, calling me Max. Breslow enjoyed teasing me about it, and it was all the more infuriating because he was ranked just ahead of me on the list.

The first three hours of the workout were uneventful. I watched as infielders and outfielders grimaced and groaned as they ran the sixty-yard dash, straining every muscle in their bodies to show they had "wheels," a scout's term for speed. One of the high school kids from California went down with a pulled hamstring after he'd run just a few yards.

"Man, that's gotta suck," one of the pitchers said with a hint of a smile while the player writhed around in agony on the outfield grass.

"Come all the way out here," another added while stuffing an enormous wad of chewing tobacco into his lower lip, "and have *that* happen. Shoulda just stayed in bed."

"Looks like we know one guy who won't be a Yankee," a third offered.

With that, everyone chuckled. They were elated that the guy had gotten hurt. One less player to compete with, they were thinking. I knew this because I was thinking it, too.

I'd been quiet the entire morning, trying to visualize myself on the mound throwing hard and striking people out. In between thoughts of fastballs, I was imagining myself on the other side of New York Bay, playing at Yankee Stadium alongside Ruth, Gehrig, DiMaggio, and Mantle. I was in the middle of doing some lower-back exercises when one of the other pitchers sidled up next to me.

"And just what's your story, partner?" It was the guy with the protuberance of chewing tobacco. For a second I thought he was referencing an old movie, in which case I'd be obliged to respond with the following lines of dialogue, but he wasn't. He was tall and lanky with a neck-beard and arms that seemed to reach down to his knees.

"Matt McCarthy," I said, extending my hand. As we shook I could feel the fiberglass mixed with tobacco on his fingertips. I'd never tried smokeless tobacco, as it was nowhere to be found in the Yale locker room. In a few months' time I would try it—in a motel in Idaho—to amuse my minor league teammates. I learned then that the fiberglass was mixed with tobacco in order to cut the mucous membranes of the cheek and gums while you chewed it—to allow the nicotine to enter the bloodstream more quickly.

"And where ya from?" he asked while the pitchers turned their attention to me.

"Grew up in Florida, went to Yale. Just graduated."

"Yale!" he said with a big smile before turning to the other pitchers. "Well, that's not the same as Harvard, is it?"

The other pitchers all laughed.

"No, but close," I said, trying to be a good sport.

"So how'd you do this year?" another pitcher asked.

"Not so great. Our team was thirteen and twenty-seven."

"No, not your team," he responded, sounding somewhat exasperated. "How did *you* do?"

"Well, I went four and three with a 3.99 ERA."

"No, no, no," he said with a smile. "We both know that don't mean shit. What did you light up on the radar gun? What'd you top out at?"

"Well," I said, trying to figure out what I wanted to say. I knew these guys were ultimately rooting against me, so I wanted to watch my words. I opted for honesty. "I hit ninety a few times, ninety-two once."

"Not bad, not bad," he said. "You a righty?"

"No, lefty," I said.

"Oh," he said. "Damn, that's good." The other pitchers quickly began sizing me up and mumbling comments to themselves. It was like being a recruit at Yale all over again. Perhaps I should've played it closer to the vest. It occurred to me that I'd been on the defensive the entire conversation and hadn't asked my tobacco-chewing friend anything about himself. So I did. He replied that he'd hit 93 miles per hour, and thus began a domino effect of one-upmanship, with each successive player claiming to have reached a higher velocity than the last.

Shortly before one P.M., the scouts turned their attention to the pitchers. One of the geriatric Yankees read out the pitching order and told us to get ready. We would each pitch two innings and I would be throwing second.

I was assigned a catcher and we walked down to the bullpen together.

"Whaddaya got?" he asked.

"Fastball, slider, change," I replied.

"One, two, three?" he asked, trying to clarify the signals we'd be using.

"Yep." This was one of the most important tasks—to get on the same page as the catcher. If he put down the sign for curve and you threw a fastball, there'd be a problem. I'd done it a few times in my career and it usually resulted in the catcher pulling me aside in the dugout to say, "If it happens again, I'm going to fucking kill you."

After a few warm-up tosses, my name was called and I jogged out to the pitcher's mound. It was then that I finally took in the beauty of my surroundings—the field was arranged such that the mound was lined up between home plate and the Statue of Liberty, which stood out in the distance behind center field. Beyond right field was a sweeping view of lower Manhattan, where the rubble from 9/11 was still being cleared.

As I toed the rubber, I realized I was naked. On this day, I knew only the feeling and not the term. In a few weeks I would discover that playing naked meant taking the field without your go-to performance enhancer. In the minors the enhancers of choice were amphetamines, or "greenies," and steroids. For me it was heavily caffeinated energy drinks like Red Bull. I'd tried one in the fall and had thrown a few miles an hour harder than usual, and with that I was hooked. But today, of all days, I'd forgotten about it.

The first player to step into the batter's box was a big left-handed hitter, the type I enjoyed facing. Left-handed hitters hate facing left-handed pitchers, I told myself. As I started my windup, I saw several radar guns pop up. I reared back and fired a fastball that was fouled straight back, a sign that the hitter just missed the pitch. My father was now sitting in the front row, trying to listen to the scouts. Normally, I'd follow up my fastball with a slider, but today I wanted to show off my velocity. I again slung the pitch as hard as my body would allow and the batter swung and missed. I threw a third fastball and let out a grunt. The batter again swung and missed and slammed his bat to the ground.

I started the next batter off with a slider that was laced to left field for a single. Won't make that mistake again, I muttered. The next batter grounded into a double play on the first pitch, and with that my first inning, all five pitches of it, was over.

I walked off the field and made eye contact with my dad, who gave me a thumbs-up. I now had a few minutes to get a drink of water and speak to my catcher.

"Look good out there," he said.

Before long I was back on the mound to face three batters who'd just graduated from high school. They'd never swung a wooden bat before and it showed. I struck all three out—on all fastballs—and walked off the field triumphantly. My line for the day: two innings, no runs, one hit, four strikeouts. But I knew that those numbers alone were not going to get me drafted.

I took off my hat and glove and found my father, who had walked over to the dugout.

"I definitely saw ninety," he said.

"Yeah?"

"Definitely. Way to go, boy."

Several more pitchers took the mound and they all looked sharp. After the last out was made, one of the coaches yelled, "All right, that's it. Take it to the dugout."

As we crammed into the dugout, there was a cacophony of metal spikes meeting concrete. The scout waited for the noise to cease and began again. "Thank you all for coming out. Overall I'd say it was a great day. The draft is three days away. Good luck. And, eh, don't call us . . . we'll call you." The scouts shared a chuckle and we were dismissed.

Walking out of the stadium I saw the group of scouts comparing notes near the concession stand. I wanted to say something, anything, in the event that it might help them remember me on draft day.

"Nice job," one of them said as I walked by.

"Thanks," I said, trying to come up with something more. "So, are the Yanks looking for any left-handed pitching this year?" I asked the question with a smile, and as soon as it came out I realized it was a rather stupid thing to say.

The scouts all looked at one another. "Kid, everybody's looking for left-handed pitching," one said tersely, before patting me on the shoulder and turning back to speak to his fellow scouts. Feelings of optimism and excitement were quickly replaced with the dread of doubt.

And with that, my tryout with the Yankees was complete. We took the Camry to Kennedy Airport and headed home to Orlando, to wait for the draft.

UNLIKE OTHER PROFESSIONAL SPORTS in 2002, Major League Baseball had no central location for its annual draft. There was no convention center, no television cameras, and no green room where square-jawed young men in pin-striped suits would wait patiently for their names to be called and their rides in professional sports to begin. Instead, the baseball draft was held via conference call on the first Tuesday in June and would span fifty rounds, with each team having roughly one selection per round. Major League Baseball had decided some years ago that only certain residents of the United States and Canada would be eligible for the draft: (1) graduating high school seniors, (2) junior college and community college players, and (3) juniors, seniors, and those who have turned twenty-one while attending four-year colleges or universities. So for me, it was my third and final opportunity to be selected.

I woke up early on draft day. It was a hot and muggy Florida day and I spent the morning indoors, reading the anemic predraft coverage in the *Orlando Sentinel* before consulting the latest issue of *Baseball America*. This would be a strong year for high school players in the draft, the magazine said. Expect big things from B.J. Upton and Prince Fielder, the son of ex–home run champ Cecil Fielder. College pitching was very weak this year, the writers agreed. With the exception of a few collegiate superstars—Bryan Bullington, Joe Saunders, and Jeff Francis—there were very few quality arms in the college ranks who deserved the seven-figure signing bonus that came with being selected in the first round.

In a few months' time, a landmark book would be published called *Moneyball*, which called into question many of the practices that scouts had used to evaluate players. It would argue that statistics such as RBIs, stolen bases, and batting average were irrelevant in evaluating players and that on-base percentage and slugging percentage were better indicators of success. It would show how these statistics were used by scouts for the Oakland A's and how this had allowed them, with their $41 million payroll, to stay competitive with the New York Yankees, who were spending more than $150 million per season. It would also argue that teams would be wise to invest their money in proven college pitchers rather than high school phenoms who were wild but could light up a radar gun. But on draft day in 2002, no such book was available.

The draft started at 1:00 P.M., and by 1:15 I'd downloaded the Internet radio system that allowed me to listen to it as it happened. My mother and father took turns sitting with me at the computer as I listened in, but they both found it to be a rather boring affair.

"With the third pick in the 2002 Major League Baseball draft, the Cincinnati Reds select player 838204, Christopher Gruler, from Liberty Union High School. With the fourth pick in the 2002 Major

League Baseball draft, the Baltimore Orioles select player 574883, Adam Loewen, from Fraser Valley Christian High School." After two rounds, I found myself alone at the computer daydreaming about the minors. Playing professionally has got to be more fun than playing in college, I reasoned. Without the constant pressure of classes and exams, I could relax and just play ball. It would be the sport at its purest, with no outside distractions.

I zoned in and out as the draft rolled along, but I always paid special attention to the Yankees' selections. After three hours and ten rounds of draft picks, I was starting to get anxious. I hadn't expected to be selected in the first ten rounds, but I was optimistic about the next ten.

My heart skipped a beat when the Yankees selected Marcus McClanahan in the eleventh round, and it nearly stopped altogether when they used their twelfth-round pick to select player 485743, Matthew Mamula. After a few more rounds I decided I'd had enough and went to find my father. Nothing cured a case of the nerves like playing catch, so I headed outside and interrupted Bernie as he was mowing the lawn.

"I can't take it anymore," I said.

"It must be awful boring listening to all that," he said.

"The Yankees took two guys with names that sound like mine. Unbelievable."

"Unbelievable," he said, wiping the sweat from his brow.

"Wanna play catch?" I asked.

He could tell I was out of sorts. "Of course."

As we started tossing the ball, I began to talk fast and furiously. First it was about the draft and then Yale baseball and then my plans if I didn't get drafted. I didn't have a job if this baseball thing didn't work out, and for the first time I began considering my options.

"I'm sure I can play in Sweden," I said with a smile.

"I'm sure you can get a job," he replied.

After a few more throws I began to ponder my future in a life without baseball.

"I guess I could put a résumé together," I said.

As these words came out of my mouth, my sister came running out to the driveway.

"Matt!" she yelled from the driveway. She was nineteen and home from college, but I still treated her like my nine-year-old kid sister. "Craig's on the phone."

"Tell him I'll call him back," I said and threw my dad a changeup.

"He says it's important. He wants to know if you're following the draft."

"Say that I was, but I got sick of it."

"He said you're an Angel," she said with a wry smile.

"What?"

She hung up the phone and walked to within three feet of me. "He wants me to tell you that you were just selected in the twenty-first round by the Anaheim Angels!"

My dad and I looked at each other and I dropped my glove. He came over and gave me a hug.

"Holy shit," I muttered.

Chapter 2

||||||||||||||||||||||||||||||||||||||||||||||

MANY DRAFTEES CHOOSE to engage in protracted contract negotiations while others agree to terms almost as soon as they're offered
a deal. I fell into the latter category. I had two things working against
me in the negotiation process: my age and my draft round. I was a college
graduate and therefore no longer draft-eligible, so I couldn't threaten to
walk away from an offer and return to school. And with each successive round, signing-bonus money decreased significantly. First-round
guys got a few million dollars, second-rounders a few hundred thousand. A player taken in the fifth round was lucky to get six figures, and
by the tenth round you could expect low five figures. I was prepared for
the minimum—a one-thousand-dollar signing bonus.

A few minutes after Craig called to deliver the momentous news, I
received a call from a scout named Biron.

"This is Biron from Anaheim," he said without the grandeur of Cesar
Presbott.

"Hi."

"I'm the scout who drafted you. I wanted to deliver the good news
myself. I saw you pitch against the Indiana Hoosiers and against Brown.
I saw a lot of you this spring and you really showed me something."

Scouts log tens of thousands of miles chasing the next big thing or
looking for that diamond in the rough. A few weeks before the draft
they start assembling their list of prospects that they eventually send
to the big-league team that they work for. Just before the draft, the

general manager, assistant general manager, and all of the scouts gather in a war room and create one massive list of all the players in the country they'd like to select. They put all the names, upward of a thousand, on massive marker boards that span several walls and they strike names, one by one, as players are selected by other organizations on draft day. It's a hectic day, and each time their team selects a player, everyone stops what they're doing to applaud, high-five, and shake hands. As the draft proceeds, scouts can lobby for one player over another, and in this case, Biron had lobbied for me. I had trouble placing him at first, but then I remembered the lone scout at Murray Stadium on an unseasonably cool day in Providence, watching me pitch my final collegiate game against the Brown Bears. I'd thrown a complete game with ten strikeouts, and I'd also hit 90.

Biron had approached Craig and me after the game and given us Anaheim Angels questionnaires to fill out. Theirs was a standard form that I'd received from about a dozen clubs; it requested my contact information and wanted to know if I'd ever suffered an arm injury. I'd never been hurt, but Craig had recently undergone elbow surgery. He wrestled with disclosing it to the scouts, as it would undoubtedly be a mark against him, and ultimately he wrote, "No prior arm injuries."

"Sir, this is the greatest day of my life," I said to Biron without hyperbole.

"It should be," he replied. "You're a tough kid. That's why I drafted you. And I think you've got the talent to make it. Now I have some advice for you: no matter what happens in the minors, don't get discouraged. You're a lefty, and lefties can hang around pro ball for years if they can throw strikes."

"Yes, sir."

"And there's another thing I tell all my draftees. Now, you went to Yale so I'm sure you're a smart kid . . ."

I smiled as I heard those words, which had been thrown my way

many times by scouts. The last time had been a week earlier by a roving scout who, instead of representing a specific team, represented all
of Major League Baseball. He'd come to New Haven to administer an
intelligence test to Craig and me. It was a test that nearly all prospects
took and it was used by organizations to determine if a player was mentally fit to play professional baseball, a concept that I'd later come to
view with more than a touch of irony. It was baseball's version of the
Wonderlic Personnel Test, which had been used by corporations and
the NFL for decades to evaluate prospective employees. The Wonderlic
was a twelve-minute fifty-question multiple-choice test, while the MLB
test consisted of one hundred true/false statements like, "Athletic competition began on earth in 1974."

"I'm sorry I had to put you through that," the man had said as he
collected our exams.

Biron continued on the phone, "I'm sure you're a smart kid, but
please don't do anything stupid once you get out there. Don't make me
look bad. You're representing a professional organization now."

"Of course."

"Now let's talk money," he said with a sigh.

"Okay," I said, "but let me get my father on the line. I know he'll
want to hear this."

"There's really not much to say," Biron said somberly as I began
looking for Bernie. I waved him into the kitchen and handed him a
separate phone.

"Hi, this is Matt's dad," he said.

"Hi, this is Biron from Anaheim. I think your son's got a bright future. I think he can play in the big leagues someday."

"Thank you."

"So here's what's going to happen. . . ." From the monotony of Biron's voice, I could tell he'd had this conversation hundreds of times.
"Your son is going to get a thousand dollars to sign. We'll mail the

contract today. He'll also be offered the standard minor league contract of eight hundred fifty dollars a month. It's what everyone gets."

"Is there any way he can get, uh, more money than that?" my dad
asked sheepishly.

"No."

"Are you sure?"

"Yes."

With that, the conversation drew to a close. My father and I
thanked Biron and I assured him I would not disappoint him or the
Angels. I hung up the phone and looked at Bernie.

"You're quite the negotiator," I said.

"You said yourself that you had no leverage to negotiate," he said
defensively.

"I'm just kidding," I said and slapped him on the belly.

"Well, let's go to the mall," he said with a big grin. "I want to buy
you an Angels hat."

He thinks I can play in the big leagues, I said to myself.

THE NEXT DAY my contract arrived; it had been overnighted from
Anaheim. In addition to the signing bonus and monthly paycheck, the
contract explained that the Angels would provide medical insurance
and airfare for any baseball-related trips, including spring training, an
end-of-season flight home, and the eventual day I'd be released. According to Article XVI, I was henceforth prohibited from engaging in
automobile or motorcycle racing, hang gliding, fencing, parachuting,
skydiving, boxing, wrestling, karate, judo, football, basketball, skiing,
hockey, or any other sport "involving a substantial risk of personal injury." If it had said I was also prohibited from using the restroom, I still

would've signed it. I filled out the half dozen green pages and mailed it back the same day.

On the way home from the post office, I decided to give my girl-friend a call. Our relationship had been on the rocks for months, and when I left New Haven it was unclear if we were going to stay together. She had casually mentioned the difficulty of a long-distance relationship and I wasn't sure how she'd take the news that I'd soon be moving to the other side of the country.

Her name was Cara and she was from a town near Minneapolis. She was tall and blond with a thick midwestern accent and she was a couple of years younger than me. She played a varsity sport at Yale and she liked to say that if push came to shove, she could beat up Breslow.

"I just got some great news," I said as soon as she picked up the phone.

"Are you coming out to visit?" she asked excitedly.

"No, no, I just got drafted. By the Angels!"

"The Angels! That's great. Where is their team?"

"California."

"Oh."

"But I won't be in California."

"Thank goodness for that. Where will you be?"

"I don't know, but I want you to come visit, wherever I am."

"Oh, Matt, I don't know . . ."

"I'll pay. Just say you'll come visit."

"Matt, I don't know if I can. I just got a job with—"

"Just say that you'll come."

"Maybe, Matt. Things are pretty crazy at home, but maybe I'll come visit."

It didn't sound particularly encouraging.

The next day I received a call from Abe Flores, manager of Baseball Operations for the Anaheim Angels. He cut right to the chase.

"This is Matt, right?"

"Yes."

"This is Abe Flores from Anaheim. You're ready to go, right?"

"Yes."

"Okay, here's the deal: the day after tomorrow you're flying out to Mesa, Arizona. You'll spend a week in what we call extended spring training and then you'll be assigned to one of our minor league teams. You'll spend the summer in Provo, Utah; Cedar Rapids, Iowa; or Rancho Cucamonga, California. Or we might keep you in Mesa. . . . I don't know. As you can imagine, this is a pretty hectic time for us. We'll figure out where to send you after we get a good look at ya."

"Sounds great," I said.

"You know," he said with a deep breath, "I really appreciate you being an easy sign. Some of these fuckers try to drag out the negotiations and they waste the whole goddamn summer. You did the right thing, my boy."

"Thank you."

"Now, when you land in Phoenix we'll have someone waiting for you at Ground Transportation."

"Who should I look for?"

"Oh, don't worry, you can't miss him. We look forward to meeting you."

Having a one-way cross-country plane ticket caused me all sorts of headaches, as the Department of Homeland Security was still tinkering with its color-coded terror-alert scheme. The day of my flight, June 8, was a yellow day for terror. I sleepwalked my way through three rounds of beefed-up security at the Orlando airport and was pulled out of line twice to have my pockets and carry-ons searched. My grogginess was to be expected—after speaking to Abe Flores I'd spent forty-eight hours reading every postdraft recap and analysis I could get my hands on. The Angels had had a very successful draft, landing prized left-handed pitching prospect Joe Saunders in the first round. These analyses focused primarily on the players taken in the first ten rounds, so there was no mention of the Angels' twenty-first-round pick.

Craig had been drafted shortly after me, in the twenty-sixth round, by the Milwaukee Brewers. I was happy he'd been selected and even happier that it had been after me. He was also offered a one-thousand-dollar bonus and had eagerly taken it.

"Congratulations," I said to him shortly after hearing his name called on draft day. He was spending the day with his parents as well, in Trumbull, Connecticut.

"Go to hell," he said before starting to laugh. "I know you're gloating down there in Florida."

"The Brewers were lucky to get you."

"You are very generous."

"Good luck out there. We've been waiting for this for a long time."

"I know. . . . Jesus, I can't wait to get back on a mound."

Two days later, after a bumpy flight to Phoenix, I exited the plane jelly-legged and went out in search of my ride. But before I could do that I had to head over to baggage claim to retrieve my duffel, which had been neatly packed with two pairs of jeans, two pairs of shorts, ten sets of socks and underwear, a CD player, one pair of khaki pants, a Mead notebook, three pens, five T-shirts, and fifteen short-sleeved collared shirts. After a few minutes of staring at the revolving carousel, I felt a tap on my shoulder.

I turned around to see a wide grin and two big ears creeping out from under a high-riding Brewers hat.

"Motivational speaker Joel Osteen!" I said to Craig.

"Fancy meeting you here," he said with a playful roll of the eyes. One of my old girlfriends at Yale—a wealthy debutante from Park Avenue—once said that to him, and he still enjoyed mocking me by imitating her.

"Oh, go to hell," I said with a smile. My teammates at Yale had ridiculed me mercilessly after Craig told them I was dating a Manhattan socialite who was a member of both the Yale Repertory Theater and the Elizabethan Club. The relationship had been doomed from the start.

"Where you headed?" I asked him.

"Just outside of Phoenix," he said while straightening his new hat. "A place called Maryvale. You?"

"Mesa."

"Long way from New Haven, huh?"

"You can say that again. Well, shit, it was great to see you. I've gotta go find my ride."

"I'm gonna bet that won't be too hard," he said with a chuckle before nodding ahead at a short, stocky man who looked like he'd just come from a shopping spree at an Anaheim Angels gift shop.

I said good-bye to Craig and approached the man with my hand extended.

"You must be Ronnie," he said. He was wearing an Angels T-shirt tucked into Angels mesh shorts as well as Angels socks. On his right arm was a rubber Angels bracelet.

"Actually, I'm Matt McCarthy."

"Oh, right. McCarthy," he said, reaching for his pocket and a piece of paper. It had three names on it, including mine.

"I'm Grant—one of the strength and conditioning coaches for the Angels. We've got two more guys to pick up. Shouldn't be too long."

"Great," I said.

Grant made a short call on his cell phone and then resumed speaking to me.

"Well, isn't that cute," he said, reaching toward me. "You got yourself an Angels hat."

The missing piece to your ensemble, I thought.

"Yeah, it was a gift."

"Isn't that precious," he replied. He was about to continue when something caught his eye.

"I think that's Ronnie," he said, pointing in the direction of an individual wearing blue jeans and a white T-shirt with a red gym bag over his shoulder. He was tall with short jet-black hair, and he bore a striking resemblance to a baby-faced Elvis.

"Ronnie Ray," he said as he approached us, extending his hand first to Grant and then to me.

"Ronnie Ray," Grant repeated, "now *that* is a baseball name."

"Yes, sir," he replied confidently.

A moment later the third player arrived. Felix Nuñez, from El Tigre, Venezuela, was a second-year player in the organization who was being demoted to Mesa after suffering through a batting slump in Rancho Cucamonga. He was six feet tall with a large, toothy smile and a flattop and he spoke no English.

"Noon-yeah!" Grant exclaimed.

"Grant!" Nuñez replied, exposing his big crooked teeth for the first time.

They shook hands and with that we were off to find the white Angels van in the parking lot. Nuñez sat up front while Ronnie and I sat in the back. Ronnie was the Angels' fourteenth-round selection—a flamethrowing eighteen-year-old from Pacific High School, in Missouri, whom I'd briefly read about after the draft. He'd had an uneven season but could light up a radar gun—topping out at 94 miles per hour just before draft day. Ronnie was just the sort of player that Michael Lewis, the author of *Moneyball,* would say you shouldn't draft.

We'd been driving along the dusty highway in silence for ten minutes when Ronnie caught me staring at some bruises on his right arm.

"Cigarette burns," he said proudly, holding his arm up closer to my face.

"Yikes," I said, pushing down on the pink mottled skin.

"Me and some buddies got a little crazy at my draft party."

"Looks like it. That must hurt like hell."

"I didn't feel a thing. I was so fucking drunk."

I glanced at Grant, who was tinkering with the radio.

"I basically had my whole high school over to celebrate."

"Must've been a wild night."

"You have no idea." He leaned closer. "I fucked some girl in my hot tub as the sun came up. It was amazing."

"Amazing."

"Oh, I love this song," Ronnie said to Grant. "Keep it."

It was one of Eminem's new songs.

"You got it, Ronnie Ray."

"So, McCarthy," Grant continued, "somebody told me you went to Yale. Is that right?"

"Yes, sir, it is."

"All right, you can drop the 'sir.' I'm not one of your cocksucking Yale professors. I'm a strength coach."

"Okay."

"Now, you're not one of those goddamn Ivy League know-it-alls, are you?"

"No, definitely not. I barely graduated," I lied. I wasn't expecting such a grilling from someone dressed like an eight-year-old.

"Is that right?" he said, looking into the rearview mirror.

"Yeah."

"Good, 'cause I hate a know-it-all."

"Me, too," said Ronnie, staring out the window.

"I didn't go to class and didn't do any work. I just played baseball."

That seemed to satisfy them and we drove fifteen more minutes in silence along cactus-lined streets to Mesa, listening to the local hip-hop radio station.

The minor league facility was a sprawling expanse of land tucked away behind a retention pond in the suburbs of Mesa. Three pristine baseball fields surrounded a large, centrally located glass-walled building and the entire complex was fenced in by orange groves. Rolling hills could be seen in the distance in all directions, but through all the dust, they appeared somewhat faded.

Grant led us into the building and gave Ronnie and me a quick tour of the facility, which included a weight room, showers, and a locker room large enough for more than one hundred players and their equipment. Last we were introduced to the clubby—a middle-aged man with curly brown hair whose job was to clean our uniforms and provide us with breakfast and lunch as long as we were in Mesa. He fitted us for uniforms, including pants, jock straps, socks, and an Angels jersey and hat. Then he handed each of us a pair of sandals.

"Gotta wear sandals in the shower. Team policy. We had an outbreak of athlete's foot a few years ago and it got pretty ugly."

"Gross," mumbled Ronnie.

"I'll take care of you as long as you're here," the clubby continued, "which hopefully won't be long."

He went on to explain that Mesa was where spring training was held every year in March and that if you were lucky you left in April to join one of the minor league teams. Players who needed more time to mature were kept in Mesa, or Purgatory, as he liked to call it.

"You don't want to stay here a day longer than you have to, trust me."

"I don't plan on it," Ronnie said confidently. "I've got a three-year plan. . . . Gotta be in the big leagues by the time I'm twenty-one."

"Good luck with that," the clubby replied.

A moment later Grant appeared.

"Looks like everything's in order," he said. "Let's get you two over to the housing complex. I'm sure you'll want to be rested for tomorrow."

Grant drove us ten minutes across town to a large, adobe-inspired apartment complex. He let me out in front of Building E, handed me a set of keys, and informed me that apartment 8 was mine. "Your roommates should already be in there," he said as I shut the door, "but make sure you knock. You never know what's going on inside these buildings."

I gave a quick knock and used my keys to enter the apartment. Before me was a large living room connected to a kitchen and dining room. It was a big step up from my dorm room at Yale. On the couch playing video games were my two roommates.

"What's up," they said in unison without taking their eyes off the television.

"Hey, guys, I'm Matt McCarthy."

"Mitch Arnold, nice to meet you," said the six-foot-nine behemoth who lay sprawled out over most of the couch. Mitch had a bad case of acne and incredibly long arms. He was undoubtedly a pitcher.

"I'm Quan Cosby," said the more moderately sized roommate, who was African American. He had a cell phone clipped to his ear and a pager attached to his belt. Around his neck was a large gold cross and on his wrist was a shiny silver bracelet. Probably a high draft pick, I thought. Quan, it turned out, had been the Angels' sixth-round selection a year earlier and had commanded ten times the signing bonus of a typical sixth-round pick. He was the 2000 Texas High School Football Player of the Year, a USA Today All-American quarterback, and the Texas State Champion sprinter in the 100 m and 200 m. He'd been offered a full scholarship by the University of Texas to become its quarterback, but ultimately turned it down when the Angels offered him $800,000.

"You got the room with Mitch," Quan said, still fixated on the video game.

"Oh, come on," grumbled Mitch. "He stays with the loser of this game."

"Fine."

I stood with my bags as they played a football video game. After five minutes I decided to sit down. Eventually Mitch prevailed.

"Yes!" he said and stuck his finger in Quan's face.

"Look's like I'm with you, Quan," I said, to no response.

I brought my belongings into Quan's bedroom and pushed my bag under the empty bed. I lay down on the bed, and before I knew it, I was asleep.

"Yo, DUDE," a voice said as I was given a gentle shake. "Get up. Time to go to work." I opened my eyes and realized it was morning. I'd slept through the night without eating dinner or changing my clothes. Thankfully Quan was there to wake me. "Come on," he said. "I'll give you a ride."

I hastily brushed my teeth and scrambled out to his brand-new Harley-Davidson pickup truck. Even at six-thirty in the morning it was terrifyingly hot in Arizona. Quan and I parted ways shortly after entering the locker room, which was full of players milling about in various states of undress. A handful were lying down on large tables being tended to by trainers, others were sitting at a wooden table playing cards, while others were sitting in front of their lockers listening to music or reading the newspaper. The large room contained six rows of lockers and mine was in the back, presumably because I was new. I was in the process of making a protein shake when Grant approached me and said he'd be taking me to get a physical at seven-thirty.

Ronnie and I were the first two draftees to report for duty. The rest were still negotiating their contracts. The two of us once again piled into the white Angels van at seven-thirty, with two veterans: Larry Bowles, a chunky left-handed pitcher from Roanoke, Virginia; and his buddy, a soft-spoken man whom he referred to only as "Pink."

"New guy?" Larry asked. He had a deep Southern accent and his eyes were bloodshot.

"Yeah. You?"

"Nah, gotta get my hand checked out," he said, and I noticed he was cradling his left wrist with his right hand.

"Hit by a ball?"

"Not quite," he said and looked out the window. A few seconds passed before he continued. "I got a call from a buddy last night. Turns out my girl back home has been cheatin' on me. I went out with Pink here and things got a little messy."

"Fourteen shots of whiskey will do that," Pink said flatly.

"When I got home," Larry continued, "I decided to do a little re-decorating."

"He punched a hole in our bathroom wall," said Pink, clearly un-amused.

"They think it might be broke," Larry said, lifting up his hand. "I gotta get it x-rayed."

Before long we pulled into a strip mall and walked into the doctor's office. Ronnie and Larry were seen immediately while Pink and I were told to take a seat in the waiting room.

"So are you here to get an X-ray, too?" I asked as I reached for the latest issue of *People*.

"No, I'm here for a physical," Pink replied.

"Oh, you're one of the new guys, too?" I asked.

"Nope, they make you get a physical when you retire," he replied genially. Pink didn't look a day over twenty-two and the idea of retiring caught me off guard. He had a slight build and was wearing a light blue Ralph Lauren dress shirt with the collar flipped up.

"You're retiring?" The words jumped out of my mouth.

"Yep, the best decision I've ever made. I can't wait to get the fuck out of here."

I was intrigued. "How long have you been with the Angels?"

"They took me in the sixth round last year. Gave me $150,000 to leave college a year early. Big mistake."

"How so?" I asked.

"You'll see," he said, leaning forward to reach for a magazine. "It's brutal out here being away from your family, your friends, your girl. Constantly moving around from one motel to another in little piece-of-shit towns."

"Huh," was all I could muster.

"You'll see. It's a different world out here."

We sat a few more moments in silence, reading our magazines, before the nurse came out.

"Brad Pinkerton, the doctor is ready to see you."

I followed Brad and received a clean bill of health. The physical was fairly extensive, but, as Quan had correctly informed me, no rubber glove was necessary. We were driven back to the baseball complex and Grant escorted Ronnie and me into the office of Tony Reagins, the Angels' Director of Player Personnel. An African-American man in his midthirties, Tony was responsible for the promotion and demotion of the roughly 150 minor league players in the Angels' organization. He was also called the Grim Reaper, because he usually wore black and he was the man you'd face if a pink slip ever mysteriously appeared in your locker. Today he was all business.

"Mesa, Arizona, gentlemen," he said from behind his desk as Ronnie and I sat across from him. "As long as you're affiliated with our organization, you'll report here on March first for spring training. Spring training, gentlemen, will end on April first, at which point you'll be assigned to one of our minor league teams. If you fail to make one of those teams and you're not released, you will remain here in Mesa for what we call extended spring training."

Ronnie and I nodded. This was clearly a speech he'd given a hundred times and he appeared bored with it.

"You do not want to be here, gentlemen. Arizona in the summer is hell. Being in extended spring training means you're on the bottom of the minor league totem pole. And that, my friends, means you're one step away from having to look for a new line of work."

We nodded again. I felt like a child in the principal's office.

"Fortunately for you guys," he continued, "there is a league specifically designed for first-, second-, and third-year players. Our team is in Provo, Utah. You may have been told you're going to Provo. Whoever told you that doesn't know what they're talking about. We're going to evaluate each of you new guys over the next week and then we'll decide who's going to Provo and who's staying here in hell with me. In the meantime, you'll compete with the guys here in extended. Good luck, gentlemen."

As if on cue, Grant opened the door to take us away.

"Did Tony scare the shit out of ya?" Grant asked after we were safely out of earshot.

"Hell, no," Ronnie said. "They didn't give me six figures for nothin'. I know I got some job security."

"And what about you, Yale? I'm sure you've got some Wall Street job if this falls through."

Before I could respond, Grant had changed the subject. "I'm gonna bring you guys over to watch today's workout. It's just a half-day today since we've got a lot of new players coming in."

Walking around the building, I could hear loud voices coming from field 3. As we approached, I saw about forty players being led through various stretches by a young man in full Angels regalia. Three-quarters of the players were Hispanic and the majority of them weren't stretching, they were taking turns smacking one another, yelling, and simulating intercourse with those who were stretching. Nearly all were teenagers.

Ronnie and I sat down in the first row of bleachers.

"Are you kiddin' me?" he said.

A few minutes later, stretching ceased and the players jogged out to their positions. The mood quickly went from playful to serious. I was jolted by the transformation. The players were incredibly talented and made difficult plays look mundane. And I'd never seen routine plays performed with such grace. The biggest surprise, however, was hearing Spanish as the primary language spoken on the baseball field.

"These guys can play," I said to Ronnie. They were significantly better than anyone I'd played against in the friendly confines of the Ivy League.

"I guess," he said.

Three hours passed surprisingly quickly as we watched the players take batting practice and play a seven-inning scrimmage. Grant appeared as the final out was recorded.

"You two should go hit the showers. That's it for the day. Be ready to get after it tomorrow."

We headed for the locker room and sauntered into the shower together. Just as the hot water was coming on, I heard a burst of noise. Fifteen dark-skinned, wire-thin teenagers were coming toward me. Ronnie and I looked at each other like two deer in headlights. They all began singing in Spanish. One began simulating intercourse with the shower handle while another pretended to film it. The two next to me began swinging their large, uncircumcised penises around like fire hoses. Unintelligible Spanish phrases were thrown around with glee. I finished my shower and began to dry off, but soon noticed the veritable gauntlet that had been set up between me and my locker. If I wished to leave I'd have to endure at least a dozen towel smacks. This was the Dominican shower that Blake would later warn me about.

"Never showering with these fuckers again," Ronnie said to me. We chose to remain in the shower until they were all finished. Fifteen minutes later, the last one was gone. Ronnie and I walked out and were met by laughter from the dozen or so American players waiting to shower.

"Gotta be the new guys," one said.

"Baptism by fire," quipped another.

"In the future, I think you'll find it best to wait and shower with us," a third said and we all laughed.

Grant found me as I was changing at my locker and brought me to a small room and had me measured for height (six-foot-one), weight (191 pounds), and body fat (10.85 percent). Quan gave me a ride back to our apartment and I was asleep by eight P.M.

I ARRIVED in the locker room the next day to find a large group huddled around a small bulletin board. The day's itinerary had just been posted. Under "Pitchers" I found my name and the words "Bullpen— 8 A.M." next to it. I had a few minutes to eat a banana and change into my uniform before heading to the large bullpen where I'd seen pitchers throwing a day earlier. With ten pitching mounds, it was five times the size of the one I used in college.

I grabbed my glove and jogged over. Three coaches were waiting for me at mound number 3. Each looked like a carbon copy of the other, forty and trim, wearing an Angels uniform, with a mustache, a large wad of chewing tobacco in the left cheek, Nike running shoes, a clipboard, a stopwatch, and a pair of Oakley sunglasses resting comfortably on the brim of his hat.

"I'm Coach Hines," said the one with the bushiest mustache. "You must be McCarthy. Can I call you Mac?"

"Sure."

The others introduced themselves and explained that they were all minor league pitching coaches.

"Okay, Mac, I want you to throw forty pitches to that catcher down there at seventy-five percent. Don't overexert yourself now. We don't want anyone getting hurt at this stage of the game." The others nodded in agreement.

I leaned over and picked up the baseball. It was noticeably different than the balls we'd used at Yale. Ivy League baseballs had high seams, which were ideal for throwing curveballs and generating movement on a fastball. The ball I was using today had flat seams, which, according to my Yale professor Robert Adair, would produce a straighter, faster pitch. He'd written *The Physics of Baseball* a few years ago and I thought back to reading his book on cold, snow-covered nights in New Haven as I rubbed my left index finger against the seams.

The pitching coaches spread out around me and one pulled out a notepad as I began gingerly tossing with the catcher. Before each toss, I'd indicate what pitch I intended to throw using signals all baseball players are taught in high school. No signal was default for a fastball, using my glove to simulate tipping my cap meant slider, and a jabbing motion with the glove represented a changeup.

The coaches all stood motionless with their arms folded. I threw the first pitch at 75 percent of maximum effort and saw one of the coaches scribble something down. Being evaluated caused me to progressively throw each pitch a little harder than the last. By the fifteenth pitch I was giving it all I had. My body language told the whole story as I grimaced and grunted with every delivery.

"Nice work, Mac," Coach Hines said after I threw my final pitch. A small smile emerged from under his mustache. "Change into your running shoes and join the rest of the pitchers on field two. They're just about to start stretching."

I walked over to the locker room, moderately pleased, and got a drink of water. I was doubled over at my locker lacing up my running shoes when a pair of snakeskinned boots appeared in my field of vision. I looked up to see Tony Reagins, dressed like Johnny Cash, standing before me.

"Walk with me," he said, and we began walking through the empty locker room to his office. A thousand thoughts raced through my head.

"I'll be honest with you," he said as he walked behind his desk. I tightened up. Rarely did enjoyable conversations begin this way.

"I just spoke with Hines, and you know what? He liked what he saw."

I nodded.

"Now, I know you only got a thousand bucks to sign. So . . ." He reached into his desk and produced a green piece of paper. "We're prepared to rework an incentives deal into your contract."

"Thank you, sir."

I quickly read over the stipulations of the offer—a $1,000 bonus for making Double-A, an additional $1,500 for making Triple-A, and $5,000 for making the big leagues.

"Looks great," I said and quickly signed it.

"The Angels . . . we're owned by Disney, you know," he continued. "Have you ever been to Disney?"

"I grew up in Orlando. I used to have a year-round pass."

"So I don't have to tell you that Disney's got some money. If you play like we think you can, well . . . the sky's the limit financially."

I left his office and had a skip in my step for the rest of the morning. I may not have been a top draft pick, but the Angels could tell I was worth more than the thousand dollars they had offered me. I spent the majority of the day doing a pitcher's most thankless job—chasing down fly balls in the outfield while others took batting practice.

Lunch was a somber affair. Two large tables were assembled in the middle of the locker room. Dominicans sat at one table and Americans at the other. I sat with Quan and Mitch, the man-child. A few more new draftees had just arrived and Grant was giving them the tour.

"Fresh meat," Mitch said while chomping on his ham sandwich and looking at the new players.

"You know what that means," said Quan.

"Every time somebody new comes in . . ."

"Somebody old has to go."

We finished our lunch in silence before hustling back out to field 2 for a review of team fundamentals.

After practice, the buzz around the locker room was that a pitcher from Double-A Little Rock who threw 100 miles per hour was being demoted to Mesa for threatening to kill his coach.

I HAD TO PINCH myself when I woke up on my third day in Arizona, as I was roused by a large spider crawling up my right forearm. I'd been warned about the scorpions in the shoes but not the spiders between the sheets.

When I arrived at the ballpark, I saw Larry Bowles cleaning out his locker.

"X-rays came back," he said while folding a pair of jeans. "Angels released me. Said they don't have no use for a guy with a broke hand."

"I'm sorry."

"Nah, man, it's fine," he said, "I gave this game all I got. Besides . . . I got some business to tend to back home."

After lunch, the name above Larry's locker had been replaced with "Saunders." This was undoubtedly for the Angels' first-round draft pick, Joe Saunders, a junior left-handed pitcher from Virginia Tech. He was the twelfth player selected in the country and considered by many to be the finest college pitcher available in the draft. I'd read extensively about him before the draft because he was the pitcher I one day hoped to be. He'd just signed with the Angels for $1,825,000.

Saunders and his entourage showed up an hour later. He was flanked by two well-built men in their thirties wearing jeans and designer T-shirts and he was being given a tour of the complex by an older gentleman in a suit. A moment later the tour ended and his associates were dismissed. Joe went over to his locker and began unloading his bag.

I walked over to introduce myself. Joe was tall with short brown hair, wide shoulders, and a doughy face. Sunglasses were resting on the brim of his Angels hat and he had long arms with large hands. His scouting evaluation on Major League Baseball's official Web site immediately came to mind:

> Extra-large frame. Durable build, large hands, strong. Build similar to Barry Zito. Smooth delivery. Fields position well. Aggressive with riding fastball. Effectively mixes in two-seamer. Slider is more of a slurve with late bite. Changeup is strikeout pitch. Improving every year. Good feel for the mound.

In contrast, mine had read something like:

> Parents are professors. Average fastball, decent off-speed pitches.

"Joe Saunders, Virginia Tech," he said as I extended my hand to greet him.

"Matt McCarthy, Yale," I replied.

"You new?" he asked.

"Yeah."

"Me, too. So, uh, what round did you go in?" he asked, still filing clothes away in Larry's old locker.

"Twenty-first."

"Oh, uh . . . hey, that's nice. Congrats."

He hadn't yet learned how to play it cool. He was like a Yalie who went around asking people what they got on their SATs.

"Congrats on going in the first round," I said preemptively.

"Thanks," he said, placing his Virginia Tech hat in his locker. It was the hat baseball commissioner Bud Selig would one day give him permission to wear in a major league game for the Angels, shortly after the Virginia Tech shootings. "My friends at school are all calling me Joe Millionaire." He was referring to a Fox reality show with the same name in which an average Joe pretended to be a millionaire.

"So, Yale, huh?" he said, sitting down on the chair in front of his locker. "I saw that movie *The Skulls*. Is that stuff true?"

"Some of it."

"Like what?"

"Well, we do have secret societies."

"Yeah? With all the money and the girls?"

"Not exactly," I said. "I think Hollywood took some liberties with the script."

He seemed disappointed. "What about President Bush . . . didn't he go there?"

"Yeah. He came and talked to our team last year."

"And his daughter . . . doesn't she go there?"

"Yes."

"Is she a slut?" he asked perfunctorily.

"Nah," I said, and he again looked disappointed. "But . . . I've seen her get high a couple of times," I lied.

A big smile emerged on his face. I'd spoken the universal language of young ballplayers.

"Nice!" he said, and walked over to a vending machine.

Today's workout had gone just like the previous two—a morning stretch followed by running, throwing, batting practice, defensive work, and an exhibition game. Our last assignment before the scrimmage was to work on pickoff moves and I paired up with Mitch for the drill.

He froze after his eighth throw to me, staring off blankly into the distance. From his facial expression I thought he'd either pulled a muscle or seen a ghost. Turning around I saw a tall, overweight bald man getting out of a truck.

Mitch walked toward me and in a hushed voice whispered, "That's Bobby. He throws a hundred."

"Bobby" was Bobby Jenks—a man who'd attained mythical status in Mesa prior to his arrival. Raised in the backwoods of Idaho, Jenks played only one year of high school baseball before dropping out of school. At eighteen he'd been six feet three inches, 280 pounds, with a 100-miles-per-hour fastball, and was considered one of the most promising talents in the 2000 draft. A projected first-rounder, many teams passed on him because of questions about his character. There were rumors that he was an alcoholic and that he had a history of violence. The Angels took a chance and signed him in the fifth round for $150,000. Bobby was a subject of intrigue for many in the baseball community; everyone seemed to have an opinion about him.

"Jenks could become something special," wrote Baseball America's Jim Callis after the draft, "and he could just as easily go down quickly in flames." Peter Gammons called him a "monster" while others compared him to the fictional Nuke LaLoosh from the movie Bull Durham. From where I was standing, Bobby Jenks looked something like a nightclub bouncer. He quickly disappeared into the locker room and after fifteen minutes appeared on the field with us.

"Well, look who it is," Coach Hines said.

"I'm here," replied Bobby flatly.

"Nice of you to join us, Bobby."

"Just trying to help the Angels win a World Series."

"You're moving in the wrong direction for that, Bobby. All right, we're about to scrimmage. Bobby, you're in charge of broken bats."

The daily exhibition game was pretty boring if you weren't scheduled to throw. Pitchers were assigned odd jobs, like tending to broken bats, chasing foul balls, and manning the radar gun. My job was to hand three baseballs to the umpire between every inning.

A bat was cracked in the fourth inning and I walked over to have a look.

"Check it out," Bobby said softly to me, holding the bat. With his big rosy cheeks and pale skin, he looked much younger than I'd expected and he certainly didn't look like a monster. He held the bat up, showing the fracture from the handle to the barrel. As he did so, I noticed a tattoo under his shirtsleeve.

"You like it?" he asked, rolling up his jersey. On his right arm was a large tattoo of a flaming vampire skull with baseball stitches. It looked ridiculous.

"Nice ink," I said, trying to sound cool.

"You like that?" he asked. "How about *this*!" And he pulled down his left sock to expose a tattoo of a wolf on his ankle.

"You have any tats?" he asked, smiling, as he examined his leg.

"Nah, but I'm thinking about it," I lied. "So you're new around here?"

"Yeah, I just got sent down from Little Rock."

"How was Arkansas?"

"It's no Idaho."

"Of course."

"Me and the coach had some personality issues," he said, looking out at the exhibition game. "He said I threatened to kill him."

"Wow."

"Yeah, I know."

"Did you?"

Bobby looked away from the field and into my eyes.

"It was just a figure of speech. I really didn't mean it."

For some reason, I believed him.

Bobby and I sat next to each other for the rest of the game, talking baseball. He's a good kid, I thought, probably just misunderstood. We went out to dinner that night, burgers at Burger King, and he told me that this demotion was a wake-up call, that he was going to take baseball seriously and stop causing so many problems off the field. And again, I believed him.

Maybe I was wrong. Just months after Bobby told me that he was ready to grow up, an article in *ESPN The Magazine* described how, after a bout of heavy drinking, he had taken a lighter and burned the backside of his pitching hand, as well as parts of both of his forearms. It also told of his fraught relationship with his former agent, Matt Sosnick, who said of Jenks:

> Imagine being in the top five in the world at what you do, and your demons are so terrible that your ability is dwarfed. That's Bobby Jenks. The worst thing that could happen is if he gets to the big leagues. If he gets to the big leagues, he'll free fall. He can't handle success.

The next day, Bobby and I were assigned to pitch back-to-back innings for our team in the exhibition game. He pitched the first two innings and hit 100 miles per hour three times. No one was able to make solid contact with his pitches and he finished without giving up a hit or a run while recording five strikeouts. He was a tough act to follow, but I convinced myself that the batters would have a hard time adjusting to my slower velocity after being geared up for Bobby. I chugged my Red Bull, took a deep breath, and took the mound ready to make my minor league debut.

Perhaps the batters *were* thrown off, because I was able to throw two scoreless innings, allowing two hits while recording three strikeouts. I walked off the field confident in my ability to play baseball professionally, and with every passing day I felt I was inching closer to the big leagues. The Provo team would be announced in two days and I thought I had a strong chance of making it.

"Day's not over," Coach Hines said to me as I filled a cup of water in the dugout. "Ice your arm, hit the weights, and run twenty foul poles."

I changed into my running shoes and walked into the clubhouse, where I found Bobby splayed out on a trainer's table reading a magazine.

"Nice job out there," I said as I sat on the table next to him.

"Yeah," he replied, not taking his eyes off of the reading material.

"Already ice your arm?"

"Nah."

I walked over to the ice machine and filled up two bags for my left shoulder.

"Do you want any ice?"

"Nope."

I applied the ice bags to my shoulder, clumsily wrapped them in gauze, and returned to Bobby.

"What are you reading about?" I asked.

"Me," he said flatly. He put down the magazine and let out a deep breath. "Everybody's got something to fucking say about Bobby Jenks."

"You're a popular guy."

"One day I'm an alcoholic, the next day I'm the second coming of Christ."

I laughed awkwardly, trying to think of how I would describe him.

"I'm a damn bargain is what I am," he continued as he rolled onto his stomach. "Hundred and fifty thousand dollars for a guy with my shit? The Angels piss ten times that much away on Dominican fuckers all the time."

I nodded.

"And what do they do? They send me to this hellhole with guys who don't even belong in pro ball."

It wasn't a stretch to imagine that he was talking about guys like me.

"How many guys can throw a hundred miles an hour?" he asked me as he tossed the magazine on the floor.

"Probably a dozen," I offered.

"How many guys on this *planet* can throw a ball a hundred miles an hour?" he said in a much louder voice as he sat up.

"I can think of one," said a large man with a mop of shoulder-length brown hair as he sauntered into the room and calmly submerged himself in a vat of ice. It was Angels reliever Derrick Turnbow, in Mesa on a rehab assignment. A year earlier he had suffered a displaced fracture of the ulna bone in his right forearm while throwing one of his 100-mile-an-hour fastballs.

"Now, I can't say that I've ever seen you hit triple digits," Bobby said playfully.

"Go to hell, Jenks," Turnbow said as he took off his hat and parted his long brown hair.

From my vantage point, Turnbow looked a lot like legendary Tigers pitcher Mark "The Bird" Fidrych, but the players in Mesa had taken to calling him Ringo, though only behind his back.

"Talk to me when you've pitched a game in the big leagues," Turnbow added.

For the next fifteen minutes we sat in silence, until Turnbow finished with his ice bath and left the room.

"They always said Ringo was an asshole," Bobby muttered to himself.

Clearly Jenks didn't subscribe to the rule that minor league guys should defer to major league players.

"Did you see his arms?" he continued. "He's so roided out it's ridiculous."

"I've seen all those supplements in his locker . . ."

"That's just for show," Bobby continued. "He's juicing."

"You think so?"

"Definitely."

I didn't know what to think. Turnbow did have the physique of an amateur bodybuilder, but I had never actually known someone who used steroids. In a few months' time I would see that Bobby's comment precisely summed up the era we were playing in. No one really knew for sure who was using steroids, but we were all skeptics and we all had our theories. If a guy hit two home runs in a game, he was using steroids. If a pitcher bumped his velocity up a few miles an hour, there was only one explanation. And naturally we were most suspicious of the players we were directly competing against. I didn't give a damn which hitters were juicing, but if you asked me which pitchers were using steroids, I could've given you a list of two dozen players without batting an eye.

And as it turned out, Bobby was right about Turnbow. One year later Derrick Turnbow was the first major league baseball player publicly identified as having tested positive for a banned steroid, 19-norandrosterone, although the ban extended only to Olympic competition and not Major League Baseball.

"I'm done icing," I said as I unwrapped the bags from my shoulder.

"Congratulations," Bobby said as he lay back down on the table.

"Any interest in hitting the weights?" I asked, knowing that there was no chance.

He shook his head.

"I'll let you in on a little secret," he whispered. "Tell 'em you have a bad back and they don't make you do a thing."

"Is that right?"

"Lift weights? Not with a bad back. Run? Not with a bad back. Stretch? You can't with a bad back. It's the life, man."

"That's great," I said halfheartedly as I exited the room and Jenks returned to his magazine. It was the last conversation I had with Bobby Jenks.

Bobby never got his act together with the Angels. Alcohol continued to be a problem for him and he showed up to more than a few games hungover. He would be suspended for a barroom brawl and would later marry a woman he met at the drive-through window of Dick's. In December 2004, the Angels washed their hands of him.

Bobby was claimed on waivers soon after by the Chicago White Sox, who were willing to spend twenty thousand dollars on his million-dollar arm. Chicago provided the change of scenery that he so desperately needed. He made the Double-A All-Star team in 2004, and in 2005 the White Sox called him up to the big leagues. Jenks played an integral role in their playoff victory over the Angels, giving the Sox their first World Series berth in nearly forty years. He would go on to pitch in each game of the 2005 World Series, recording the last out as his teammates charged the mound to celebrate their first title in eighty-eight years. In 2006, he was named to his first All-Star team, the same year that Derrick Turnbow made his first All-Star team, as a Milwaukee Brewer.

Chapter 3

||||||||||||||||||||||||||||||||||||||||||||||||

MY SKIN CAN'T TAKE much more of this, I thought as I slung my duffel bag under the bus. It was a few minutes after four-thirty A.M. and my sunburned body illuminated the aisle as I looked for an open seat. The Provo list had been posted and I'd made the team. Most of the new draftees had by now arrived and many were on the bus to the airport with me. Quan and Joe Saunders would be joining me in Provo while Mitch the Man-child and Ronnie Ray were left behind in hell.

As it turned out, Ronnie's three-year plan never came to fruition. He had trouble adjusting to the daily grind of minor league baseball and never figured out how to harness his blazing fastball. His career gradually stalled and "Single-A Ronnie Ray," as he later came to be known, never advanced beyond Single-A with the Angels, despite his great baseball name.

We were heading to the airport to take a six-thirty A.M. flight from Phoenix to Provo. As I leaned back in my seat, I heard one of the veterans, my future confidant Blake Allen, talking with Saunders. Blake had spent the previous season in Provo before injuring his arm.

"Where we're going," Blake said before spitting tobacco into an empty Gatorade bottle, "there ain't nothin' to do. Don't get me wrong, the place is beautiful—mountains, rivers, crap like that—but there's absolutely nothin' to do. You can't buy alcohol, you can't even buy caffeine. There ain't no bars and everything closes at ten."

Joe shook his head in disapproval.

"It's a college town," Blake continued. "BYU is right there—but the college kids don't act like college kids. They don't drink, don't smoke, don't party. It's absolutely mind-bogglin'."

"Are you fuckin' with me?" Joe asked.

"I wish I could say I was," Blake said seriously.

"I don't get it."

"Mormons."

"Can't say that I know many Mormons."

"They're all Mormons!" Blake continued. "Somethin' like ninety-nine percent. The church runs the goddamn town. We can't even play home games on Sundays 'cause the church says so!"

"Unbelievable."

"This team of ours—the thirty of us on this bus—we'll probably double the number of non-Mormons livin' in Provo."

"And they hate us being there," another veteran chimed in. "They just see us as a bunch of troublemakers."

"Which is not an unfair assessment," Blake said cheerfully. "And you don't even want to know what they think of the Dominicans."

"How about the girls?" asked Joe.

The two veterans looked at each other and smiled.

"Unbelievable," they said in unison.

"Amazing," said another player who'd been listening.

"But you and your million-dollar arm can't get nowhere near 'em, Joe," said Blake mirthfully.

"Why not?"

"Because they're Mormon! You're just a heathen with a fastball, my man."

Soon we were at the Phoenix airport. I should explain that flying is not the normal means of transportation for a minor league ball club. Tony Reagins had booked us a flight to Salt Lake City because from

Mesa, the bus ride to Provo would've been sixteen hours due to a long detour around the Grand Canyon.

Utter chaos was the only way to describe the team check-in at the airport. No one was able to explain to the Dominican players why their bags were repeatedly being emptied and searched. Two young Dominicans, Erick Aybar and Alberto Callaspo, tried to physically prevent one security guard from doing so, and it almost cost us our flight. A handful of security guards rushed to the scene to restrain the players. We were traveling without a coach and without anyone in the vicinity who spoke Spanish well enough to pacify the players, so anger on both sides continued to escalate. A shouting match in two languages quickly ensued and a small crowd gathered around.

"Well, I haven't seen this before," Blake said to me, clearly amused.

Our trainer, Clayton Wilson, a heavyset man with short dark hair who'd briefly played football at Texas A&M, was the only nonplayer traveling with the group. He was eventually able to step in and explain to the Dominicans in broken Spanish that this was a standard procedure, and order was gradually restored.

"I had to deal with a lot of Mexicans in Texas," Clayton said to us proudly as we boarded the plane.

But the episode left me scratching my head. How much did the Angels really have invested in us if they couldn't spring for a translator? Would the Dominicans just be left to fend for themselves all season?

It was a seventy-minute flight to Utah and I spent the majority of it chatting with a second-grade teacher from Phoenix. She was pushing forty, with long blond hair and long tan legs emerging from a light blue dress. Eventually I mentioned that I was on my way to Provo.

"Provo!" she exclaimed, "I grew up in Provo. It's the most beautiful city in the world!"

"I've heard that."

"Provo!" she said again. "I met my husband in Provo. We both went to BYU. There isn't another city in the world like Provo. You're going to love it there."

"Someone was just telling me that," I said.

As we exited the plane she tapped me on the shoulder and said, "Have the best time in Provo. I'm so jealous you're going there."

Our trainer led us through the Salt Lake City International Airport, past store after store hawking discount relics from the Winter Olympics the city had hosted four months earlier. We grabbed our bags and boarded another bus, and as we got settled, a dozen players simultaneously reached for their tobacco.

"I thought I'd never make it through that flight," Joe said to me as he pinched some tobacco into his cheek.

"That felt like ten hours," said another.

I marveled at the Rocky Mountains as we drove Interstate 80 toward Provo. The fifty-mile trip was surprisingly quiet—most players donned headphones while a few spoke quietly on cell phones. Most of the Dominicans were asleep, apparently worn out from the tussle in the airport. We were still without coaches and Clayton stood up as we pulled into the parking lot of the Days Inn Provo.

"All right, guys," he shouted over a few Dominicans in the back of the bus. "The Angels are gonna put you up in this hotel for three days while you look for housing. You've got a few options. One: you can stay with a host family. You'll stay at their home, likely for free, and they'll cook for you and some will even clean your shit for you. But these fuckers are Mormon, so be prepared for that. Two: if you don't want to live with a family, we've got a deal with an apartment complex and it will only cost you $150 a month, but it's unfurnished. I haven't seen the place, but shit, that's cheap. And if those two don't suit you, you can live in the Courtyard Marriott for $40 a night, or

$20 a night with a roommate. It's right next to the field and there's free continental breakfast. Now, drop your stuff off and be back on the bus in twenty minutes."

Thirty minutes later we were headed down Canyon Road to Larry H. Miller Stadium, home of the BYU Cougars baseball team in the spring and the Provo Angels in the summer. It's a beautiful twenty-seven-hundred-seat stadium located at the base of the Wasatch Mountains with six spires behind home plate supporting a white roof that's illuminated for night games. The field is named for a Utah businessman who owns the Utah Jazz, a car dealership, and Larry H. Miller Megaplex Theaters. He would gain national attention in 2006 when he pulled *Brokeback Mountain* from his theaters.

A staff member gave us a tour of the stadium and later the clubhouse, which was a white concrete room shaped like home plate with blue lockers surrounding the perimeter. I located the locker with my name above it and found it fully stocked with three different Provo Angels hats (two blue, one gray), two Provo Angels shirts, a full uniform, and a Provo Angels jacket. There was also a questionnaire that would be used for the media guide, with fill-in-the-blank statements like, "People don't know how much I like . . ." and, "If I could have dinner with one person, it would be . . ."

I sat down on the chair in front of my locker and filled out the paper with a Provo Angels pen. After a minute I looked up and took in my surroundings. In front of me were thirty new teammates from all over the world who were anxiously milling around the room. This was my chance to be on a winning team again, I thought as I looked at the names above the lockers. It was also an opportunity to prove that Biron—the scout who drafted me—was correct when he said I could play in the big leagues someday. On this day it seemed we were all on equal footing with the Angels, and from what Tony Reagins had said, every one of us was going to have the same opportunity to succeed.

I would soon learn that wasn't exactly true.

I'd been assigned the number 21 but was hoping to get 20, my old college number. I walked over to Josh Gray, the Angels' thirteenth-round selection in 2000, who'd been given that number. He was from Oklahoma and had a blond beard. He led the nation in home runs as a high school senior but lost leverage in the negotiating process with the Angels when it was revealed that he'd lost his college scholarship offers due to poor grades. He had a tired look in his eyes, clearly frustrated to be back in Provo for the third straight year.

"Hey, Josh," I said, "would you mind trading numbers with me? I got twenty-one and I was hoping . . ."

"No."

And that was that.

Another staff member came into the locker room and asked us to change into our uniforms for pictures that would be used for the media guide. Several players made a beeline for the sink and began primping. Again I wondered about the Dominicans. How did they know where to go and what to do? Was someone translating for them? Did they speak English better than they let on? Or did they just follow the herd and hope for the best?

I was sitting at my locker, filling out my questionnaire, when I felt a nudge on my left shoulder.

"You're Matt, right?" said the soft-spoken person sitting at the locker next to mine. He was five feet ten and muscular, with shoulder-length blond hair tucked behind his ears and tan forearms that had recently been shaved.

"Yeah."

"I'm Brian. People call me Sunshine."

So this was Sunshine. Quan had told me in Mesa about a player named Sunshine who'd be joining us in Provo. He said he'd been thrown off two junior college teams for fighting—once with a teammate and once with a coach. He'd been acquired by the Angels as a free agent, and word around Mesa was that his signing had been done as a favor to someone and that the Angels had no intention of using him as anything other than a bullpen catcher.

"Nice to meet you."

The glazed look in his eyes gave him the appearance of being stoned. Quan and Mitch had enjoyed speculating on Sunshine's drug habits while playing video games.

"This is all pretty cool, isn't it?" I said.

"It sure is. I can call you Matty, right?"

"Sure."

"Hey, Matty, where you gonna live?"

"I guess I'll try to stay with a host family, but I heard only a couple volunteered this year. That apartment sounds great, but I don't want to have to go out and buy furniture. I'll probably just stay in a hotel until I can find something."

Sunshine's glazed eyes lit up. "Me, too!"

"Yeah, the price is pretty reasonable . . ."

"We should be roommates," he interrupted.

I was not one of the cool kids on the team, so I was frankly a bit skeptical of his offer. I tried to let him down easy.

"The thing is," I said, searching for words, "I have some strange sleep habits. I'm up all night."

"Me, too!"

"The other thing is . . . I'm not such a good roommate. I talk on the phone a lot and I'm not a real people-person."

"Matty," he said, looking deep into my eyes, "you've sold me. I think your personality's fine. I'd be happy to live with you."

I started looking through my locker. "I, uh . . ." but I couldn't find the words.

"Matty," he said, putting his arm around my shoulder, "say no more.

I'll swing by your room after dinner and we can move into the Marriott."

Resistance was futile. I had a new roommate.

A moment later, a forty-eight-year-old man wearing a white and blue Provo Angels uniform entered the room. He had thin arms and legs and a craggy, weathered face and he looked remarkably like Don Imus.

"Everybody, shut the fuck up!" he bellowed, and everything came to a screeching halt. We all sat in the chairs in front of our lockers and listened intently.

"I'm Tom Kotchman," he continued, while pacing in the center of the room, "and I'm your manager. I've been with this organization for nineteen years. Longer than any other coach in this goddamn organization." He was chewing on a toothpick and appeared to be ticked off. "I've got a few rules that you're all gonna live by. One: Be on time. If you're late, don't bother showing up. And I mean that. Just stay the fuck home. Two: Play hard. If you're not gonna play hard, stay the fuck home. And three: Don't fart on the bus." He gave a hint of a smile and everyone chuckled. "I mean that," he continued after the laughter died down. "We've got some fifteen-hour bus rides and I don't want to be smelling your ass all the way to Montana."

He spoke for a few more minutes about dress codes, the other teams in our league, and how to handle ourselves in an interview. "No matter what happens on the field or what is said in this clubhouse, I will never make you look bad with the media. If you give up a home run and we lose the game, I'll take the blame. I will never, ever throw one of my players under the bus."

Kotchman walked across the room and took some of Blake's chewing tobacco.

"You guys know my kid?" he asked, looking around the room. He was referring to his son, Casey Kotchman, the Angels' first-round selection the previous year. He was rated by *Baseball America* as the top prospect in the entire organization and many were already penciling him into the lineup in Anaheim as a future Hall of Fame first baseman.

"The Angels offered me a coaching job with the big-league club. I could be their goddamn first base coach if I want to. I could stand there with a stopwatch all day and eat fancy fucking food and stay at the nicest damn hotels. But I turned 'em down. And you wanna know why? Because I want to work with young people and I want to develop players. I don't give a shit about the finished product. I want to make people better."

Several players nodded, as if to acknowledge his sacrifice.

"Last thing," he said. "It's against league rules to leave the bench in the event of a fight. That said, I expect all of you to be in the thick of things if a brawl ever breaks out. You've got to protect one another."

We all looked around. For the first time, the individuals in the room felt like teammates. He started to leave, but stopped just short of the large blue door. "And for you city guys," he said with a smile as he raised his arm, "this is how you make a fist."

SUNSHINE AND I MOVED into the Marriott that night and I stayed up late watching baseball and listening to him talk. He prattled like a man who needed to get a few things off his chest. Many of the stories involved his relatives, some of whom he described as drunks, others as Mafia-connected. With every new story it seemed he was trying to outdo the last. It was hard to know how much of it was true. He described his sexual trysts in Mexico and his stops at various junior colleges and how they all seemed to end with a physical altercation that wasn't his fault. He asked a bit about Yale, but mostly he wanted to

talk. I fell asleep around two A.M. in the middle of his story about diving with sharks in Australia.

I woke up early the next day, well before Sunshine, because I
wanted to explore Provo. I picked up a map of the city and a brochure
for Brigham Young University in the lobby and set out on foot. I found
myself gasping for air as I walked down the street: sitting at nearly five
thousand feet, Provo was the highest altitude I'd ever lived at. Pitchers
suffer at increased elevation, I could hear Professor Adair saying, because long fly balls turn into home runs.

I was hoping to reconcile what I'd heard about BYU students with
the brochure in front of me. BYU students are required to adhere to a
strict honor code, it said, that forbids extramarital relations, alcohol or
drug consumption, and cheating. The code also requires that students
be religiously active, wear modest clothing, and avoid outlandish hair-
styles. It was a far cry from Yale, where the university sponsored dances
like "The Exotic Erotic" where the less you wear, the less you pay to
get in.

I saw a large Y that appeared to be painted on the side of a mountain, and it reminded me of Yale, so I decided to walk toward it. I
learned that this was Y Mountain and that the Y, standing 380 feet
high and 130 wide, was one of BYU's most cherished symbols. It was
made of whitewashed concrete and had been on the mountain for almost one hundred years. After inspecting the Y, I decided to turn
around and walk to the Mormon temple.

Walking down the street, I noticed that Provo looked like any
other town in America—with one exception: everyone was white.
Well, 89 percent of the population was white, according to the 2000
U.S. Census. Before long, I was standing in front of the temple. With
its broad base and tall, piercing spire, it looked a bit like an old television with an antenna. I walked up to the front entrance, where I was
told I that the temple was for Mormons only and that I wouldn't be

allowed in. The elderly man at the door explained that the architec-
ture represented the fiery pillar that the Lord used to guide the Israel-
ites through the wilderness under Moses. "You know, from the book of
Exodus," he said.

I stepped away from the temple and took a seat on a bench. In a few
hours I had to be at the field for Media Day. I began thinking about
what I wanted to say, how I would compliment the city of Provo and
discuss the beauty of the temple and the magnificence of the Y. Be
original, I told myself. Every athlete uses the same clichés, but I was
going to be different.

At 3:45 we gathered in full uniform in the third-base dugout in
preparation for the interviews. At 4:00, representatives from the local
newspaper and radio and television stations appeared on the field. Like
patients in a waiting room, we sat restlessly as they huddled on the
pitcher's mound. One of the men emerged and came over to us with a
message. "We would like to see Joe Saunders for interviews. The rest of
you are free to go."

Embarrassed, we got up and walked back into the clubhouse. Players immediately began cursing Saunders.

"They want to talk to him just because he's a first-rounder. Fuck
him."

"What the fuck has *he* ever done as a professional?"

"He's a first-round draft pick. Big deal. He's never even thrown a
pitch in pro ball."

"Fuck him."

We changed out of our uniforms and into practice attire. Kotchman wanted us back on the field in thirty minutes for our first team
practice. When we returned to the field, Saunders was still conducting
interviews. Kotchman gathered the team together on the pitcher's
mound and started to bark instructions when he noticed Joe was missing. Someone pointed to Joe, sitting in the third-base dugout with a

rotund, bald man with bushy black eyebrows from the local radio station. Joe was smiling and speaking into a tape recorder when we all
looked over. Kotchman covered his mouth with his hand and muttered
something unintelligible.

He walked over to the two of them and with a smile said to the reporter, "The sooner you get your *fat* ass out of here, the sooner I can do
my job!"

The man's eyes grew wide and he shut off the tape recorder. Joe got
up and jogged over to join the rest of us on the field while the reporter
waddled away in a huff. He didn't dare say anything back to Kotchman, who was now sauntering over to us.

"Jesus fucking Christ!" he screamed. "Joe, if you ever pull that shit
again . . . I will personally see to it that you are unable to have children. Do you understand me?"

"Yes, sir."

"Jesus fucking Christ!" he repeated. "If you start pulling that prima
donna bullshit I will personally stick my foot so far up your ass you'll
wish you'd never been born."

"Yes, sir."

"I don't give a *fuck* if you were a first-rounder!"

Tom Kotchman had been quite the ballplayer in his youth. He'd
been working his way up the minor league ladder like all of us, Sunshine said, when he was hit in the head by a pitch and never fully re-
covered. After he retired, he was hired by the Angels to become one of
their Florida scouts as well as one of their minor league managers. He
truly enjoyed developing players and he resented Joe because, well, Joe
didn't need a lot of developing. Most scouts believed Joe was ready to
pitch in the big leagues when he was still in college.

The following year in spring training, I would meet Tom Kotchman's
son, Casey, the Angels' first baseman. He was quiet, courteous, and

soft-spoken—the antithesis of the typical first-round draft pick and of his father. He'd signed for $2 million, but didn't talk about his money, and he drove a Volkswagen Beetle "because my dad would've killed me if I bought something flashy."

Practice was a monotonous affair for the pitchers. We did a few fielding drills but spent most of the time in the outfield chasing down fly balls during batting practice. Afterward, Sunshine and I walked to T.G.I. Friday's with Kelly Sisko, a left-handed pitcher from Westville, Oklahoma. He was tall and thin with short blond hair and crooked, tobacco-stained teeth.

"We'll have three shots of whiskey and three Bud Lights," Sisko said to the waitress as she handed us the menus.

"All right, boys," she said, "but that's it for the next hour."

"Excuse me?" Sisko replied, taking a sip of his water.

"Two drinks an hour, gentlemen. House rules."

"It's not enough that they dilute the fuckin' things. Jesus Christ," said Sisko as the waitress walked away. Sisko was referring to the fact that in Provo you could purchase only three-two beer—beer that was 3.2 percent alcohol, compared with the rest of the country, where it was closer to 5 percent.

Sisko started in on a story about his family's farm in Oklahoma while I looked around the restaurant. I felt like I was an extra in a Swedish tourism video—nothing but blue-eyed, blond-haired, smiling faces milling around the room.

"I've been drunk the past fourteen nights in Mesa," continued Sisko proudly. "It looks like I'm gonna have trouble makin' it fifteen."

"I'm sure we can find a place that'll serve an inbred fuck like you," said Sunshine, smiling as he read the menu.

The waitress soon returned with our drinks and I noticed that several people turned to stare at us as we raised our shot glasses and Sisko made a toast to us "being in the most bizarre place on earth." Before she walked away, Sunshine struck up a conversation with our waitress that bordered on embarrassing.

"So are you local or from around here?" he asked.

"Uh, I'm not sure. Both?"

"Yeah, you are, I *knew* it!"

He told her he was a baseball player and was new to the area and she told him a few places he should visit in town. As she walked away, he turned to me and winked.

"Why are you wasting your time?" I asked dismissively. "I'm sure she's Mormon."

A large, mischievous grin emerged.

"Have you ever heard the term 'Jack Mormon'?" he responded.

I hadn't.

"It's someone who looks Mormon . . . and acts Mormon . . . and even tells you they're Mormon and goes to the temple and shit."

"But . . . ?"

"But they drink and have sex like the rest of the world. They just do it without anyone knowing," said Sunshine.

"Really?" I said naïvely.

The waitress returned with our food and told Sunshine she'd love to come to one of our games.

"Matty, my boy," he said, taking a sip of his beer and putting his arm around me, "you may have gone to Yale, but you have a lot to learn."

Sunshine left his number on the bill and received a call from the waitress around eleven P.M., after she'd finished her shift.

"I knew it!" he said as he hurriedly put on a pink long-sleeved dress shirt and a pair of Diesel designer jeans. In an instant he was gone. I nodded off to sleep and found him sitting on the bed next to me in a towel the following morning.

"Jack Mormon?" I asked.

"Jack Mormon," he confirmed. "She made me promise not to tell anyone. It was hilarious."

"Hilarious," I agreed.

At 12:45, Sunshine and I walked to the field and boarded the team bus to Panda Express for a "Meet the Owners" luncheon. One by one, players tossed their makeshift spittoons into the trash as we filed into the empty fast-food restaurant and were escorted to an equally empty backroom where the two owners were waiting for us. They were both lawyers, a man and a woman in their midforties who'd always dreamed of owning a baseball team. As we sat down, they stood up. They were well dressed and looked like they'd just come from the office.

"I'd like to welcome you all to Provo," the man began. "We are incredibly excited to have you here and we're expecting the best season yet for the Provo Angels!"

He paused for applause but there was none.

"Before we get started with lunch, I wanted to talk a little bit about the logistics of playing here. First, we may ask you from time to time to make public appearances in the community. This may be an autograph-signing session or an appearance to promote one of our sponsors—like spending a morning at a car dealership or something. For those of you who are new to the area, I just want to remind you that Provo is an incredibly conservative and religious town. You will be under a microscope for the duration of your stay here. We've had some incidents in the past and it reflected very poorly . . ."

Sunshine winked at me.

"What Jim is trying to say," the female owner interrupted, "is don't do anything to embarrass us. Don't curse and don't get into fights. Don't carouse and don't chase after girls. Now, let's have some lunch!" The two owners laughed awkwardly and sat down.

Waiters quickly brought out our meal—a hearty helping of General Tso's tofu, a meal I'd had many times at Yale. The tofu craze, it soon became apparent, had yet to reach minor league baseball.

"What is this shit, tofu?" one player asked loudly and everyone laughed.

Everyone was picking at the food and eating around the tofu.

"I never met the man," Sunshine said, stabbing a piece of tofu with his fork and holding it up to me, "but I can assure you that the general never ate tofu."

After lunch we packed into the bus with Coach Kotchman and headed down the street to Utah Valley State College. It was Sunday and we were prohibited from using our own facilities in Provo so we had to leave town and head to the neighboring city of Orem. Tomorrow was Opening Day and it would be my last chance to prove myself before the starting lineup was determined.

A few minutes before practice was to begin, I found myself standing next to Kotchman, whom I still hadn't introduced myself to.

"What's up, bitch?" he said to me with a stern look.

"Not much, Coach, I'm . . ."

"Don't call me 'Coach.' I don't call you 'Player,' do I? Call me Kotch."

"Yes, sir. Kotch, I'm Matt McCarthy."

"I know that. You think I don't know that? Nice to meet you, Matt." He was now smiling.

Quan, Joe, and Sisko walked over toward us.

"What's up, bitches?" he said to them with his arms extended like a pastor delivering a homily. It was comforting to know I wasn't the only bitch on the team.

"Let's go!" ordered Kotch, and all thirty players quickly gathered around him. "I want to introduce you to your other coaches," he said, pointing at the man standing next to him. Kernan Ronan, a slender man of about forty with thin lips and wire-framed glasses, was the pitching coach. He'd made it to Triple-A with the Giants but an injury had permanently sidelined his career. In medical school I'd meet a man by the name of Paul Farmer who was the spitting image of Kernan. Farmer was the subject of the best-selling book *Mountains Beyond Mountains* and was one of the world's leading authorities on infectious diseases. He and Kernan couldn't have been more different, despite their similar facial features.

"And this is Black Magic," Kotchman said, pointing to our African-American hitting coach, James Rowson.

Kernan rounded up the pitchers and brought us over to first base.

"Here's the deal," he said, pushing his glasses up on his small nose. "Tomorrow is Opening Day. Hector Astacio is going to be our Opening Day starter."

A wide grin emerged on Hector, a nineteen-year-old from Hato Mayor, Dominican Republic. He was the cousin of Mets pitcher Pedro Astacio and had been signed by the Angels as a sixteen-year-old.

"We've decided Hector is starting the first game, but we haven't decided who's starting games two, three, four, and five. That's what we're going to try and figure out today."

We were going to use a five-man starting rotation, which meant that there would be five starters and eight relievers. I'd been a starter all through college but it was doubtful that I'd be able to remain one in the minors.

"Everyone is going to throw twenty-five pitches today and then I'll talk to Kotch and we'll decide who's going to be a starter and who's a reliever."

One after another, we got up on the mound and threw to a catcher.

I remained surprisingly calm during the audition. No one was using a radar gun, so I just focused on throwing strikes.

"Nice work," said Kernan after I had finished. "Were you a starter in college?"

"Yes, I was."

"When's the last time you started a game?"

"Last month."

"And how many pitches did you throw?"

"About a hundred."

"And do you think you could start this week?"

"Absolutely."

I sized up my competition as one pitcher after another took the mound. Most threw harder than I did but many were wild, even bouncing some pitches to the catcher. And when each finished, Kernan asked them the same questions he'd asked me.

At the end of practice, Kotch rounded up the team and told us to run three laps around the field because someone had picked up a resting baseball with his glove instead of his bare hand. "I know it's a little thing, but it drives me nuts. I'm going to teach you guys the right way to play the game, so help me God."

We regrouped after the jog, all panting heavily.

"Not used to this elevation?" he asked triumphantly. "It'll toughen you girls up. Now, here's the starting lineup for tomorrow . . ."

He proceeded to read the batting order and finished by announcing that Hector would be the Opening Day starter. "The other starting pitchers will be Holcomb, Williams, Marquez, and McCarthy."

I flinched when I heard my name. I had my hopes, of course, but I hadn't really expected to be named a starting pitcher. My paltry signing bonus alone seemed enough to relegate me to a career of pitching out of the bullpen, but perhaps I had underestimated myself. I slapped my left thigh and immediately thought of calling my parents and Breslow. The big leagues seemed one small step closer.

Sitting on the bus back to Provo, I heard a number of players discussing the pitching assignments.

"This is total bullshit."

"The coaches don't have a clue what they're doing."

"I've been a starter my entire life."

"And who the *fuck* is McCarthy?"

Chapter 4

||||||||||||||||||||||||||||||||||||||||||||||

MOST PROFESSIONAL LEAGUES begin their seasons in early April, as the lilacs are emerging from their dull roots, but the Pioneer League is different. Opening in mid-June and lasting until mid-September, the league is designed for players who've just been drafted and is famous for its particularly grueling schedule of seventy-six games in eighty days. To make matters worse, the eight-team league is spread out across the western United States and Canada and all travel is done by bus. The Southern Division included the Provo Angels, Idaho Falls Padres, Casper (Wyoming) Rockies, and Ogden (Utah) Raptors; while the Northern Division was comprised of the Billings (Montana) Mustangs, Great Falls (Montana) Dodgers, Missoula (Montana) Ospreys, and Medicine Hat, Alberta (Canada) Blue Jays.

Around nine A.M. on Opening Day I received a call from Steitz. He was marooned in Beloit, Wisconsin, playing for the Brewers' Single-A affiliate in the Midwest League, and he wanted to wish me luck with the season. An hour later, Breslow called.

"Looks like we're rivals," he said.

"Haven't we always been?"

"No, I'm playing for the Ogden Raptors. It's like an hour away from Provo. Our teams are rivals."

"What are the chances?"

"So how are things in Mormonville?"

"Pretty good . . . I just got named one of the starting pitchers."

"Really?"

"Yeah." I took great pleasure in hearing the surprise in Craig's voice. "I'm the only lefty in the starting rotation."

"What about Saunders?"

"Somebody said they baby all the first-rounders. Don't let them play for like a week until they get their bearings and everything. How about you?"

"They put me in the bullpen, but it's all good. . . . As long as I get in the game I don't care if it's the first inning or the seventh."

"Exactly."

"Well, I'll be seeing you in a few days."

"Is that right?"

"We play each other in four days."

I did a quick calculation. "I'll be pitching against you guys!"

"Great, I hope we tear you to pieces!" he said before hanging up the phone.

Baseball, the old saying goes, is a game of failure. But on Opening Day, everyone has a blank slate. Gone are the painful slumps and disappointing defeats of the previous season and in their place are an unbridled optimism and the sometimes irrational belief that this year, for once, everything will come together. For many, Opening Day is the happiest day of the year. It marks the time before the aches and pains of the season set in, before the mental aspects of the game begin to toy with your psyche—it's the time when, in theory, baseball can still be fun. For me, it was a chance to be on a winning team.

Home games were to start at 7:05 P.M. except on Mondays, which the Mormon Church had designated "family night." As such, our games were to begin at 5:05 P.M. so that our fans could make it home in time for dinner with their loved ones after the game.

We arrived at the field at noon and the mood in the clubhouse was decidedly different. Players who normally ignored each other were talking baseball and slapping high-fives. Guys competing for the same position were trading tips, and, most shockingly, a few American players were trying to interact with some of the Dominicans, though it looked more like a game of charades than an actual conversation.

Kotch came in at 12:30 and the room fell silent. He had a solemn look on his face and quickly began what would be a two-hour meeting. In the first hour we received a detailed scouting report of our opponent—the Casper Rockies. Since I was pitching on Friday in Ogden, I didn't listen too intently as Kotchman reviewed the strengths and weaknesses of each opposing batter. The second hour dealt with our signs, bunt plays, pickoffs, and base running. Clayton put us through some stretches from 2:30 to 3:00 and we took batting practice until 4:15. With a little less than an hour before game time, we were told to go back into the clubhouse and relax.

At 4:30, Clayton entered the clubhouse beaming with excitement.

"You boys are in for a treat!" he said as we ate peanut butter and jelly sandwiches. "In about ten minutes you're all going to head down to the right-field corner. There are thirty biker dudes on Harleys waiting for you. You're each gonna hop on the back of one of those bikes and they'll drive you around the field from right field to third base. You'll be dropped off at third. From there, you'll walk to home plate, grab the microphone, and introduce yourself to the crowd."

We all smiled. This sounded a bit ridiculous and a bit fun—I'd never been on a Harley before.

"But please, for the love of God, don't say anything stupid. Remember, we're in Provo and these people walk around with sticks permanently jammed up their asses."

After a team photo with our mascot, an overgrown Saint Bernard named Charlie (it was a play on *Charlie's Angels*), we went through with the introductions. The fans, all 1,971 of them, got a big kick out of it and no one managed to say anything stupid. After "The Star-

Spangled Banner," the mayor walked out to the mound and threw out the first pitch.

After all of the preliminary hoopla, the actual game turned out to be a sluggish affair—at least from where I sat. Because I was not pitching, I was given the assignment of filming each of our hitters from the corner of the dugout as they took their at-bats. In theory it was a simple task, but it was made much more difficult because each hitter had a separate tape and I hadn't learned everyone's name yet.

The lead changed hands several times, with the Rockies jumping out to a 7–4 lead on a double by Ryan Shealy, a six-foot-five first baseman from the University of Florida who now plays for the Kansas City Royals. We were able to score two runs in the bottom of the ninth before our third baseman struck out to end the game.

Walking back to the clubhouse, I was interested to see how my teammates would react to the loss. I'd heard that in the minors, no one cares if you win or lose—that it was all about personal performance. The clubhouse, it turned out, was silent. Gone were the laughter and high fives. They had been replaced by an overwhelming feeling of gloom. Most sat with their heads in their hands and I began to wonder if they were putting on a show. It was only one game, for God's sake. We did this all the time at Yale.

Kotchman entered ten minutes later to address the team. I was expecting sound and fury but what we got was a soft-spoken, fair analysis of the game.

"I saw a lot of positives out there," he said. "We made some mistakes, but for many of you this was your first professional game. You guys played hard and ya did good. Keep your heads up."

We hit the showers—Dominicans first, of course—and made plans for a team dinner at Applebee's. Exiting the stadium we encountered a throng of nine-year-olds in search of autographs. One youngster approached me with outstretched arms holding a ball and a pen.

"Hi, there," I said as he came to a stop just inches from my leg. "Would you like an autograph?"

"Yes. Yes, sir."

I was grinning from ear to ear. In my four years at Yale I had never been asked to sign a thing.

"Who should I make it out to?"

"To my best friend."

"Your best friend? What's his name?"

"His name is Sporty."

"Sporty? That's an interesting name."

"He's my hamster."

I smiled and pressed the pen to the ball. My first autograph, and it was to a rodent.

"So TELL ME what you think of this idea," Sunshine said to me as he stared at himself in the large mirror in the center of our hotel room. He was wearing a canary-yellow bathrobe with his initials embroidered on the back. "My girlfriend bought a car from some dealership in Arizona two months ago. Turns out it's a total piece of shit and breaks down on her all the time."

"Okay," I said, eating some of last night's leftovers.

"She went to the dealership to complain and they basically said it wasn't their problem. They said it was fine when it left the lot."

"That's too bad."

"So here's the plan."

"The plan . . ."

"I told her to drive the car to Mexico and just leave it there. With the keys in it and everything." His face was flush with excitement.

"We'll do it in the off-season so I can follow her down there and drive her back to Arizona. What do you think, smart guy? Pretty good plan?"

"What is the plan?"

"We'll report it as stolen and the insurance company will give us a big chunk of change."

"Oh, you mean insurance fraud."

Sunshine looked perplexed. He was still staring at himself in the mirror.

"No, Matty, no. Not insurance fraud."

"I'm pretty sure that's fraud."

"It might be, Matty," he said, stroking his long blond hair, "but I think it'll work. But I'm gonna need your help." He fastened his robe and sat on the bed next to me. "We really complement each other well," he said, putting his arm around me.

I muted the television.

"Thanks, Sunshine."

"That's why I want you to be my alibi."

Sunshine explained my role in the caper—something about my renting a time-share in Tijuana—for the next twenty minutes as we left the hotel and walked the mile or so to the ballpark. When I entered the clubhouse, Kernan was standing in front of my locker.

"Be ready to pitch in relief tonight," he said. "It'll be a good way to get your feet wet for your start on Friday."

He caught me off guard and within minutes I was sitting on the toilet. Whenever I get nervous, my bowels start acting up. It had happened only a few times in college and I had hoped I'd grown out of it.

Rather than spending the game in the dugout filming our hitters, I watched the game from the bullpen with the other relief pitchers. Being in the bullpen, it turned out, was a lot of fun. There was no coach there, so no one paid much attention to the game and nobody talked about baseball. Instead, the conversation hovered around the sexual conquests of a few lotharios on the team and the chances that any one of them could score with a Mormon. It was like being back at Kangaroo Court at Yale.

We jumped out to a six-run lead in the first inning, which meant there was a slim chance that any of us would be called on to pitch in a pressure situation.

"Looks like a light night for the bullpen," said Brett Cimorelli, a tall, broad-shouldered twenty-year-old with a shaved head and a crooked smile. In medical school I would discover the term for his ailment—Bell's palsy. He was one of the most religious players on the team, keeping a Bible in his locker, and he was incredibly sensitive about his smile. Brett spent half the year with the Angels and the other half serving as the field-goal kicker for Florida State University. He'd missed a crucial field goal in the National Championship Game a year earlier and had been widely maligned in the media.

"It really tested my faith in God," he once said to me while we were talking about it. "I've read the Bible every night since I was a little kid, but I stopped reading it for a good month after I missed that kick."

Before I knew it, the Rockies had scored two runs and the bases were loaded. Conversations about girls were cut short and I saw Kernan looking at us from the dugout. He was trying to decide whom he should signal to start warming up. Before the first game, Kernan had assigned gestures to each of us so he wouldn't have to jog down to the bullpen to tell one of us to get ready. If he wanted Justin Fuller, he'd rub his stomach as if he were full. If he wanted Anthony Reed, he'd pretend to read a book. For Heath Luther, he'd extend his arms like Superman in midflight (in reference to Superman's nemesis Lex Luthor). Sign selection had been a group effort and players took great pride in coming up with one that stuck. When Kernan wanted me, he'd pretend to shoot a bow and arrow because a sportswriter once referred to my pitching mechanics as employing a "bow and arrow–like arm action." In case you're wondering, it wasn't a compliment.

The next batter reached base on a single to right, and with that, Kernan was shooting the arrow in my direction. Then he spun his index fingers around each other quickly to indicate that I should get ready in a hurry. Sunshine was serving as the bullpen catcher and I started throwing to him in a hurry. "Let's go, let's go," I said to him after he took a few seconds to throw the ball back to me. I was getting nervous and praying that my bowels would stay in check.

The next batter walked and Kernan again looked at me. I tipped my cap to indicate that I was ready. Kernan relayed that to Kotchman, who strolled out to the mound. On his way, he pointed to the bullpen, indicating that he was making a pitching change. I took a deep breath and jogged out onto the field. The lights seemed much brighter on the field than they did in the bullpen. Kotchman was waiting for me at the mound. He handed me the ball and said, "Relax."

I nodded.

"You know the situation. Bases loaded, no outs. Now, go get 'em." He slapped my butt and walked off the mound.

I tried to ignore the two thousand screaming fans, but I found it difficult. The most I'd played in front of at Yale had been about a hundred. The supportive fans of Provo were now all chanting, "Let's go, Matt! Let's go, Matt!"

The foremost thought in my mind was "throw strikes." I couldn't walk the first batter I faced, as it was a cardinal sin for a reliever to have control problems. My first pitch was a fastball on the outside corner.

Smack! The ball barely missed my ear as Florentino Nuñez, an eighteen-year-old from Santo Domingo, Dominican Republic, laced a single up the middle and two runs scored. Welcome to the minors.

Flustered, I decided to avoid the outside corner and throw an inside fastball.

Whack! The ball was ripped 380 feet for a double off the left-field wall. Two more runs scored. Battered but not broken, I decided to change my plan of attack. I fed the next two hitters a steady diet of sliders, inducing two groundouts. Regaining a bit of confidence and wanting to establish my fastball, I threw two more fastballs that resulted in back-to-back hits. I got the last batter to pop out on a change-up. Clearly, my fastball wasn't fooling anyone.

I walked off the field and into the dugout with my head down. This was not the first impression I was hoping to make.

"You're going back out there," Kotchman said to me.

I sat in the dugout trying to make sense of what had happened. The catcher, Alex Dvorsky, and his bulging forearms took a seat next to me. He was from Cedar Rapids, Iowa, and in the year I played with him, I never heard him speak about anything other than baseball.

"You gotta pitch by color," he said, putting his hand on my knee.

"Huh?"

"Dominicans and blacks can't hit curveballs," he said earnestly. "Throw the Americans fastballs and changeups."

It was the first time I heard this advice but it wouldn't be the last. The next inning, I took Dvorsky's advice and it paid off. I retired all three batters in order and came off the field feeling a bit better about my night, though still disappointed.

"That's it for you, kid," Kotchman said as I walked into the dugout. I'd pitched two innings and given up five runs. Two were charged to me and three were charged to the pitcher before me.

In accordance with team policy, I returned to the clubhouse and hopped on the stationary bike for half an hour. That was followed by a brief weight-lifting session and then it was back to the showers. I was changing into my street clothes as the final out of the game was recorded. We'd come out on top, 16–8.

Kotchman was upbeat in his postgame speech and didn't bother to mention my poor performance. He was trying to keep morale high. Walking out of the stadium, I faced another round of autograph seekers.

"Who are you?" each child would ask as he handed his ball to a different player.

"Matt McCarthy," I said to one as I scribbled my name.

"Oh, yeah, I remember you," one of the older kids said. "The outfielders tried real hard to catch all those balls that were hit off you . . . but they were just hit so far."

"And hard!" added another, handing his ball to me.

Sunshine came over and, as he was apt to do, put his arm around me.

"Let's go get something to eat," he said. "The peanut gallery can be brutal."

WE ROUNDED OUT the series with the Casper Rockies by winning the next two games and it was in the locker room that Kotchman reflected on our first four games.

"This was a good series for us. You guys played well, for the most part, and were able to take three of four from a good ball club. We play Ogden tomorrow, and if there's one team in this league I wanna beat, it's them. They're our arch-fucking-rivals."

We all nodded. It was a bit odd being told who our rivals were.

"They'll draw about five thousand people when we come to play," he continued, looking around the room. "They got the rowdiest fans in the league and the drunkest fans in the league. You ain't in Provo anymore. There's no two ways about it. . . . It's a hostile fucking environment."

He paused and reached for a pinch of tobacco. "They'll make banners about ya and they'll throw stuff at ya. They don't care. So you better come ready to play." He walked around the room for a while making eye contact with each player. Then he walked over to a table in the center of the room and slammed his fist onto it.

"If there's one team in this goddamn league I wanna beat," he said through gritted teeth, "it's those bastards from Ogden! I take it person-ally every time we lose to those sons-a-bitches."

And with that, he walked out of the room. I grabbed my wallet and moseyed over to Blake.

"What's the deal with Ogden?" I asked.

Blake looked around the room and laughed when he confirmed that Kotchman was indeed gone.

"Have you ever seen Kotch with his hat off?"

"No."

"Do you know why?"

"I don't."

"It's because he's going bald. He's got this whole comb-over thing going on and he never takes his hat off."

"So."

"If you notice, Kotch never comes out to join us for the national anthem. He goes inside the clubhouse or into the bathroom. Any-where so he doesn't have to take his hat off during the song in front of thousands of people."

"I see."

"The fans in Ogden picked up on this last season and started heck-ling him about it. It drove him nuts, but he would never show it. They said all kinds of crazy shit and kept it up throughout the year. At the end of the season, we were playing a game at their place and a mes-sage appeared on the JumboTron right before the game. It said "HEY, KOTCH, WHY DON'T YOU JOIN THE REST OF US FOR THE NATIONAL ANTHEM?"

"Wow."

"Needless to say, there's been bad blood ever since. After the game, Kotch flipped out. I'd never seen someone so mad. It was the craziest postgame speech ever. He flipped over tables and shit."

"Jesus."

"You're starting against Ogden tomorrow, right?" he asked, punching me lightly on the shoulder.

"Yeah," I said gingerly.

"Well, don't put too much pressure on yourself," he said, smiling to himself. "It's only one game."

I JUMPED OUT OF bed the next morning. I was still riding high from being named one of the starting pitchers and I couldn't wait to take the mound that evening against Breslow's team, the Ogden Raptors, which was the only unbeaten team in the league. I called Craig after breakfast to see how he was doing.

"Haven't pitched yet, but Ogden's pretty cool. Better than Steitz described it."

"Of course it is. New England will always be his home. By the way, how's he doing?"

"I haven't heard from him, but the word around the organization is not good. I think he's lost his fastball."

"I'm sure he'll find it. Have you heard this stuff about our teams being rivals? Our coach hates you guys."

"Yeah, it's pretty funny."

"I guess, unless you're on our side and have to deal with him flipping out."

"I gotta warn you, we have the best hitter I've ever seen—Prince Fielder. Batting practice for him is like a home run derby. And he's only eighteen."

"Great."

At one P.M., Sunshine and I walked to the field to board the bus to Ogden. It was our first road trip and before we could leave we were each assigned a piece of team equipment to take with us. Kelly Sisko and I were dealt the trainer's trunk, the most cumbersome piece of equipment known to man. Because the handles were broken off, we were forced to kick, push, and drag the sixty-pound trunk (which contained every bandage and muscle stimulator on the market) about a quarter of a mile before loading it onto the bus. When we were all settled in our seats, Kotchman got up to address the team.

"You all know how much I hate the team we're playing today," he said, looking like he'd just taken a bite into a lemon. "What they did last year was unforgivable." He slammed his left fist into his open right palm. "We must win today!"

I stared at the headrest in front of me. I was terrified of letting the man down.

Kotchman signaled to the bus driver and we started on our journey to Ogden. Then he reached into his bag and pulled out a movie. There were two types of movies we could watch on the bus: stand-up comedy acts and professional wrestling. Today's selection was *Chris Rock: Bigger and Blacker.*

Once in Ogden, we entered the visitor's clubhouse from behind center field. It was a far cry from the comfortable room we'd grown accustomed to in Provo. We unloaded our equipment in a small, dank faux-wood-paneled room that had been recently used to store spare lawnmowers. There was a smell of gasoline and many players began covering their noses with their shirts.

"Let's get out on the field," ordered Kotchman. "Batting practice begins in thirty minutes."

As I got up to leave, Kotchman pointed at me. "McCarthy, you stay in here and relax. It's a big game tonight."

So I was left to relax alone in the makeshift clubhouse, amid the sedative powers of gasoline vapors. Before I knew it, I'd fallen asleep in my chair.

Kotchman stormed into the clubhouse at six o'clock, an hour before game time.

"McCarthy, let's go over the scouting report."

"I'm ready."

"Now, usually I give a fairly detailed scouting report, but Ogden doesn't need one."

"All right."

"I'm sure you've heard of Prince." He was referring to Prince Fielder, the eighteen-year-old son of former Tigers All-Star slugger Cecil Fielder. *Baseball America* rated him the top power hitter in the draft, but at five feet eleven and 286 pounds, many teams had worried about his weight. The Brewers were willing to take a chance and signed him to a $2.4 million contract.

"Everyone's scared of Prince," continued Kotch, "but here's the thing. . . . The kid can't hit! They're scared of him because of his daddy."

I nodded.

"He looks more like a linebacker than a baseball player. He's got breasts, for God's sake. Do not be afraid to pitch to him. He's got a slow bat and he doesn't hit the fastball well. Bottom line . . . he's a cripple at the plate."

This was not the scouting report I'd expected and had a hunch it had something to do with the JumboTron incident.

"The rest of the players . . . they got nothin'. It's really a weak lineup. And that's it. Go out there and throw strikes. They really don't have many quality hitters."

This scouting report couldn't have been more different from the hour-long player-by-player scouting report that we'd received for the Rockies.

"All right, I'll go after 'em."

"I'm gonna let you throw three or four innings tonight, so give me everything you got."

"Absolutely."

And with that, our meeting was over. He got up, walked into his makeshift office, and shut the door.

After what seemed like days of waiting, I finally walked onto the field to begin my warm-up tosses in the outfield. The Ogden fans, living up to their reputation, immediately began heckling me.

"Why don't you go have a beer, you fucking Mormon!"

"I hope you burn in hell, you stuck-up Mormon asshole!"

"Go back to Provo . . . and bring all your wives with you!"

I smiled at the last comment and the fans must have noticed, because I was heckled about my wives for the rest of the game.

At 7:00, the national anthem was played and all eyes turned to Kotchman. This time Kotchman joined us along the first-base line, and when he took off his cap, all fifty-one hundred in attendance cheered, including Breslow, who was standing on the third-base line. After the song he gave me a quick nod and returned to his dugout.

My legs felt like jelly as I walked out to the mound amid the heckling. Dvorsky had just reminded me to "pitch by color," and I agreed. The first batter was Mario Mendez, a twenty-year-old from Las Barias, Dominican Republic. Dvorsky put down the sign for three straight sliders and Mario missed each one, whiffing badly on strike three. Next up was Callix Crabbe, a diminutive second baseman from the Virgin Islands. I'd never thrown six straight sliders to start a game, but that's what Dvorsky called and I got Crabbe to ground out. This game was going much better than my previous appearance. The next batter was yet another Dominican, Manuel Melo, a lanky outfielder from Cagua, Venezuela. I threw him a first-pitch changeup, something

I'd never done before, and he popped out to left field, ending the inning.

"Prince is leading off next inning," Kotchman said to me as I entered the dugout. "Go after him."

When Prince lumbered to the plate, I did a double take. He was nearly as wide as he was tall. I threw him four consecutive fastballs and he took each one of them, running the count to 3-1. Dvorsky called for another fastball, but I shook him off, opting instead for a slider. The slider missed and the umpire called ball 4, awarding Prince first base.

"Goddamn it!" Kotchman yelled from the dugout. There's an old baseball adage that you should never walk the first batter of an inning because he'll inevitably score, and Fielder was no exception. When I came off the mound at the end of the inning, the Raptors were ahead 1–0 and Kotchman was furious.

"You walked him on a *slider?*" Kotchman said, sticking his finger into my chest.

"Yeah."

"Why the fuck did you throw him a slider?"

"He'd just seen four fastballs. I wanted to mix it up."

"You wanted to mix it up," he said incredulously.

"That was the plan."

"I think you're scared."

"I'm not scared."

"Yeah, I think you are." Kotchman was raising his voice and everyone in the dugout was now watching.

"I don't like to throw the same batter the same pitch five times in a row."

"Because you're a pussy."

I had to stick up for myself but I also realized he was my superior and I wasn't going to win this one.

"I'm not a pussy."

"Jesus Christ! Be a man and challenge him."

"It won't happen again. If you want Prince to see five fastballs, I'll give him five fastballs."

It was still 1–0 when Prince came to the plate again. I threw him two high fastballs and quickly fell behind, 2-0. I started my windup and delivered a third fastball and Fielder took a hellacious cut, sending the ball to deep right field. It landed just below the top of the wall and Prince had himself a double. I finished that inning without any more damage and retired the lineup in order in the fourth, striking out the last batter I faced. I knew it was my final inning and I came out of the game trailing, 2–0.

I received a few handshakes when I came into the dugout, including one from Kotch.

"It's still early," he said and walked away. It left me wondering if he was referring to the game or the season. I went to the clubhouse and went through my usual postgame routine. When I emerged from the shower, it was the seventh inning and we were winning, 6–3. Players were all smiles in the dugout as it looked like we would beat our supposed rival.

But then the wheels came off. Our relief pitchers gave up seven runs in the eighth inning and we lost, 10–6. Everyone walked solemnly from the dugout to the clubhouse, where I was waiting with the fumes.

Kotchman was the last to enter the clubhouse.

"Fuck!" he screamed, kicking a cooler, sending ice and Gatorade all over the room. I froze in my chair. He punched the side of a locker and kicked the cooler again, sending it flying into the wall. Then he slowly leaned over and picked up the cooler and threw it across the room. We were all taken aback. I held my breath as he strutted back and forth like a toreador. He took a deep breath and began criticizing each player individually, starting with those closest to him.

"Hancock! This ain't fuckin' T-ball anymore," he said, addressing our third baseman. "If you keep playing like that you'll find your ass out on the street!"

"Cosby! You've gotta learn how to bunt. You ain't a power hitter, son. Learn how to fucking bunt!"

I was next.

"McCarthy, I thought you pitched scared to Fielder, but then I saw Bailey's performance," he said, turning to the pitcher who came after me. "And he was even more scared than you were. Bailey, what the fuck were you doing out there?"

I got off easy.

Then Kotchman took off his jersey and spiked it in the center of the room. Several players jumped back, as though the uniform might bounce up and hit them. He started to yell something else, but stopped in midsentence and walked out to the bus. The room was silent and everyone had blank looks on their faces. I had never seen a coach so upset; Stuper would never have behaved this way. The two pitchers who'd given up all the runs in the eighth inning had their heads in their hands.

After a few minutes, Dvorsky stood up.

"We just gotta go after it tomorrow. Every day's a fresh start."

The bus ride back to Provo was a long one. It rained the entire way and no one said a word, not even the Dominicans. An hour and a half felt like two days. We pulled into the parking lot of our stadium at 12:15 A.M. and unloaded. As we were cleaning up the bus, the driver offered to take us back to the various hotels we were staying at. We put our uniforms in the wash, and as the last player was climbing back onto the bus, Kotchman emerged.

"Get off the bus," he said without emotion. His face was pale and his eyes were bloodshot. "You guys are walking home."

And that's exactly what we did.

"WE PLAY SIXTEEN GAMES against the Raptors this year," Quan said in a low voice as we pulled into Lindquist Field in Ogden the next night. With a sweeping view of the Wasatch Mountains in the distance, it looked remarkably like our field. He put down his handheld video game and looked me. "Is Kotch gonna go nuts every time we lose to them?"

"I think so," I whispered.

"I don't have to put up with this crap." And he was right. With the full scholarship at Texas waiting for him, he was one of the few players who had something to pursue if baseball didn't work out.

When a coach beats up on a team, his players usually do one of three things—rise to the challenge, implode, or disengage—and Quan was starting to do the latter. He was one of the fastest and most athletic players I'd ever seen, but there seemed to be one problem—he wasn't very good at playing baseball. He struck out far too often and he didn't have a strong grasp of the fundamentals of the game. It came as no surprise when I saw him playing football for the University of Texas a few years later, making a crucial reception in the National Championship Game, helping his team win the title.

There would be no pregame speech today. Instead, Kotchman simply walked into the dreary cellar of a clubhouse, tacked the starting lineup to a bulletin board, and walked out. He was giving us the silent treatment. Kotchman was widely respected in the organization, but these did not seem to be the actions of a stellar coach. It occurred to me that all of this could be an elaborate ruse on his part, to see who could perform under pressure, and that ultimately he didn't really care about Ogden. That this really was about developing players.

If that was the case, his strategy didn't seem to be working. Astacio had a difficult time with the Raptors, giving up three runs in the first inning. When he walked into the dugout, Kotchman glared at him and said, "I need better from you."

In the next inning Erick Aybar made a hard tag on Prince Fielder for the third out, and when Aybar led off, he was hit with a 90-mile-per-hour fastball between the shoulder blades. No one thought much of it as it was likely retaliation for a hard tag on their best player. But that all changed two innings later when Aybar was again hit with the first pitch he saw.

"Did you guys see that?" Kotchman said. "Are you kidding me? Fuck!"

A few of my teammates yelled at the pitcher, but he didn't acknowledge them.

"Astacio," Kotchman said from across the dugout, "I want you to bean the leadoff hitter next inning. Do you hear me? Hit him in the ribs with the first pitch."

Hector didn't respond.

"Did you hear me?"

Hector took a deep breath and quietly said, "I'm not going to hit anyone." It was surprising to hear perfect English coming out of the mouth of a Dominican.

"What did you say?"

"I said I'm not going to hit anyone."

"What?"

Kotchman could hardly believe his ears.

"That's not how I play the game."

"Listen to me," Kotchman said as he walked toward his pitcher. "You are going to hit the next batter you face or I'm taking your ass out of the game. Do you understand?"

The third out was made and Astacio jogged out to the mound without responding to Kotchman's demand. I couldn't wait to see what would happen. I understood where Kotchman was coming from—teammates had to stick up for one another—but I respected Astacio for having the balls to stand up to him.

The dugout was aflutter with speculation as Astacio threw his final warm-up tosses. We all looked on as Kennard Bibbs, an outfielder from Houston, Texas, stepped into the batter's box.

Astacio wound up and delivered a fastball right down the middle for strike one.

All eyes turned to Kotchman, who shook his head and called time-out. He walked out to the pitcher's mound and took the ball from his pitcher. His day was done. No one greeted Astacio when he entered the dugout—not even Clayton, whose job it was to wrap the starting pitcher's arm in ice. Astacio grabbed a bag of ice and headed for the showers.

When I walked into the clubhouse an inning later to use the restroom, I saw Astacio sitting alone at his locker with his head in his hands.

"*Hola*," I said awkwardly. It was my first attempt at a conversation with a Dominican.

"Hi," he said, looking up at me briefly before averting his eyes. His black cheeks were puffy and it looked like he'd been sobbing.

"Kotch put you in a tough spot out there."

"I know what he was trying to do," he said softly. "I'm not stupid."

"Yeah."

"I know we have to stick up for one another. I know that."

I nodded.

"And now there's thirty guys out there who think I only care about myself."

"Don't beat yourself up over it," I said, patting him on the shoulder.

He sat hunched over in his chair, stiff as a board.

"It's just that . . . that's not the way I play the game. I'm not out to hurt people."

He looked into my eyes as I searched for the right words.

"That's good, man. No one's gonna fault you for that."

"You never know what can happen when you hit somebody," he said and his gaze returned to the floor. "I've seen guys who never re-cover. I couldn't live with that. If I ended someone's career because a coach told me to . . ."

I thought of Sunshine's story about Kotchman—how a high fast-ball had ended his career—and I wondered how he could seem so un-troubled about having Astacio hit someone.

"I think people will respect that. I do."

"You do?" he said, looking up at me.

"Sure."

"It's just that . . . Kotchman isn't who I answer to at the end of the day. There's a lot of people who come before him."

"You mean God?"

"Yes, I mean God," he said, sounding somewhat annoyed. "I have to answer to God and my family before I even think about Tom Kotch-man."

"That makes sense."

"I know how this team works. I know what you guys think of us. We're the Dominicans and you're the Americans. I know what it means to be a second-class citizen. But you guys don't know anything about me. You think we're a bunch of idiots with gold chains who only care about ourselves."

"That's not true."

"Well, I did what I thought was right," he said as his eyes welled up, "and now I have to live with it."

"You did what you thought was right. People will understand."

I walked out of the room knowing that no one would understand.

With the score 11–2 in the eighth inning, Kotchman decided to send a message to our struggling pitching corps by bringing Sunshine in to pitch.

It had been difficult for Sunshine to get warmed up in the bullpen. He was the bullpen catcher, and when it was time for him to get ready to pitch, there was no one there to catch for him. Undaunted, Sunshine played catch with me for a few minutes before jogging out to face his first hitter.

He looked almost comical on the mound. He took off his hat several times to run his hands through his long blond hair before finally toeing the rubber. With his stocky, muscular build, he was the antithesis of the typical pitcher. To me, he looked more like a professional wrestler.

"This should be interesting," Brett Cimorelli said to me in the bullpen as Sunshine began his windup.

"I can't believe Kotch put him out there," said another.

Sunshine fired six straight fastballs and got the first batter to ground out and the second batter to strike out.

"Well, I'll be damned," said Blake.

It was now Sunshine's turn to face Prince Fielder.

"Be ready, boys," said Sisko before accidentally spitting some tobacco onto his shoe.

Sunshine threw a fastball down the middle of the plate and Fielder swung through it. He took off his cap and again ran his fingers through his hair. He stepped back on the mound and threw another fastball that Fielder fouled off down the left-field line. Sunshine quickly got back on the mound for his third pitch—another fastball—which Fielder hit weakly to the shortstop for an easy out.

I jogged down to the dugout to congratulate Sunshine. He'd pitched to Fielder the way Kotch wanted me to—and it had worked.

"Nice job with Prince," I said as Sunshine reached for a cup of water.

"Thanks. Which one's he?"

"Prince Fielder."

"One of the guys I just pitched to?"

"Do you know any of the guys you just faced?"

"No," he said, happily drinking his cup of water.

"The big fat kid!" I said.

"Oh, yeah, that big fat kid. He should mix in a salad every once in a while."

Six years later I thought back to Sunshine after reading an article in the *New York Times* about Prince Fielder's new diet. He had just become a vegetarian and was now debating the merits of edamame beans versus cucumber aioli.

Ignorance is bliss, I said to myself as I walked back to the bullpen. Perhaps there was some wisdom in Sunshine's approach to pitching and maybe he was right, maybe I did have a lot to learn.

Despite his success, this would be Sunshine's only appearance all season.

We were finally put out of our misery in the ninth inning when the last out was recorded. Having lost, 11–2, we knew we were in for some postgame fireworks from Kotchman. I was just hoping he wouldn't throw the water cooler in my direction.

We all sat silently at our lockers. After half an hour of waiting in the methane-infused room to be yelled at, it became clear that Kotch was not going to address the team. So we took our showers and headed for the bus, where we found Kotchman sitting in the front seat reading a magazine.

There were no assigned seats on the bus, but everyone always sat in the same place. Coaches and staff were in the front, followed by white

Americans, black Americans, and Dominicans in the back. I usually sat up front with the white Americans, though sometimes I'd break the color barrier and sit with Quan.

About twenty-five minutes outside of Provo, we all heard a loud commotion coming from the back of the bus. Several of the players were arguing in Spanish and we all turned around to see what the fuss was about. It was the first time anyone had spoken on the bus after a loss. The yelling soon turned to laughter and the episode was over in a matter of minutes.

When we pulled into the parking lot in Provo, Kotchman got up and quietly walked to the back of the bus.

"Junior," he said calmly to our backup catcher from Bonao, Dominican Republic, "what was the score tonight?"

Junior was one of three bilingual players on the team.

"Eleven to two," he replied.

Kotchman slammed his hand into a headrest.

"Then why the fuck were you talking?"

Junior sat expressionless.

"It doesn't take any goddamn talent to shut the hell up."

Junior nodded.

"Jose," he continued, suddenly calm again, "what was the score tonight?"

"Eleven to two," said the six-foot-six pitcher from Puerto Plata, Dominican Republic.

"Then why the hell were you talking?"

He continued this line of questioning with each Dominican player, using a translator when necessary. Then he threw a bag down the aisle of the bus.

"If you assholes lose tomorrow," he said soberly, "I'll run you so hard you'll wish you'd never been born."

I tiptoed off the bus, happy not to have been hit in the crossfire.

THE NEXT DAY WAS the final game of the series with the Ogden Raptors. Down two games to none, we were just trying not to get swept. But a number of Ogden fans brought brooms to the game to remind us of that embarrassing possibility.

Matching Ogden run for run, the score was tied, 4–4, through nine innings. I was hoping to see Breslow pitch, but he was never brought into the game. We scored two runs in the top of the eleventh and held on to win, 6–4. The win improved our record to 4-3, but, more important, it meant that we wouldn't have to dodge water coolers in the clubhouse or run to the point of submission.

"No speech," Kotchman said as we sat at our lockers. "Just shower and get on the bus. We gotta get moving."

It was six P.M. and we had a six-hour bus ride to Idaho to look forward to. We were about to begin a four-game series with the Idaho Falls Padres and I was slated to start game 3.

The mood on the bus was decidedly upbeat as most players talked on cell phones, played cards, or watched the feature presentation, *Andrew Dice Clay Live! The Diceman Cometh.* I spent the first part of the ride staring out the window, mulling over what little I knew about Idaho. My thoughts turned to Sun Valley and Ketchum and Hemingway. From there my thoughts drifted to Yale, where I first learned about the controversy surrounding the naming of Idaho. When Congress was considering the creation of a new territory in the West in the early 1860s, an oddball lobbyist named George Milling proposed "Idaho," which he said was derived from a Shoshone language term meaning "gem of the mountains." Thirty years later the land would become the state of Idaho, despite Milling's admission that he simply made up the name. But my memories of reading about Idaho in Sterling Library were abruptly interrupted by Kotchman, who was now standing in the center aisle with a big smile on his face.

"Call me the Diceman," he said, doing his best Andrew Dice Clay impression. He was holding his toothpick like a cigarette and had his collar flipped up. I'd never seen him so jubilant. Card games were halted and cell phones were closed.

"Hickory, dickory, dock, some chick's been sucking my cock . . ."

Everyone started to giggle, especially the Dominicans.

"Clock struck two, dropped my goo, dumped the bitch down the next block!"

A riot of laughter erupted. Kotchman walked by me and reached out his palm. I slapped his hand.

He was now walking up and down the aisle, slapping high fives, yelling out "Oh!" and pretending to fight with some of the Dominicans. He wasn't yet finished with his Diceman act.

"Panties? You shouldn't be wearing panties, darling. D-D-Don't you read the gynecological reports! You get that . . . that . . . that moisture build-up which leads to . . . you know . . . the yeast thing."

Players were up on their seats, howling with laughter.

"I mean, you're making bread down there, baby. And after the guy eats a loaf and a half, he gets full!"

Kotchman gave a few more high fives and shed the Diceman routine as he returned to the front of the bus.

"We'll be pulling into the hotel around midnight," he said in his usual stern voice. "Get some food and go to bed. We got a big game against the Padres tomorrow. Nothing good happens after midnight. I mean that."

It was now dark out so I decided to get some sleep.

We made it to the Idaho Falls Comfort Inn around twelve-thirty A.M. and quickly unloaded the bus. I'd been assigned a room with Leonardo D'Amico, a Dominican player from Maracay, Venezuela, who spoke no English. We walked to our room in silence, and after dropping off our bags he pointed to a bed and left. I found Sunshine and we went out in search of food. An hour later, I was alone in my room, slowly falling asleep as I watched a show documenting the life and times of Billy Bob Thornton.

D'AMICO'S SNORING woke me up early, so I decided to do some sight-seeing. The town was rather small, but there must have been fifteen car dealerships and at least that many car repair shops. And between them was sprinkled the occasional fast-food joint and discount clothing store. It was a far cry from Hemingway's Idaho. I made my way down to the town's biggest attraction, the Snake River, and took a seat. It was about thirty feet across and the water appeared black with a swift current.

We'd been playing for a week and I really hadn't stopped to take it all in. Sitting before the winding expanse of water, my mind started to wander. I'd pitched in two games with mixed results, but I now felt confident that I could perform at this level, although I wouldn't be able to use my fastball as much. I was certain I could handle the grind of playing in a different town every few days, and the bus rides really weren't so bad. My coach was probably crazy, I decided, but he wanted the best for us. I thought about my teammates—the strange mix of Southerners and Dominicans—and how we really were two separate teams playing for the same maniacal, mercurial manager. And I didn't see how we could ever come together to be anything more than that.

I took a leisurely lunch by the river before returning to my room to take a nap. It was 2:00 and D'Amico was still sleeping, so I set my alarm for 4:00 and joined him. At 4:45 we boarded the bus and took the short ride to McDermott Field. From the parking lot the stadium appeared very old—it was built in 1940—the kind of park they'd use when Hollywood wanted to make a film about baseball from a bygone era. The

outfield wall was made of wood paneling and there was no padding to
protect players who crashed into it. The bleachers were all rusted, and
paint was chipping from nearly every corner of the stadium.

We brought our equipment to the visitor's clubhouse, but the first
players to enter told the rest of us to wait outside. Two inches of brown
water blanketed the locker room because a pipe had recently burst.
How recently, no one knew—and why the water was brown, we could
only guess.

Aside from the water, the clubhouse was in terrible condition.
Wires dangled from the low ceiling, the foundation was cracking, there
were only four showers to accommodate thirty players, and the entire
room tilted to the left. Kotchman surveyed the scene.

"Change in the dugout," he said curtly.

We waded through the brown muck to reach the dugout—a six-
foot-high cage large enough to house a team of ten or twelve, not
thirty. We had to duck each time we entered or exited the dugout, with
Saunders having to learn the hard way.

Surprisingly, I heard nary a complaint from my teammates. It made
me wonder if I was a snob or if they were simply used to playing in such
conditions.

Coming into the series, the Idaho Falls Padres had a record of just
1-6 while we found ourselves at 4-3. From his pregame speech, Kotchman was clearly expecting us to have our way with them.

"If you guys lose today," he said as we all squeezed like sardines into
the tiny dugout, "I'm bringing your asses out here tomorrow at eight
A.M. and we'll do some running."

Someone groaned. It was probably Quan.

"Does someone have a problem with that?"

No one responded.

"I'll run you motherfuckers so much tomorrow you'll be begging for
your release."

The game was close until the eighth inning, when they pulled away and won, 5–1. As soon as the game ended, I saw Kotchman walk over and say something to our equipment manager, Smitty, who'd been seated in the first row of the stands.

"Well," he said, slapping a clipboard into the fence, "I'll see you pieces of shit out here bright and early tomorrow morning. Better bring your running shoes."

He started to leave the dugout, but he'd forgotten to tell us something.

"And another thing. Don't bother to bring your uniforms over to Smitty's room tonight. I told him not to wash your uniforms. You guys stink and I want you to be reminded of it tomorrow."

THIS TIME KOTCHMAN'S BARK proved to be worse than his bite. We showed up bleary-eyed at eight A.M., expecting to run all morning, but were told to run eight laps around the field and get ready for batting practice. As always, batting practice proved to be a colossal waste of time for the pitchers, as we stood in the outfield for two and a half hours chasing down fly balls.

The workout ended at eleven-thirty and I was soon back in my motel room wondering what I should do until game time. I still wasn't used to the large expanses of free time in the middle of the day. D'Amico had gone out for lunch with the Dominicans, so I was left alone to watch television. Around one o'clock I heard a knock on my door. It was Blake. He wanted to go down to Snake River and was looking for someone to join him. I was happy to get out of the room.

"How ya likin' it so far?" he asked as we walked under gray skies down the highway.

"Pretty good so far. I wish I could have a few pitches back, but . . ."

"Ya live and ya learn."

"Yep."

"Places like this remind me of Alabama," he said, looking at a used-car dealership by the highway.

"You know, I lived in Alabama."

"Bullshit," he said, giving me a wide-eyed grin.

"I did. Oxford, Alabama."

"You sure don't sound like it."

"I lost the accent, I guess."

"Bull . . . shit. Are you messin' with me?"

"I swear. Five years in Oxford and five years in Birmingham."

"I met my wife in Oxford."

"It's a great town."

Actually, I couldn't say for sure if it was a great town. I'd lived there when I was quite young and the only thing I'd learned about it was that in 1961 an angry mob of its citizens had attacked a bus of Freedom Riders who were advocating civil rights, which prompted JFK to provide federal protection for their ride to Jackson, Mississippi.

"It is a great town," he agreed.

Soon we were at the river and Blake was looking for rocks to skip.

We each threw a couple in silence before we heard the first rumble of thunder in the distance.

"God, I miss my wife," he said, as much to himself as to me.

"Yeah," I said before throwing another rock.

"You married?"

"No."

"You have no idea, man."

"You're right."

"Some days I wonder what the hell I'm doin' out here."

"Yeah?"

"Actually, most days I wonder what I'm doin' here. My arm is killin' me, I've already had surgery, I'm on the disabled list, and there's no end in sight. I could stay on the disabled list forever."

"It's better than having a real job," I offered.

"You think so?"

"Sure."

"I don't know, man. Travelin' from town to town. Playing with a bunch of illegal immigrants and a crazy fuckin' coach. Missin' my wife, missin' my kid. Not seein' my kid for half the year. You're tellin' me that's better than being home with my family."

"No, I'm not saying that."

"It's weird, man. You spend your whole life livin' one way and thinkin' one way. You have everybody telling you you're the next big thing. And you believe it. And come draft day, somebody cuts you a huge check and says you're gonna be a big leaguer one day. And you believe it. You believe every word of it and it becomes who you are."

"Sure."

"But then you play awhile, you see what the competition is, and you start to wonder."

"I've been out here a week and I wonder."

"And then you stop believin'."

"Yeah."

"And then you get angry."

"Angry?"

"Yeah, angry. Angry that you been lied to. Angry that you gotta play baseball for some maniac coach who treats you like shit. Angry that half your team is a bunch of migrant farmworkers who have more money than you do. Angry that this game is keepin' you away from everyone and everything you care about."

I nodded.

"But I tell you what, as soon as I retire . . . I know I'm gonna be kickin' myself."

We stood a few more minutes in silence before Blake said he needed to get some tobacco from a convenience store.

"You want some?" he asked as he surveyed his options in the 7-Eleven.

"Nah, I'll pass . . . maybe next time."

"You never tried the stuff, have you?"

"No."

"And you're from Alabama?"

"I know. I didn't get the full experience."

We walked back to the motel amid light rain and an imposing sky. An hour later I was back in my room watching television with Blake when a commercial for New York governor George Pataki's reelection campaign came on. Why this was airing in Idaho, I'll never know.

"He was our commencement speaker," I said to Blake, who didn't respond.

The commercial ended with a statement from Pataki's daughter Emily.

"She was one of my classmates," I continued.

"Oh, yeah? You date her?"

"No."

"Was she a slut?"

"I don't think so."

"But you're not sure?"

"I guess we can never be sure, right?" We both laughed.

Governor Pataki had given the commencement address in New Haven just a few weeks earlier, speaking about globalization and its implications for the twenty-first century. He called on all of us, as new Yale graduates, to embrace globalization and to think about how we could play a role in the new global economy. If Pataki could see me now, I thought, as Blake turned the channel to *America's Funniest Home Videos*.

We arrived back at the Padres' dilapidated field to find that we had three new teammates. All were undrafted free agents who'd been passed over in the draft and were offered contracts by the Angels afterward. All three happened to be pitchers, raising the number on our squad to sixteen. It was like finding out I had an extra set of in-laws.

The three new pitchers sat alone in the dugout as we jumped to an early lead against the Padres. We cruised to a 7–1 victory and Kotchman was in a much better mood as we got on the bus.

"You guys played good," he said with a hint of a grin, "but we've still got a long way to go. Some of you are struggling right now . . ."

He paused for a moment, trying to fight back a smile, but it was no use.

"It might be time for some of you to go out and get yourself a slump buster. Gotta be at least two hundred and fifty pounds . . . so you don't even know you're in there."

Kotchman thrust his hips and the bus erupted in laughter.

I had just come across the term *slump buster* in *Maxim*. Curt Schilling had been asked about it and explained it like this: "If you're struggling with your hitting or any aspect of the game, there's a way that baseball players believe you can relieve your negative karma. You go out and fornicate with a woman who might be of less than appealing visual quality, I guess is the way to put it. The key to slump busting is alcohol intake before the excursion."

My girlfriend was two thousand miles away, but this option seemed extreme.

After the game, we went out as a team to dinner at Denny's. As soon as we sat down, a group of players began taking turns trying to spot female customers who would qualify as slump busters. In the middle of the meal, Felix Nuñez got up and met a woman in the parking lot. She wasn't obese, but she wasn't particularly attractive. We could all see him talking to her from our booths.

"What the hell can they be talkin' about?" asked Sisko.

"He doesn't even speak English," said Blake.

"I'll tell you what he's doing," said Kotchman merrily. "He's taking my goddamned advice. Go ugly early, gentlemen. No sense waitin' all night for the girl of your dreams."

Chapter 5

||||||||||||||||||||||||||||||||||||||||||||

I WAS TENSE when I woke up the next morning. I would be making my second start of the season that evening and my bowels were already acting up. I spent an hour on the toilet before I could even think about breakfast. After a bowl of Cheerios, it was back to the toilet. In medical school I would learn that I suffered from irritable bowel syndrome, but at this point, I just thought it was a case of the nerves.

Kotchman again gave his pregame oration from the cramped dugout.

"It would be in your best interest to play well today," he said, looking down the row, making eye contact with every player. "Donny Rolen is going to be here for tonight's game. For those of you who don't know, he's the director of scouting for the Anaheim Angels. He's the one who made the final call when it came time to draft each and every one of you."

He paused.

"If you play poorly today," he continued, again looking down the row at each one of us, "you'll make him look bad. That would not be a good career move."

I was beginning to think that Kotchman's plan was to put slightly more pressure on us each day. And it seemed to be working, as his speech sent me straight for the toilet.

As I emerged from the cramped stalls, I ran into Tim Becwar, a talk-show host from KOVO 960 AM in Provo. He was the host of the

Angels' daily hour-long pregame radio show and he traveled with us on the bus. Tim was a balding, thin man with glasses, and he was always impeccably dressed. He had a rich baritone voice and enjoyed an occasional drink and he was a favorite among the players, who'd dubbed him Backdoor Becwar, despite the fact that he wasn't gay.

Tim was glowing as he came over to me.

"Wait till you hear this, Matt."

"What's up?"

"We had this caller during the show today . . ."

"The crazy Mormon lady?"

"No, not the crazy Mormon lady. But a woman called in and she asked for your number."

"My number?" I said.

"She wants to know if you'll live with her."

"She wants to know if I will live with her."

"Yes! She's offering to be a host family, but only for you."

"Just for me."

"Yes."

"Is she single?"

"No. She's got four kids. She's in her midthirties and she lives two miles from the ballpark."

"Looking for a father figure?" I asked, only half-jokingly.

"No! The husband's sister went to Yale or something and they've offered to host you for the summer. Free of charge. And they said they'd provide food and transportation."

"Really?"

"I know how much you guys make. You should take it."

"Are they Mormon?"

"Of course."

"You still think I should . . ."

"Here's her number," he said, shoving a Post-it note into my hand. "Call her if you decide to do it."

It was getting close to game time so I had to find Sunshine to get warmed up. As we threw the ball I told him about the offer to live with the Mormon family.

"You should definitely take it," he said.

"Are you sure? I feel bad ditching you at the Marriott."

"Matty, it's a great offer. Take it. I'll be fine."

"You're not just saying that?"

"No."

It occurred to me how close we'd gotten in such a short period of time. This was the guy I initially tried to avoid living with and now I felt bad about leaving him.

"I'm on a pitch count tonight," I said. "Kotch said I can throw sixty pitches. I'm hoping to go five innings."

"Definitely five innings, Matty."

The game began at 7:15 amid heavy winds and light showers. Despite the slick ball and playing surface, I felt on top of my game as I faced the Padre hitters. The first three innings raced by as I struck out four batters and allowed one run. As I got up to head out for inning number four, Kotchman stuck his arm out to block me from leaving the dugout.

"You're done, kid. Nice job," he said.

"It's only the fourth," I said, trying not to be disrespectful.

"Yeah, but you've already thrown fifty-three pitches."

"So I've got seven more."

"No, sir, I always err on the side of caution."

"Kotch, I got another inning in me."

"You've got a long career ahead of you. No need to rush things. Now, go ice your arm."

I threw my glove into my bag and grabbed a bag of ice. In the spectrum of temper tantrums, mine was tame. But still, it was the first time in a long time that I'd thrown a glove after being taken out of a game. I wanted nothing more than to go back out to the mound and show Kotchman what I was capable of.

I came out of the game with the score tied and thus I was ineligible to receive my first professional victory. Clayton wrapped my left arm with six plastic bags of ice—two for the shoulder, two for the back, and two for the elbow—as I stood with my hands on my hips, muttering expletives under my breath. I sat uncomfortably in the tiny dugout for the next three innings as the ice slowly melted.

As my temper and left arm gradually cooled, I tried to put my outing in perspective. I'd now pitched in three games, and made steady progress with each appearance. I was pleased that Kotch had said something positive about my performance and I was glad that I'd pitched well in front of our scouting director. I still wasn't where I wanted to be, but I was getting more comfortable with the crowds and the traveling, and the hitters were no longer crushing my fastball. The team was playing well and I would've been eligible for my first victory if only I'd pitched another inning.

And then the wheels came off. Our relievers gave up three runs in the bottom of the ninth and we lost, 6–5.

There was no postgame speech and there were no showers. We boarded the bus quickly and sat in silence as we drove back to the motel. Once in the parking lot, Kotchman stood up and addressed the team.

"There are thirty guys on this team," he said quietly, "and to be honest, most of you will never play in the big leagues. In fact, only a few of you even have a shot. Most of you will kick around in the minors for a few years and wash out. There'll be a pink slip in your locker before you know it."

He was looking out the window and he appeared unsteady on his feet.

"You play this game for such a short period of time and it kills me to see some of you not giving it all you've got. It fucking kills me."

His voice was now quivering. I looked down at my shoes.

"I want you guys to be winners on the field and off the field!"

He slammed his fist into a headrest and I looked up.

"If you play hard for me, I will do anything for you. Anything! And to see some of you just going through the motions . . . it kills me. You're disrespecting the game!"

I thought Kotchman was about to burst into tears. It was agonizing to watch.

"Am I upset that we lost today? Sure. But I'm more upset that some of you don't seem to give a damn about anything other than yourselves. Someday someone's going to take this game away from you, and you're gonna spend the rest of your life wishing you'd just played a little harder."

It was hard to believe that this was the same man who delivered the stand-up routine a few days earlier. Gone was the freewheeling Tom Kotchman; in his place stood a tired, rigid man running on raw emotions. He addressed us for forty minutes, delivering an impassioned homily that took us through his experiences as a player, his failures in life, and what he viewed as his chance at redemption through his players. I'm not sure what the Dominicans took away from it all, but I walked off the bus feeling a new sort of connectedness to this curious man.

KOTCHMAN'S SPEECH TURNED OUT to be lost on many of my teammates as they went out and played an uninspired fourth and final game against the Padres. We took it on the chin, 12–4, and it dropped our record to 5-6. It was the first time we'd been below .500 since Opening Day. The game ended at 10:30 P.M. and we were told that the bus back to Provo would be leaving at 12:30 A.M., so we had two hours to return to the motel, shower, check out of our rooms, and eat dinner. We would be facing the Ogden Raptors tomorrow night in Provo.

We were all dreading the bus ride back to Provo. Kotchman hadn't yet spoken to the team and we knew he'd want us to be silent for the duration of the six-hour trip. He was the last one to get on the bus and didn't say a word as we left the parking lot and headed for Interstate 15. The lights on the bus were turned off and everyone grew quiet.

An hour later we pulled into a rest stop in Blackfoot, Idaho. The lights came on and Kotchman stood up. He was ready to talk.

"We've been going at it for almost two weeks now," he said, brushing some crumbs off his shirt, "and I know you guys haven't gotten your first paychecks yet. Money can be tight and I don't want anyone to be put in a bind. Does anyone need money?"

The bus remained silent.

"I'm serious. Does anyone need money?"

I was down to $109.83 in my bank account but I wasn't about to ask Kotch for anything.

"This is not a joke. This team . . . we're a family. This is the last time I'm gonna ask: Does anyone need money?"

"I'm runnin' a little short," said a meek voice from the back of the bus. It was Junior Guzman.

"Who is that? Junior?" Kotchman asked as he started walking to the back of the bus. "How much you need, Junior?"

"Can I get fifty bucks?" he said humbly.

Kotchman whipped out his money clip, counted out the money, and handed it to him.

"Anyone else?"

"I'm short a hundred," said Jose Torres.

Kotchman turned around and handed Jose five twenty-dollar bills.

One player after another proceeded to ask Kotchman for money. I estimated that he gave out four hundred dollars at that rest stop and he didn't make a note of any of it.

"I'll trust that you'll all pay me back," he said as he exited the bus and headed for the restroom.

I fell asleep around three A.M. and was woken at six-thirty by Kotchman yelling, "Get up!" as we pulled into Provo. I soon found myself in an awkward spot. I'd told Sunshine that I was finished with the Marriott but I hadn't yet contacted my host family. It was too early to call them, I figured, so walked over to Sunshine with my tail between my legs.

"Think you can stand being my roommate for one more day?" I asked.

"Sure thing, Matty."

We checked into the Marriott at seven and spent the next three hours ordering room service and watching *SportsCenter* six times. We both fell asleep around ten, nine hours before our rematch with Ogden.

NINETY MINUTES into my slumber, I was woken by the sound of my cell phone.

"Is this Matt?" a woman asked.

"Yes."

"Oh, hi, I'm so glad I reached you. I hope you don't think this is weird, me calling you like this, but the radio guy, Tim, he gave me your number."

"No, it's fine," I said, still groggy. It did seem a bit weird.

"Okay, great. Well, my name is Sarah. Did Tim tell you about me?"

"Yes, he did. That's so nice of you to offer."

"My husband, Jeff, is the Provo Angels' number-one fan. We have season tickets and he takes the kids to almost every game. We've got four little ones here and they love the Angels just about as much as Jeff does."

"That's great."

She went on to tell me that she was a stay-at-home mom, and that her kids ranged in age from eighteen months to eight years, and that her husband was a pediatrician in Provo. After some more small talk, she popped the question.

"So what do you think . . . do you want to live with us?"

I could tell that someone on the other end had picked up a phone and was now listening in. I listened for a moment to see if it was one of her kids.

"Shh!!!!" I heard the voice say.

"I'd love to," I said finally, and immediately I heard the sound of children celebrating on the other end.

"He said yes!" I heard Sarah say.

I thanked her for the opportunity to stay with her family and offered to do anything around the house to minimize the inconvenience, but I'm not sure she heard me.

"Where are you right now?" she asked.

"At the Marriott."

"All right, we'll be there in thirty minutes to pick you up."

I jumped into the shower, gathered my belongings, and bade Sunshine farewell.

"Good luck, Matty."

"It's been fun rooming with you."

"Sure has. Just don't go and turn into a Mormon."

"I don't think that'll be a problem."

"I don't know. I heard they can be *very* persuasive."

We shook hands and I brought my duffel bag down to the lobby, then I picked up the Provo *Daily Herald* and sat outside on a bench and waited for Sarah. Exactly thirty minutes after I'd hung up the phone with her, a large, shiny white Jeep Grand Cherokee pulled into the parking lot. From it emerged Sarah Glenn, a slender woman of thirty-five with tan skin and light brown hair with blond highlights. She looked just like the actress Lori Loughlin.

She was wearing all white with black sunglasses and my first thought was that it was some sort of religious attire, like the men who wear white for Kabbalah. As she drew near, her beauty struck me.

"Matt?" she said.

She was radiant.

"You must be Sarah," I replied, undoubtedly grinning from ear to ear.

"It's so nice to meet you."

"It's so nice to meet you, too. I can't tell you how much I appreciate your offer to take me in."

"Oh, it's nothing," she said, waving her hand. "We're happy to do it."

I flung my bag over my shoulder and walked to her car. As I opened the trunk, I was greeted by three smiling faces and a baby.

"Hi, Matt McCarthy," they said in unison.

"Hi, guys," I said awkwardly.

Sarah and I sat in the front as we drove down Interstate 89 to her house, passing Utah Valley Regional Medical Center and the Riverside Country Club before turning into her neighborhood. The kids listened intently as I talked to Sarah about my time at Yale and my brief experiences in the minors. Eventually, I decided to turn back and break the ice with the kids. I looked back at Michael, an eight-year-old with sandy-blond hair and big blue eyes who was wearing a Provo Angels T-shirt and hat.

"So who's your favorite baseball player?"

"Well," he said, looking at his mom, "my favorite players are Barry

Bonds, Ken Griffey Jr., Mark McGwire, Manny Ramirez, Alex Rodriguez, Ichiro, Derek Jeter, Nomar . . ."

His mother turned around to cut him off.

"Jason Giambi, Sammy Sosa . . . and you."

"And me?" I said.

"Yes."

"Well, thank you. Maybe we could toss the ball around when we get home."

"That would be awesome!" he said and proceeded to fidget for the rest of the ride home.

"That's Steve Young's house," Sarah said, pointing to the former quarterback's large house and stables. "He's one of our neighbors. He's wonderful."

I quickly realized that Sarah's family lived in one of the swankiest neighborhoods in Provo. All of the houses had multiple levels, large beautiful yards, and several new cars parked in the driveway.

I shook my head in disbelief as Sarah pulled into her driveway. Her enormous house looked like something out of *Lifestyles of the Rich and Famous*. It was three times the size of any house I'd ever lived in, with a white picket fence, flower gardens, and a large basketball court behind the driveway.

I brought my bag into the foyer and Sarah made lunch for me and the kids. After a hearty helping of macaroni and cheese and Kool-Aid, I was shown my room. Actually, I had an entire wing of the house to myself. It included a large bedroom—larger than my room at the Marriott—a bathroom, a living room, and a big-screen television. Sarah told me all about her family, including her husband, whom she had met while they both attended BYU. He'd gone on to medical school in Texas and done a residency at Stanford and now worked as a pediatrician in private practice in Provo. Later on in my own medical career, as I pondered the decision to go into private practice, I would think of the Glenn family and their palatial estate. She concluded the tour in my bedroom by saying, "If you need anything, just ask. And I should tell you, in case you weren't sure, we're LDS."

I drew a blank.

"Latter-day Saints," she continued.

"Oh, of course, of course. Great."

I had no idea what it meant to be LDS. Was that the same as being Mormon?

"So how should I get to the field each day?" I asked as she began dusting a lamp.

"Oh, right, thanks for asking. Follow me."

She led me to the garage, where I found her white Jeep and a white Ford Expedition.

"We just bought it a month ago," she said excitedly.

"It looks brand-new," I said, looking at the Expedition.

"I just love it. . . . Oh, wait, no, not the car," she said, pointing to the corner. "The scooter. It's all yours."

Following the path of her index finger I saw a small neon-green Vespa motor scooter. It was sparkling and had a matching lime-green helmet. I immediately thought of the ridicule I would endure from my teammates when they saw me driving up to the field on a little scooter.

"This is great!" I said.

A minute later the kids burst into the garage and bailed me out. They insisted that Sarah drive me to the game so they could come along.

We played Ogden that night and beat them, 4–3, with a come-from-behind ninth-inning rally. After the game, the kids and their father were waiting for me outside the clubhouse. Jeff was a tall, upright man in his midthirties, with a slight build and glasses. He came over and introduced himself as I was signing more autographs for pets.

"Oh, Matt, it's so nice to meet you."

"Nice to meet you, too. Thank you again for allowing me to stay with you."

"It's our pleasure!"

As we rode back to the house, I was reminded of postgame car rides with my own father. Jeff asked a bit about the season so far and told me that he'd played a year of baseball at BYU before going on his Mormon mission to Costa Rica.

"With all the things to do in college," he said, "it's amazing that you stuck with baseball for four years."

"Yeah," I said, wondering if he regretted his decision or was critical of mine. For a moment I was reminded of dances and famous speakers I'd missed, of the afternoon classes I couldn't take because of baseball, and of those spring semesters that blurred together.

When we got home, Jeff put the kids to bed and poured two large glasses of milk—one for me and one for him. This must be the Mormon equivalent of having a beer, I thought. We stayed up for another hour talking about BYU and Yale, college baseball and Costa Rica. This is the kind of guy I would've been friends with in college, I thought as I finished off my drink.

"I'm not sure if Sarah told you," he said as he cleaned the glasses.

I was prepared for an explanation of the LDS comment.

"But we're going to California tomorrow . . . for a weeklong vacation. That's why we were so excited we got in touch with you. I'm taking the entire family to Newport Beach. You'll have the whole place to yourself, so make yourself at home."

I was falling in love with the Mormons.

"I'll leave you a key to the house and to the Jeep."

"Thank you. I don't know what to say."

He started to laugh.

"You don't have to ride the motor scooter. Sarah tried to get me to drive it, too, but I won't touch the darn thing."

I WOKE UP the next morning alone in my McMansion. The family was gone and had left a note for me on the kitchen table indicating where I could find cereal, peanut butter, jelly, and fruit juice as well as the keys to the house and the Jeep. "Be back in a week," it read, "so make yourself at home. Our house is your house!!!"

God bless the Mormons, I said to myself as I opened the stocked refrigerator. I made myself a sandwich and decided to take a look around the house. Besides the kitchen, the first floor had a mahogany-paneled office, a large living room, an entertainment room, and the master bedroom, which I took a quick peek into. The upstairs had four bedrooms (one for each of the children), a second entertainment room with a home movie theater, plus my wing.

At 10:45, I drove the Glenns' Jeep into town for our morning weight-lifting session. The Angels supplied each of us with a membership to the local gym, 24 Hour Fitness, and we were expected to lift twice a week under the supervision of our strength coach. Upon arrival each day, Clayton would hand us a checklist of lifts to perform. One day was devoted to the upper body and the other to the lower body. Everyone was expected to lift, except for that day's starting pitcher. For position players and relief pitchers, this often meant lifting on game days. It was something I'd never done in college and I didn't want to start now. But I had no choice. Absence, tardiness, or failure to perform any of the lifts resulted in a twenty-five-dollar fine, which represented roughly 12 percent of my total net worth.

Today was the second day of a six-game home stand and many

players had relatives or girlfriends in town. Coincidence or not, eight of my teammates missed our morning lift.

Clayton took the absences in stride.

"Doesn't bother me," he said with a mischievous smile. "It just means an extra two hundred dollars in my pocket." And that was it. At Yale there would have been a "players only" meeting to discuss the absences followed by a lecture from the coaches about priorities followed by a team punishment, like a Monday six A.M. run through the streets of New Haven. Here it was pay your fine and move on. If you couldn't perform on the field, the Angels would find someone else.

At Yale, this policy never would have worked. My college teammates were always trying to find extra time to accomplish everything that was expected of them and some just couldn't handle the stress of turning in a paper, taking an exam, and playing in a game on the same day. Others played well but could read the writing on the wall and started making backup plans for life after baseball. Turning down a competitive summer baseball league for an internship with Morgan Stanley was never criticized. It was almost expected. Paying to skip the weight room would've gotten out of hand very quickly.

Today's game was one that we'd all been eagerly anticipating—it was the professional debut of Joe Saunders. The coaching staff had handled him with great care, prohibiting him from pitching in a real game during the first two weeks of the season so he could comfortably acclimate himself to his new environs while the rest of us had been thrown into the fire. While we were chasing balls during batting practice, Joe would toss delicately in the bullpen, and during games, Joe would sit in the stands with a radar gun or in the dugout with a clipboard, charting pitches.

"Not too hard," Kernan would say to him in the bullpen. "Don't want to hurt your arm." Or, "Take it easy, Joe, just take it easy." The

Angels had spent close to $2 million on his left arm and I have no doubt they made that clear to Kotchman and Kernan. But it put Kotchman in an awkward position—he didn't want Joe to act or be treated differently than anyone else, but he had to treat him differently. He would probably lose his job if Joe got hurt on his watch. Handle with caution, it seemed to read on the back of Joe's uniform.

Clearly, Saunders's treatment bred more than a little resentment in the clubhouse. At the end of the day, it really didn't matter if my thousand-dollar arm got injured. No one was going to call Biron and ask what happened if I didn't make the big leagues. But if Joe failed, heads would roll.

I had mixed emotions about the whole thing. On the one hand, keeping Joe out of games meant more opportunities for me, but his presence was also a constant reminder of my shortcomings. I wasn't six feet three and I didn't throw 95 miles per hour with a great changeup.

Joe had arrived in Provo a relatively levelheaded kid. He loved playing cards before the game and was frequently found chatting with just about any American on the team. But in the past few days, he'd begun talking more and more about his agent and his new endorsement deal with Nike. He'd casually slip into a conversation that he had more pairs of shoes than he knew what to do with or that it was nice having his name sewn into his glove. During a card game he told everyone he was going to buy a Cadillac Escalade in the off-season and a house in Florida, for tax purposes. No one had said anything in response, but his arm and his money were mocked when he got up to use the restroom. So truth be told, I can't say I was rooting for the guy in his debut.

When I got to the Provo clubhouse at three o'clock, I found a group of players huddled around a table in the center of the room. They were all reading an article in the Provo *Daily Herald* previewing the matchup between fellow first-rounders Prince Fielder and Joe Saunders. The article disclosed how much each player had signed for and referred to both as future stars in the big leagues. Joe hadn't arrived at the park yet, so players took turns with potshots.

"Don't you think it's a bit premature to be calling him a future big leaguer?" said Heath Luther, a short left-handed relief pitcher from Fort Wayne, Indiana. Heath was barely five feet eight with freckles and the softest fastball on the team. He'd signed with the Angels as an undrafted free agent and was perpetually paranoid, telling anyone who'd listen that it was just a matter of days before he'd get his pink slip. He had every reason to hate Joe.

"He hasn't even thrown a pitch in the minors and they're already saying he's ready for Anaheim," said Brett.

"This really pisses me off," continued Heath. "This kind of crap just paves the way for guys like Saunders to make the big leagues and it makes it that much harder for everyone else."

"How so?" I asked from the seat at my locker. Everyone reading the article lifted their head and looked over at me. "If he's not good enough, these articles will make it that much worse for him, and if he is good enough . . . well, then the article's right."

"That's not the point," said Heath defiantly. "Everyone's gonna have a good game sooner or later, right?"

"Sure."

"When Joe has a good game, the coaches or writers or fans or whoever will nod their heads and reaffirm what they already know to be true . . . that Joe's a star in the making."

"Okay."

"But when one of us does good, people will think it's luck or something because we're not one of the chosen few predicted to make the big leagues."

"And if Joe does bad," said Blake, picking up where Heath left off, "they'll just chalk it up to him having a bad night. But if one of us goes out and gives up six runs, well . . . that's what people expect because nobody's countin' on us to make it anyway. It's all a self-fulfillin' prophecy."

"Listen, I understand what you're saying," I said, holding the attention of the room, "but Joe's one guy. One guy they spent two million bucks on. That's one spot on the Angels' twenty-five-man roster."

Heath was unconvinced.

"What about last year's first-round pick? They've already penciled in Kotch's kid at first base. And the first-round pick before that? And the one before that? And then you start talking about all the second- and third-round picks who they've signed for hundreds of thousands of dollars. Those are the guys the Angels are counting on. Not us."

A number of players nodded as I tried to think of a response.

"Maybe you're right," I said.

"Don't forget, Matt," Heath added while pointing at me, "the Angels have taken a left-handed pitcher with their first pick two of the last three years."

A moment later, Saunders entered the locker room and put the discussion to rest. Players quickly dispersed and began changing into their uniforms. Saunders smiled when he saw the newspaper open to the article about him.

"You guys see that?" he said, speaking to no one in particular. "They're saying it's gonna be a huge matchup tonight, me versus Prince."

We were all watching him smile as he read the article.

"The fat boy has no chance tonight!" Saunders said before grabbing his hat and leaving the clubhouse.

"I hope Fielder hits a five-hundred-foot monster home run off Joe," Luther announced to the dozen of us in the clubhouse.

"Me, too," said Brett, quietly.

At 6:30, Clayton led us through our pregame stretch. It was at that time that I noticed a dozen men, including Tony Reagins dressed in black, standing by the bullpen watching Saunders warm up.

"That's the Angels' entire front office," said Blake, who saw me star-ing at the group. "Scouting director, general manager, assistant general manager, director of Player Personnel, manager of Baseball Operations, director of Player Development, you name it. All the ones who decided to go with Saunders as their number-one pick. They're here to check up on their investment . . . see if they got their money's worth."

Saunders took the mound at 7:00 and received a hero's welcome from the hometown fans. He tipped his cap to the crowd before the first pitch and then got down to business. He got the first two batters to ground out and the next batter reached on a single before the clean-up hitter, Prince Fielder, came to the plate. The crowd was buzzing when Fielder's name was announced and it got even louder when it was men-tioned that his father was in attendance, seated behind home plate in the first row. Cecil Fielder stood after his name was announced and waved to the adoring crowd. A line soon formed in his aisle for auto-graphs.

At this point, Prince and Cecil were still very close. Cecil had ne-gotiated Prince's $2 million contract two weeks earlier and Breslow informed me that Cecil was always milling around the Ogden club-house, giving advice and occasionally taking batting practice with the team. But they would have a very public falling out a year later. Trump Plaza and Casino would file a lawsuit against Cecil for failing to pay gambling debts, and Prince became furious with his father for taking a $200,000 commission on his own son's signing bonus, which Cecil had also negotiated.

Saunders stepped off the mound and started rubbing his left palm on his pants leg. When we played cards, Joe's hands would get repul-sively sweaty and, unbeknownst to him, we would use that as a sign that he had a bad hand. He reached for the rosin bag to dry off his left hand even more. He may have talked a big game in the clubhouse, but Joe Millionaire was nervous.

Saunders decided to challenge Fielder with the first pitch, a fastball down the middle. Fielder took a mammoth swing, but missed the ball. The crowd gave a collective sigh of relief after the ball hit the catcher's mitt. He threw another fastball for strike two, and in the crowd I saw Tony Reagins give a nod of approval.

But the next three pitches all missed badly, with the third one narrowly missing Fielder's head. Someone in the crowd screamed as Fielder ducked out of the way. Prince gathered himself and gave Saunders a long stare before returning to the batter's box for the payoff pitch. Joe threw another fastball, but it missed high for ball four. Fielder had won round one.

Saunders struck out the next batter and then retired the side in the second. After two innings of work, Saunders was pulled.

"You've thrown twenty-seven pitches," Kotchman said to him from across the dugout. "That's plenty for tonight. Don't want to hurt that precious little arm of yours." Kotchman clearly made the comment in jest, but I saw a number of heads shaking in the dugout after he said it.

We went on to win the game, 9–4. The drama of Joe's first start obscured the fact that our record improved to 7-6, putting us in a tie with Ogden for first place. There were twenty-five games remaining in the first half of the season, and the winner of the first half was assured a spot in the playoffs.

WHAT WAS SUPPOSED to be the third game of our home stand was rescheduled and moved to Ogden due to the Sunday religious observances of Provo.

"Fuckin' Mormons," said Heath as we walked into our clubhouse. "Always cramping our style."

"I know," I said, thinking of the palace I now called home.

As we were packing up our equipment, Kotchman came into the clubhouse.

"Drug-test guy is here today. Piss for the guy and get on the fuckin' bus."

With that introduction, a short, heavyset man wearing khaki pants and a polo shirt came into the room. He moved a table in front of the bathroom stalls and told us to form a line. We were asked for the last four digits of our Social Security number and had to sign two waivers authorizing the drug test.

"Finally," said Sunshine as we waited in line.

"Yeah, finally," said Luther.

The American players assembled in the front of the line and I had to wait only a few minutes before it was my turn.

"So what are you testing for?" I asked the man as he handed me my vial.

"Drugs," he said. "Keep the door open and piss in the cup. I'm watching all of you."

"Thanks."

"My wife would be so proud," he said to himself, looking at the dozen cups of urine before him.

Twenty minutes later we were on the bus to Ogden.

I was starting tomorrow's game, so I had a different pregame routine than the rest of my teammates. I was to jog six laps around the stadium while Clayton led the team through stretches and sprints.

Kernan flagged me down after I'd completed two laps.

"What's up, Kernan?"

"Hey, Mac, uh, I forgot to tell you something. Listen, Jamie Steward is coming down from Cedar Rapids tomorrow. He needs a little extra work and he's gonna take your spot in the rotation."

"Oh," I said.

"So you don't need to do any more laps. You're gonna be in the bullpen as long as he's here."

I'd never heard of Jamie Steward but I hated him as much as I'd ever hated anyone. Walking back to the dugout, I thought of Stuper and his mantra "Control that which you can control." It would not be the last time something like this would happen.

I watched the game from my new home—the bullpen—and was again struck by the lack of connection with the game. It was like sitting in the stands, except I was forced to wear a uniform. The conversation again centered on girls, but this time the stories weren't as juicy.

We traded home runs with the Raptors early on and I began to notice the obvious lack of emotion on either side. The winner of this game would move into first place, yet when a batter hit a ball out of the park, no one even congratulated him after he'd rounded the bases. In college, we would've rushed out to home plate to celebrate. But in this league, and in this organization, wearing your heart on your sleeve seemed to be viewed with contempt. I wondered what long-term effect that had on people.

We scored a few runs in the ninth and held on to win the game, 6–4. It was our fourth straight win and it gave us sole possession of first place. Everyone was in good spirits on the bus ride back to Provo.

"Good job today, men," Kotchman said from the front of the bus. "You know I hate those assholes in Ogden. I liked the way we played today . . . but I'm sick and tired of us having to fight and scrap to stay above .500. Let's go out and win ourselves eight, nine, ten games in a row!"

The team erupted in a cheer and there were high fives all around, even between Americans and Dominicans. It was a stark contrast to the muted emotions I observed during the game. Suddenly everyone spoke the language of First Place.

Back in Provo, a half dozen of us went over to Sunshine's hotel room to have a few drinks and watch the ESPN *Sunday Night Baseball* game of the week.

I was the last to leave, as I wanted a chance to catch up with my old roommate.

"Room looks good," I said.

"Thanks, Matty. It's not the same without you, but I'm getting on."

"I'm sure you've got a different waitress in here every night."

"Almost."

"Hey, Kernan told me I'm out of the starting rotation."

"That's not fair, Matty. You've been throwing good."

"I thought I'd been doing all right."

"Say, Matty, today was a big day."

"Yeah, we're in first place."

"No . . . I mean today was the drug test."

"Yeah, wasn't that big of a deal."

"Matty, it is a big deal. They only test us twice a year. Once in spring training and once during the season."

"Nice, so we can go out and smoke some weed. Great."

"Not exactly."

"What . . . coke? You know that's outta my league."

"No, Matty, no! I know you were a biochem major at Yale or whatever, but I'm a bit of a chemist myself."

"Oh, yeah?"

"Yeah."

I felt like this was the beginning of a long conversation that I wasn't prepared to have after a long day and a few drinks.

"Let's talk tomorrow," I said. "I gotta get back to my place."

"How's that workin' out for you?"

"Pretty good, Sunshine. Pretty damn good."

IT WAS NOW July 1, and that meant my first paycheck. My excitement had nothing to do with the symbolism of receiving money to play ball; I just needed the cash. I'd racked up a fairly substantial bill at the Marriott with Sunshine and I had to pay it off.

We were to be paid twice a month from July 1 to September 15. After that, we were on our own. There were no paychecks in the off-season and those of us who'd signed tiny contracts would have to get jobs.

Smitty came into the clubhouse a few hours before the game while we were all playing cards.

"Paychecks," he said, and the game quickly dissolved. We all formed a lined behind him, with the Dominicans in the back.

I devoured my envelope as soon as it was handed to me. I couldn't wait to see the actual amount, which turned out to be $320.46. It was a bit less than I'd expected, but I'd forgotten to account for taxes. The best part, I found, was seeing the Walt Disney corporate logo at the top of the check. As someone who used to have a year-round pass to Disney, I took great pleasure in finally getting some of my money back, although it was bittersweet, considering the amount.

From the paycheck, Blake informed me, we were required to pay thirty-five dollars to Smitty for the pregame snacks that he'd been providing as well as for laundry detergent. So I was really taking home $285.46, or $571 per month.

It was also an important day for another reason—July 1 was the deadline to cut the roster down to thirty players, and at the moment we were carrying thirty-one. Sunshine said he was worried because he'd played only one inning, but I reminded him that as the team's only bullpen catcher, he was one of the few indispensable members of the team.

"I know it's me," Heath said as he walked around the locker room. "I'm definitely a goner. May as well give me the pink slip now."

A few players took turns trying to allay Heath's fears, but it was done halfheartedly. No one would've cared if he was cut.

An hour before game time, Sunshine came over to me at my locker.

"Blake's on the disabled list," he said, beaming with excitement.

"I know."

"Blake's on the DL," he repeated.

"He's been on the DL all season."

"Turns out we can carry thirty *active* players, but Blake's not active. We don't have to cut anyone."

"That's great!" I said, giving Sunshine a hug.

"Hey, don't tell Heath," he said with a mischievous grin. "I want him to sweat it out a little longer."

Tonight's game was the first of a three-game set against the Padres. It was Monday, which again meant "Mormon Family Night" and a 5:00 start time. Once again, players took turns bashing the Latter-day Saints.

"I'm sick and tired of working our schedule around the damn Mormons."

"Twice a week they mess with our schedule. We can't even play home games on Sunday? Are you kidding me?"

"Why couldn't I have been drafted by the Dodgers? They have a team in Vegas."

While this was going on, I sat down to play poker with Blake. Ten minutes into the game, he unexpectedly stood up.

"Jamie Steward," he said with a big smile. "How the hell are ya?"

"Great to see you, Blake," said the short left-handed pitcher from New Jersey. He looked a lot like Heath, but less paranoid.

"Welcome to the ball club. This is Matt McCarthy."

We exchanged pleasantries before Blake and Jamie continued their conversation. They'd been teammates in Provo last year but this year Jamie was promoted to Cedar Rapids while Blake was kept in Provo.

"Cedar Rapids is so much better than this shit hole," said Jamie. "You can actually get a beer after the game and the girls will talk to you."

"Imagine that."

"Yeah, I'm betting I'm not here long. Hopefully I'll throw a few games and get the hell out."

Good, I thought.

Jamie made his way around the clubhouse and introduced himself to the other American players, not bothering with the Dominicans. As he was doing so, Kernan came in to give Jamie the scouting report for the game. They sat down next to me and talked about each opposing hitter and his various strengths and weaknesses. It was the scouting report Kernan should've been giving me and I grew surprisingly angry as their conversation proceeded.

Five minutes before game time, we stood on the top step of the dugout to hear yet another aspiring singer belt out "The Star-Spangled Banner." The quality of the performance usually ranged from passable to awful. Some would forget the words while others were overmatched by the arrangement of the piece. Many were off-key, but they all sang their hearts out. We heard the song every night of the week and enjoyed judging the warblers. Kernan would time the song with his stopwatch, deducting points if its duration it was more than two minutes (average was ninety seconds). Tonight's songbird was a pale, chubby girl from Provo High School who belted out the song in record speed—just seventy-five seconds—because she'd forgotten two full lines, and was visibly upset when she finished.

"Somebody forgot about the rocket's red glare," Brett said to me with his crooked smile.

"She shoulda just stayed in bed," said Josh Gray, and I was immediately brought back to my workout with the Yankees and the image of the poor kid with the pulled hamstring writhing around on the ground.

The singer walked off the field with her head down and this served to energize my teammates.

"That was awful!" said Sisko, giving Blake a high five.

"She's the one who needs a pink slip," said Heath, still worrying that his number was up.

I watched from the bullpen as Jamie Steward threw the last of his warm-up pitches. I couldn't help but be critical of each one. He doesn't look good at all, I thought to myself. And he acts like Provo is beneath him.

"Weren't you supposed to start tonight?" asked Anthony Reed, a tall, tan relief pitcher from Walters, Oklahoma. He'd just signed for $150,000 but would retire the following year in spring training, just like Pink.

"Yeah, Steward took my spot," I said.

"Well, you got a better shot of making the bigs as a relief pitcher anyway."

"Yeah, I guess that's true."

This was the second time in three days that I was actively rooting against one of my teammates, and it was no coincidence that both were left-handed pitchers in the starting rotation.

My wish came true as Steward was pounded for eight hits in the first two innings, with several balls smacking off the way for extra-base hits. In all, Jamie pitched five innings and allowed six runs, leaving the game with the score 6–2.

I walked down to the clubhouse in the sixth inning to use the facilities, and as I did, I heard Kotchman yelling at a few Dominican players in the corner of the dugout.

"Eight A.M. wasn't early enough for you motherfuckers? If we lose tonight I'll have your asses out here at six A.M. tomorrow. Do you hear me?"

They didn't respond, but at least they didn't laugh.

As I was walking by, Kotchman grabbed me by the arm.

"If it stays close," he said with his nose just a few inches from mine, "you'll pitch the eighth and the ninth."

I nodded and jogged down to the bullpen to begin my warm-up—ten minutes of stretching followed by ten minutes of light tossing at a progressively longer distance, up to 120 feet.

Kotchman's threat seemed to work as we scored six runs in the bottom of the seventh, and when I took the mound in the eighth, we held an 11–7 lead.

I felt confident as I strode out to the mound. There was something about Steward's struggles that had invigorated me. My fastball had more zip on it and I had better command of my changeup and slider. The eighth and ninth innings were a breeze—I didn't allow a run—and as the final out was made, a pop-up to right field, I pumped my fist in the air, saying, "Hell, yeah!"

I walked off the mound with my head held high and made a bee-line for the locker room. When I noticed that I was alone in the room, I spiked my glove in front of my locker and threw my hands in the air like I'd just scored a touchdown. A moment later Sunshine entered.

"Matty!" he said with arms extended.

"Sunshine!"

"You looked great out there, Matty."

He gave me a bear hug and turned on the CD player that sat on a table in the corner of the room. We both began singing along with "Damn It Feels Good to Be a Gangsta."

"I can do this," I said as much to myself as to him.

I gave him another hug and tried to pick him up off the ground.

"I don't think I've been this excited since I lost my virginity," I said.

"What was his name, Matty?"

"You're a bastard," I said with a smile and we both laughed.

"I *am* a bastard, Matty. It's true! I'm also taking you out to dinner tonight to celebrate," he said as players started filing into the room, "and if you're lucky, I'll buy you an adult beverage."

Kotchman spoke to us for about ten minutes after the game, but I heard only five words come out of his mouth. Near the end of his speech, he glanced in my direction and said, "Nice job out there, McCarthy."

It was two insignificant innings at the end of a meaningless game, but I couldn't have felt more vindicated. I went to the Olive Garden that night with Sunshine, Heath Luther, and Alex Dvorsky.

"Talk to me, Dvorsky," Sunshine said as we devoured our third basket of breadsticks. "You make up your mind yet?"

"I don't know . . . I think so. I think I'm in," he said, dipping his bread into tomato sauce. The usually chipper Dvorsky was conflicted about something.

"This is the time to do it. You know that. We're not gonna be tested again this season."

"I know."

"You're sure you want to talk about this in front of McCarthy," Heath said firmly.

"He's cool," said Sunshine, looking at me as if to say, "You're cool, right?"

I nodded. I had no idea what they were talking about.

"You've got two options," continued Sunshine. "You can go through me or you can take your chances with someone else."

"I had no problems using my source," Heath said fitfully.

"Sure," said Sunshine, "but I'm cheaper. And I can have your shit in two days. Otherwise it takes two weeks. That's a lot of lost time."

There was a long pause.

"Money isn't the issue," said Dvorsky before letting out a deep breath. "I'm hitting the cover off the ball. I'm second in the league in batting average and third in hits. I'm second in walks and I haven't made an error or had a passed ball all season."

"You're playing better than anyone else on the team," I said, trying to contribute something.

"That's what makes this so fucked up," said Heath, trying to goad Dvorsky.

"What?" I asked.

Dvorsky looked at Heath and Heath looked at Sunshine. Dvorsky leaned in close to tell me his secret.

"Kotch pulled me aside the other day. He said, 'You're doin' a good job and all, but we don't need a catcher who hits singles. We need a catcher who drives in runs and hits the ball out of the park.'"

"He said that?" I asked, somewhat taken aback. This sounded like another one of Kotchman's mind games, just trying to ratchet up the pressure level. He didn't want Dvorsky's success at the plate to go to his head. "Success breeds complacency," he'd once said to us. He had to keep the heat on his best player.

"Yeah. And it's true. They got plenty of guys who can hit singles. I can read the writing on the fucking wall."

"Don't they always say power comes later?" I asked, trying to cheer up my battery mate. "That eventually the singles become doubles and the long fly balls become home runs?"

"I know, I know, that's what every scout says, that 'the power will come.' Well, it ain't come soon enough for Kotch."

"He needs to be on the juice," said Heath. "Kotch practically told him that himself."

From everything I knew about Kotchman, this was impossible to believe. Kotch's methods were sometimes a bit bizarre, but I never saw any evidence that he would condone, much less encourage, the use of steroids. He cared too much about his players to roll the dice with their health.

Even so, Dvorsky's head was down as he stared into his empty plate. His reaction reflected the dilemma that many players in baseball faced at the time, when the whiff of steroids was always in the air. What might have been nothing more than an innocent suggestion from a coach that a player needed something extra to make the big leagues could be misinterpreted as a coded message to look for chemical assistance.

"I don't know."

"Yes, you do. You do know," said Sunshine. "You're just afraid to make a decision. It's like fucking Shakespeare. Do you want to play in the big leagues or not? Simple as that."

"I still can't believe he pulled me aside like that. I'm hitting .340."

"It's bullshit is what it is," mumbled Heath.

"What do you think, Mac?" said Dvorsky. "You went to Harvard or Yale or whatever . . . give me some Ivy League advice."

Six eyes turned to me. Heath's glare seemed to say, "Watch yourself."

"It seems pretty black-and-white to me," I said, choosing my words carefully. "There's gonna be a price to pay for any benefit on the field." I felt like I was the lead character in an after-school special.

"So?" said Dvorsky defiantly. "I drink liquor. Is that bad for me? Yes. I chew tobacco. Is that bad for me? Yes. I smoke cigarettes. Is that bad for me? Of course. So you're tellin' me there's something which is just as bad for me, except it will make me play better. Why the hell shouldn't I take it?"

"I think the side effects are worse."

"Really?" said Heath, still glaring at me. "All that other shit will give you cancer. You're telling me this shit will give him something worse than cancer?"

"Well, no, but it'll shrink your nuts," I offered.

"But it won't shrink the shaft!" said a giggling Sunshine.

"Listen to me," said Dvorsky, again leaning close and looking into my eyes. "I would give my left nut right now for one day in the big leagues. One day! Do you understand what I'm saying?"

"Of course he doesn't," said Heath.

"Don't ask my opinion if you don't want to hear it," I said, staring back at Heath.

"I didn't ask your opinion, you arrogant fuck. Dvorsky did."

"Listen," I said, turning to Dvorsky, "this is what I'm saying . . ."

"You don't have a fucking clue," Heath interrupted. "If you get cut tomorrow you go back to your job on Wall Street or your Ivy League law school. What happens to me . . . or Dvorsky?"

"I don't have any job lined up . . ."

"Fuck you. You go back to New York and become a consultant. What happens to me? I go back to a shit town and get a shit job." Heath's voice was getting progressively louder and several families were now looking over at us. "How dare you try to tell Dvorsky what he should and shouldn't do. Go to hell."

"All I'm saying is that it's a slippery slope."

"A slippery slope to the big leagues," said Sunshine.

"Forget about it," said Dvorsky. "We'll talk about this later."

Someone changed the subject to Mormon girls and we talked about that for the remainder of the meal. Afterward, I offered to give Sunshine a ride back to the Marriott.

"I had no idea," I said as we drove along the base of the Wasatch Mountains, "about the steroid thing."

"Gotta stay competitive, Matty. Heath was ready to beat your ass."

"I coulda taken him . . . that paranoid asshole. So tell me, what are you guys using?"

"I don't have to tell you this all stays between you and me," he said, running his fingers through his hair.

"Of course."

"It's called Deca. Short for Deca-Durabolin. You can get it in two or three ten-week cycles between now and spring training. Before the next drug test."

I would later come to know Deca by its chemical name, nandrolone, a drug I'd consider recommending to postmenopausal women fighting osteoporosis.

"I had no idea. How many guys are using it on the team?"

"I know of five white guys and one Dominican. But I wouldn't be surprised if all the Dominicans were using something."

"Jesus."

"Just inject it into your ass or thigh and forget about it," he said, exiting the car in front of the Marriott. "Thanks again for the ride, Matty."

"Well, if it isn't Backdoor Becwar," I said as I walked into the clubhouse the next day. He was standing at my locker with a notebook.

'You know I hate that name."

"I know. I'm sorry."

"So how's the host family working out?"

"Not bad," I said, fighting back a smile.

"Any crazy Mormon shit?"

"No, they've been great. I love the Mormons."

We both shared a laugh. How easily my allegiance had been bought.

"Hey, you want to do an interview for the pregame show today?"

"Sure, it'll be my first one."

"Don't worry, I'll be gentle," he said. "I'll meet you in front of the dugout at four P.M."

"Can we make it four-thirty? I'd love to miss batting practice."

"Sorry, Matt. Gotta do it at four."

"All right, see you then."

I spent the next twenty minutes thinking of clever things to say for the interview. I was hoping to avoid all the stupid clichés you typically hear from baseball players, but I didn't want to say anything controversial.

"You better keep last night's conversation to yourself," Heath mumbled to me as he walked by my locker.

"Actually, I'm doing an interview with Becwar in an hour. I was thinking of telling him about it on-air."

"Fuck you," he said, walking away. It was strange having an enemy on the team, but I was in no mood for reconciliation.

"WE'RE HERE TODAY with Matt McCarthy, a left-handed pitcher for the Provo Angels," Becwar began in his deep voice. We were both wearing headphones and holding separate microphones in the stands above the third-base dugout.

"Thanks for having me, Tim."

"Now, Matt, you were a starting pitcher at the beginning of the season, but you've recently been moved to the bullpen."

"That's right. I've gotten to throw a couple of games as a starter and a couple as a reliever."

"Which one do you like better?"

"Oh, it doesn't matter to me," I lied. "I'm just happy to be out here, putting on a uniform every day."

"What's the transition to the bullpen been like?"

"It hasn't been too tough, Tim. Somebody hands you a ball and you try to get people out. It doesn't matter if it's the first inning or the eighth. Your focus is still the same."

I was a little nervous and tempted to start spewing platitudes about pitching.

"You had a quality performance the other night in relief . . . a scoreless eighth and ninth in a comeback victory against the Padres. Can you talk a bit about that?"

"Well . . . I definitely have to give credit to the guys in the field behind me. I've never played with better players defensively. Dvorsky calls a great game behind the plate and Kotchman's a great guy to play for. . . . He really wants to win."

I wasn't going into uncharted territory with comments like these.

"Speaking of the guys in the field behind you . . . how do you like your new teammates?"

"They're all a great bunch of guys. We really get along great. We spend a lot of time together—in the clubhouse, on the bus—and they keep it fun."

Was this stuff really coming out of my mouth?

"And what's it *really* like to play for Tom Kotchman?"

"I've never played for a man who cares more about his players than Kotch."

"He's coming up on his one thousandth career victory as a minor league manager. Do you guys have any celebration planned for him?"

"Actually, I didn't know that. I'll have to ask the guys. We should do something for him, shouldn't we?"

"Definitely, Matt. Now, I understand you're a long way from home out here in Provo. That you actually went to Yale before signing with the Angels."

"That's correct."

"I imagine the minor league lifestyle is a dramatic change from life in New Haven."

"Well, Tim, not really. I used to stay up late chasing girls in college, too."

Silence.

"Kidding, of course," I added.

"Oh, right. Kidding, of course," he said. "Well, I want to thank you, Matt, for taking the time to speak to us here at KOVO and we wish you luck tonight against the Padres, and we wish you luck with the rest of the season."

"Thanks for having me, Tim."

It was the only radio interview I'd do all season.

We won again that night, taking our winning streak to five games. It occurred to me that we hadn't lost a game since I ditched Sunshine for the Mormon ménage.

THE TOPIC ON EVERYONE'S lips the next day in the clubhouse was the radio interview Alex Dvorsky had done earlier that morning in Salt Lake City. Though less than an hour from Provo, Salt Lake City was a world away. The majority of its citizens were not Mormon, close to 20 percent lived below the poverty line, there were two large Spanish-speaking communities (Rose Park and Glendale), and it's been rated one of the top fifty gay-friendly cities in America. It was as close to a normal city as you could find in Utah.

Dvorsky's interview had started off simply enough. He was asked a few questions about his stellar performance on the field, the transition to minor league baseball, life in Provo, and the Angels organization. But after a few softballs, the interview took a different turn, becoming something like a segment on Howard Stern. Dvorsky described it to us in the locker room.

"So tell our listeners, Alex, do you live with a host family?" one of the hosts had asked.

"Yes," said Dvorsky.

"Have you . . . ever been intimate with the lady of the house?"

". . . No."

"Are you sure, Alex?"

"Yes."

"How about the daughter? Is there a daughter at your house?" asked the other host.

"No, sir. I have a girlfriend back . . ."

"Because I have a daughter at home," continued the host, "and I'm sure she'd just love to have you stay at our house."

Dvorsky didn't respond.

"What about the rest of your teammates? Any hanky-panky?"

"I'd prefer to talk about baseball."

"Anyone been able to corrupt the young Mormon girls of Provo?"

The interview continued in this manner for a few more minutes before Dvorsky told the hosts that he'd had enough. He left them on-air in the middle of the interview.

Everyone had an opinion about the story, but we all hushed as Kotchman entered the room.

"What happened to Alex this morning was despicable!" he said as he paced around the room. "It was a complete and total ambush. Those two guys down in Salt Lake are pathetic." Kotchman's hand was shaking as he reached for a toothpick in his back pocket. "Needless to say, none of you, including coaches, will ever speak to them or their station again. And in the future, you are going to need my permission before you agree to do any interview of any kind. I don't care if it's a high school newspaper or ESPN. None of you should ever be put in a position like that."

He looked around the room to make sure he'd conveyed the gravity of the situation.

"Some of you probably think what happened this morning is funny. That it's all a big joke and I should relax. Well, fuck you. It makes the team look bad, it makes the city look bad, and, most of all, it makes the organization look bad."

With that, he left the room, and we were left to discuss his latest edict.

"Kotch needs to lighten the fuck up," Heath barked.

"I'm sick of being told what I can and can't do," Sisko said after a few moments of silence. "I have to ask permission to talk to a newspaper? I don't think so."

"He's just looking out for us," said Quan, before walking out of the room.

"Self-righteous asshole," said Blake, loud enough that Quan might've heard it. "Just because he keeps a Bible in his locker and wears a cross around his neck, he thinks he can tell us what to do. Quan can go to hell as far as I'm concerned."

Quan was a quiet presence in the clubhouse and a crowd favorite, but Blake hadn't yet joined the fan club.

"He goes to chapel on Sundays. Big fucking deal," Blake went on. "It doesn't mean anything if you act like a jerk to your teammates."

"I don't see it," I said. "He doesn't say much of anything to anyone."

"It's not what he says," said Hancock, butting into the conversation. "It's how he says it. He walks around here like he's better than everyone."

Quan returned to the room and the conversation was cut short.

Tonight was the final game of the series with the Padres and the final game of the home stand. After the game, we would head to Casper, Wyoming, to begin a series with the Rockies. We all wanted to win tonight because a loss would mean seven hours of silence on the bus ride to Wyoming.

A few minutes before game time, Kotchman gathered us all together for some additional news.

"In case you didn't know, when we go on a long road trip it's my policy to fly the next day's starting pitcher to the place we're going. I don't want my starter sitting on a bus for ten hours, getting five hours of sleep, and then going out on the mound."

He straightened his cap and folded his arms.

"The Angels don't cover this. I pay for the ticket out of my own pocket. You can thank me later."

Say what you want, but the man wanted to win.

"So, Holcomb," he said, pointing at the tall, blond pitcher from San Jose, "you'll take a shuttle to the Salt Lake airport in the fourth inning. I've got a flight already booked to Casper for you."

Idaho Falls jumped out to an early lead, but we rallied late and were up, 9–3, going into the seventh. In the top of the inning, the Padres' star hitter, Omar Falcon, a cocky catcher from Miami, hit a moon-shot over the left-field wall for a solo home run. As he trotted around the bases, he pointed to the sky, and when he reached home plate, he did a little dance, bobbing his head and shaking his shoulders. It was no secret what would happen next.

Our pitcher, Jeff Marquez, also cocky and from Miami, threw the next pitch between the shoulder blades of the following batter. The batter fell to his knees and let out a low-pitched moan. The Padres' bench erupted with anger, calling for Marquez to be thrown out of the game, but the umpire only issued a warning. Several players on our team yelled back, but that stopped when Kotchman glared into our dugout.

Kotchman called time-out and walked slowly out to the mound to speak with his pitcher. From the bullpen, we could hear him yelling at Marquez, though he stood only inches from him.

"You hit Falcon the next time he comes up! You hit Falcon! Not the next guy!"

Everyone in the stadium could hear it.

Falcon did not bat again, but we did beat the Padres, 12–4. The win was our sixth in a row and we were euphoric in the clubhouse after the game. Latin music was played loudly and players were singing and slapping high fives. An Angels employee briefly interrupted the revelry to bring us fifty leftover hot dogs from the concession stand's "Weenie Wednesday" promotion.

I took my hot dog over to my locker and began to undress. That was when things got interesting. When I turned around, I saw the dark, naked bodies of two young Dominicans hovering around the hot dogs. Erick Aybar was our flashy eighteen-year-old shortstop from Bani, Dominican Republic, and Alberto Callaspo was an equally talented nineteen-year-old from Maracay, Venezuela. They were inseparable and spoke no English—the most one of them had ever said to me was "Why-ya-ya-ya-ya-yeah!" after I'd pitched a scoreless inning the week before.

Gradually more of my teammates turned to watch as Aybar's and Callaspo's naked bodies circled the food. We all knew they were up to something no good. Two naked heterosexual teenagers don't stand that close together for that long next to a box of hot dogs without something happening.

Suddenly, Callaspo took one of the hot dogs out of its bun and deep-throated it. Then he took the bun and put it around Aybar's flaccid penis and poured ketchup on it. Jaws dropped—Aybar was a willing participant. Then Callaspo bent over and pretended to eat the Dominican penis hot dog. When he did that, we all screamed, "Noooo!"

Getting the reaction he'd desired, Callaspo turned to a few of us and said, "I no gay. You gay!" and burst into a fit of laughter. I had underestimated him—he did know a bit of English. Callaspo slapped

Aybar on the ass and the two laughed all the way to the shower. As I turned back to my locker, I briefly made eye contact with Astacio, who had a pained look on his face.

Aybar and Callaspo turned out to be two of the best players on our team. Despite Blake's prediction about the fate of Dominicans, they quickly advanced through the Angels' system and were in the big leagues just after they were old enough to drink. Aybar was named the Angels' starting shortstop in 2008 while Callaspo took the field for the Kansas City Royals.

Energy was still high when we pulled out of the parking lot just before one A.M. We watched *WrestleMania VIII*, followed by *Wrestle-Mania IV*, before lights-out at four. We pulled into the Casper Motel parking lot at nine A.M. and I went straight to bed. We would open our series with the Rockies in ten hours.

I WOKE UP at three P.M. to a loud banging on my door. Fearing I'd overslept, I had a moment of panic as I raced to answer the door. D'Amico was gone, probably staying with one of the Dominicans, and he certainly wouldn't have taken the time to wake me for the game. I swung the door open and found Brian Williams and Brett Cimorelli standing before me.

"Did you hear?" said Brian.

"What? I'm not late, am I?"

"No."

"Is the game canceled?" I was still in a daze but coming out of it quickly. It was a feeling I'd later grow accustomed to in the hospital—being paged in the middle of the night, feeling confused and terrified while trying to gather my bearings.

"No."

"Then, what?"

"There was a shooting at an airport in L.A."

"LAX?"

"I don't know . . . the airport in Los Angeles. They're saying it could be terror-related."

Brett nodded gravely.

"They're saying it could be part of a July Fourth terrorism plot."

"Is today the fourth?" I asked. All the days were beginning to blend together.

"Yes," said Brian emphatically as he walked into my room. Brett followed behind him and turned the television to CNN.

"Breaking news," the anchor said. "A gunman opened fire today at Los Angeles International Airport while standing in line at the ticket counter of Israel's El Al Airlines, killing two and wounding four others before he was shot dead by a security officer."

"Jesus," I said under my breath. This was a time when September 11 was still fresh in our collective memories and any shooting, or anything out of the ordinary, seemed like it could be the beginning of a terrorist attack.

"It's gotta be terrorists," said Brett.

"The identity of the shooter is not known at this time," the anchor continued, "but he is thought to be of Middle Eastern descent."

"Definitely terrorists," said Brian. "And it's no coincidence that it was done on Independence Day. They're saying a baseball stadium might be next."

"Really?" I asked.

"Yeah, if you're gonna attack on the nation's birthday, why not attack its national pastime?"

Brett put down the remote and looked at me.

"Do you think we're safe here?" he asked solemnly.

"Here in Casper, Wyoming?" I asked.

"It's not out of the realm of possibility, Matt," said Brian. "It's a possibility."

"Definitely a possibility," added Brett.

We continued watching until 4:30, when we had to board the bus to the field. As I was walking down the aisle to my seat, Kernan grabbed me by the arm.

"Take a seat," he said.

"What's up, Kernan?"

"Remember that conversation we had a few days ago . . . about making you a reliever and moving you to the bullpen? Well, I want you to forget I ever said it."

"Okay."

"We liked what we saw out of you the other day and we've decided to move you back into the starting rotation."

"Great. When's my next start?"

"Tomorrow."

"Perfect."

"Good," he said, putting his hand on my knee. "Don't disappoint me now. We're putting you back in the starting rotation because we think you can win us some ball games."

I thanked him for the opportunity and returned to my seat. Leaning back, I was again struck by the image of Stuper telling me to control that which I could control. Still, I was incredibly encouraged.

Twenty minutes later we pulled into the Rockies' home—Mike Lansing Field—named for a mediocre big leaguer who'd grown up in Wyoming. With just a handful of aluminum bleachers and a chain-link fence, it looked like a high school park. Instead of bringing our equipment to a clubhouse, we were directed to a trailer behind right field.

The Casper crowd was treated to a host of Independence Day festivities. There were fireworks after every inning, and the Rockies' mascot, Hobart the Purple Platypus, raced children around the bases between innings. Why Hobart the Purple Platypus? Because Hobart is the capital of Tasmania, where platypuses are common. And why a platypus? Because Casper, Wyoming, is on the North Platte River. Seriously.

We kept our winning steak alive, beating the Rockies, 11–6. I returned to my empty room and turned on CNN. The shooting at LAX was not the work of a terrorist; rather it was an isolated incident by a deranged Egyptian man. I shut my eyes and had only one thought: I better not lose tomorrow. I better not be the one to end our winning streak.

Chapter 6

||||||||||||||||||||||||||||||||||||||||||||

THE NEXT DAY I heard the pitter-patter of rain outside my window all morning as I lay in bed. I hated to pitch on rainy days, so I was hoping that the storm would pick up and the game would be canceled. For a while I thought my wish was going to come true, but at three P.M. I received a call from Clayton informing me that we would be playing the game, rain or shine. With seventy-six games scheduled in eighty days, there simply wasn't time to drive back to Wyoming for a makeup game.

When I began my warm-up tosses at 6:30, there was only a light drizzle. The ball would be slick, but not unbearably so. Fifteen minutes before game time, Kernan ambled over to me.

"How you feeling, kid?"

"Great!" I lied.

"That's what I like to hear. You know these hitters. You've faced them before."

I immediately thought of my first appearance in a Provo uniform against the Rockies, when every pitch I threw was crushed.

"Yeah, I know these guys. I feel good."

"Good. Listen, Kotchman decided to tinker with the lineup tonight. He's giving Dvorsky the night off. Junior Guzman is going to be your catcher tonight."

"Okay, thanks, Kernan. I'll talk with him before I go out there."

It seemed a bit strange that Kotchman would tinker with the lineup in the middle of a six-game winning streak. Dvorsky was playing the best baseball of anyone on the team, but as I'd recently learned, Alex Dvorsky and Tom Kotchman had their own strange relationship. Then again, maybe Kotch just wanted to give his catcher a night off.

I spoke briefly with Guzman before the game about my pitches and our plan for each hitter. He spoke English just well enough for me to realize that he wasn't really listening to me. I walked away thinking about something Blake had told me a week earlier.

It was a Sunday in Provo and we'd been walking by the Mormon temple just as one of the services had ended. Passing by, we saw hundreds of well-to-do Provoans and their beautiful children spilling out onto the street in their Sunday best.

"Can you imagine being a Dominican in this town?" he said, shaking his head.

"I can't."

"I mean, can you imagine being dumped in this town, with all of those people," he continued, gesturing to the mass of people exiting the church. "It boggles my mind."

"Where do they all live . . . all the Dominicans? They don't have host families, do they?"

"Ha. Are you kiddin' me? Host families? You think they'd let Dominicans into their house?"

"I don't know."

"They rent two three-bedroom apartments up the hill and all pile in there," he said, pointing toward the Wasatch Mountains behind our field. "Ten guys in two apartments with no furniture. I think they like it that way."

"Sounds awful."

"It's better than what they're used to."

"Well, to their credit they stick together."

"To a fault."

"Yeah. I guess they don't really have to bother learning English if there's enough Dominicans around."

"You know they cheat, right?"

I shook my head.

"They steal signs. And they give our signs to Dominicans on other teams."

"No. Come on."

"It's true. If the catcher is Dominican and the hitter is Dominican, the catcher will whisper to the batter what pitch is coming . . . if the pitcher is American."

"Oh, come on, I don't believe that. Since when are you a conspiracy theorist?"

"It's true. Watch for it. Somebody told me that last year and I looked for it. Dominicans always hit better when there's a Dominican catcher."

"Are you serious?"

"Watch for it, that's all I'm sayin'."

"What if everybody's Dominican—the pitcher, catcher, and batter? Then what happens?"

He smiled at me before looking away.

"I don't know, man. I don't know what the tiebreaker is. Maybe it comes down to country of origin or some shit."

Blake tended to be a reliable source of information, but I didn't believe him on this one. And today, taking the mound with a Dominican catcher, I couldn't afford to believe him.

When I took the mound in the first inning, we had a 1–0 lead. As I was throwing my final warm-up tosses, it became clear that I was not on top of my game. My fastball was sluggish and my slider wasn't moving. There was a moment of panic as I feared that I was about to throw batting practice to the Rockies, but I regained my composure, remembering that I'd pitched many games in the Ivy League without my best stuff. The first time it had happened was against Princeton when I was a freshman. Right before the game I had pulled Breslow aside, trembling.

"I can't go out there. I'm throwing seventy miles an hour. I can't control my changeup and my slider isn't breaking. I mean it. I can't go out there."

He looked at me and put his hands on my shoulders.

"Hey, pilots don't just fly on sunny days. You're gonna have to work for it today."

Breslow was right then and he's still right, I thought, as the first batter lumbered to the plate.

Pitchers don't just pitch on sunny days, I told myself as I delivered my first pitch—an outside fastball that was drilled to right field for a single. The ball came back to me soaking wet from traveling through the outfield grass. I switched balls with the umpire and proceeded to strike the next batter out on three pitches. I walked the following batter, and that brought Ryan Shealy, the league leader in home runs, batting average, and RBIs, to the plate. With runners at first and second with one out, I was hoping to get a ground ball from Shealy to induce a double play.

My first pitch to Shealy was an inside fastball that nearly hit his left leg. The crowd booed as he jumped out of the way. I tried to surprise Shealy on the next pitch with a changeup away, but I missed my spot and he wasn't fooled. He smacked the hanging changeup 450 feet over the left field wall for a three-run home run.

I began to panic. My arm felt like shit, the ball was wet, my catcher might be a traitor, and I was going to be responsible for ending the winning streak. I was just praying that my bowels wouldn't move while I was on the mound.

Shealy stared at me as he rounded third base and continued to stare as he stomped on home plate. Should I bean him the next time he comes to the plate? I wondered. It would be better than allowing another home run. But he was six feet five, 240 pounds, and if he did charge the mound, I knew I'd be in trouble.

I temporarily righted the ship by retiring the next two batters to end the inning. With one inning in the books, we were down, 3–1. Kotchman said nothing to me as I entered the dugout, instead choosing to take out his frustration on Callaspo, who'd failed to run hard to first base in the top half of the inning.

With the score still 3–1, I took the mound for my second inning of work. This game is still salvageable, I told myself as I toed the rubber.

Picking up where I'd left off, I gave up back-to-back hits to start the second. The next batter reached on an error by our third baseman to continue my collapse in Casper. Kernan made a few hand gestures down to the bullpen and quickly there were two pitchers warming up to take my place. I'm not going to make it out of the second inning, I said to myself.

I struck out the next two batters and that brought Vladimir Bello, a five-foot-eleven outfielder from Santo Domingo, Dominican Republic, to the plate, with Ryan Shealy salivating in the on-deck circle.

There was a runner on third and I needed to get Vladimir out to end the inning. I didn't want to face Shealy again with men on base. I threw Vladimir two fastballs and he swung and missed both of them. Wanting a strikeout, I followed the fastballs with a slider. The pitch broke sharply—the first one of the day to do so—but it hit him on the left ankle.

"Take your base," the umpire said as Vladimir dropped his bat. The score was 5–1 and Ryan Shealy was now stepping into the batter's box.

Kotchman called time-out and walked through the light rain out to the mound. He kept his head down and said nothing as he approached me. He stuck out his hand and I gave him the ball. My day was done. It had been a horrendous outing—1 ⅔ innings, 5 runs, and probably a half dozen hits. But I wasn't off the hook yet—the two runners on base were mine. I jogged off the field to cheers from the Casper faithful, who were thrilled that I'd breathed a little life into their last-place team.

Kotchman brought in Ozvaldo Lugo, a quiet, little-used, moon-faced reliever from Miami, to face Shealy, who took the first two pitches, watching them miss wildly high and away. Shealy took the third pitch from Lugo and deposited it over the left-field wall for yet another three-run home run.

I sat with my head down in the dugout for what seemed like eternity. There was no one there to give me a pep talk, to tell me it would all work out. Kotchman said nothing the entire game, and we eventually lost, 8–4. The winning streak was snapped and I'd blown my opportunity to rejoin the starting rotation. I was dreading the speech Kotchman would give and what he'd say about me. But I would have to wait for his commentary because when we returned to the bus, we found it stuck in two feet of mud behind the stadium. We gathered behind the bus, all thirty-one of us, and tried to push as the driver pressed on the accelerator. It was no use. The bus was stuck and we were sprayed with mud every time we pushed. We waited for an hour in the darkness as rain continued to fall, and eventually a tow truck arrived and dragged the bus to solid ground.

I was still in a daze as Kotchman delivered his postgame speech. I listened for my name or some comment about the pitching letting us down, but there was none. I did manage to catch his parting words.

"All good things must come to an end. You guys played well during the streak. You got a little taste of what it feels like to be a winner. You've got two options from here. . . . You can let tonight's game affect you tomorrow and for the rest of the season, or you can move on and start a new winning streak tomorrow."

I immediately began praying for a new winning streak. I sure as hell didn't want to be the guy responsible for losing the game that sent our

team into a tailspin. We left Casper just before midnight and pulled
into Larry H. Miller Stadium at eight A.M.

WE WERE NOW nineteen games into the season, and as minor league
events go, tonight's was a big one in Provo—it was Larry King Night at
the ballpark.

"Who the hell is Larry King?" asked Josh Gray as we played a round
of poker in the clubhouse.

"No idea."

"Don't know, don't care."

"He's a boxing guy—a promoter or something. Use to work with
Mike Tyson."

"Oh, yeah? The black guy with the crazy hair?"

"Yeah."

My teammates were more than a little disappointed when Larry
King's tiny, white shriveled body came into the dugout a few minutes
before game time.

"That's Larry King?"

"I thought he was black."

"This guy looks like a little raisin."

"What's this guy famous for anyway?

"He's a talk-show host," I said.

"Is it a sports show?"

"No."

My teammates quickly lost interest in the old man and turned their
attention to Shawn Southwick, Mr. King's sixth wife, who'd accompa-
nied him to the game. She was a tall, thin, beautiful blonde nearly
thirty years his junior who was walking through the dugout, trying to
find a cup of water as thirty-one pairs of eyes stared at her ass.

"She's pretty hot," Sunshine whispered. "What's she doing with an old dude like that? He could be her grandpa."

"He's pretty famous," I whispered back.

"Oh."

Also with the Kings were their two young sons, Chance and Cannon. We all lined up in a long row in the dugout, and as Shawn and Larry moved down the row with introductions, Cannon trailed behind, trying to punch each one of us in the groin. A few of my teammates were brought to their knees just minutes before game time.

"That little bastard!" mumbled Matt Brown, a baby-faced third baseman from Idaho, as he lay doubled over on the dugout floor. "I'm gonna kill that little shit."

After the introductions were complete, the King family left the dugout. Shawn walked to home plate to sing the national anthem while a doting Larry looked on from the front row. We all lined up on the third baseline and removed our caps—except Kotchman, of course—as she began singing.

"She sounds great," I whispered to Kernan.

"Yeah, best this year," he replied from the corner of his mouth.

"You think so?"

"Definitely. The woman can sing."

But halfway through the song, something seemed off.

"Whoops," said Kernan.

"What?" I asked.

"She held that last note too long."

"You think?"

"Yeah . . . she's lip-synching."

"No!"

"Yes!"

"No, Kernan, say it ain't so."

Word quickly spread down the line that she wasn't really singing, and with it came a sense of outrage, which may or may not have been tongue-in-cheek.

"How can you come in here and lip-synch 'The Star-Spangled Banner'?"

"What an arrogant jerk."

"Yeah, this isn't the Super Bowl—it's a minor league baseball game. Sing the damn song."

When Shawn was finished, Larry took over, serving as the public-address announcer for the first few innings of the game. He made a few snide comments about our opponent, the Ogden Raptors, and then launched into a long story about how he met Shawn, a devout Mormon and graduate of BYU. The fans cackled as he told of his reaction when Shawn suggested that he, Larry King, a Jew, go on a Mormon mission with her. While the fans enjoyed his story, the players were not amused. He repeatedly spoke while pitches were being delivered, batters were swinging, and crucial plays were being made. Several players even had to call time-out and step out of the batter's box to let him finish a joke.

Between innings, all anyone could talk about was how, specifically, they were going to murder Larry King. A number of options were discussed, but the majority settled on strangulation.

In the end, both the fans and the players got what they wanted. The fans were entertained and we won the game, 12–7, thus preventing the start of a losing streak. My dreadful performance the day before would likely be just a blip on the radar of a long season. The win moved our record to 13-7 and gave us sole possession of first place.

SOMETIME DURING THE TRIP to Wyoming, I noticed that a new word had entered the team vernacular. My American teammates were no longer referring to the Hispanic players as "Dominicans," but instead simply as "Coños." It was a few days before I asked someone about the name change, and in the interim I'd noticed that the Dominicans were always saying the word *coño* and that it was included in just about every conversation.

"Why do you call them the Coños?" I asked Sunshine during a game of Texas Holdem in the clubhouse.

"Honestly?"

"Yeah."

"Because everybody else does."

I figured I'd try my luck elsewhere.

"What's with calling them Coños?" I asked Anthony Reed, who was sitting nearby, reading the newspaper at his locker.

"Ya got me," he said, without looking up.

"Brett?" I asked.

"I got nothing," he said.

It was amazing to me that this word had entered our lexicon but no one could trace its origin or knew its meaning.

"It means 'fuck' in Spanish," said Heath, hanging up his phone. "They say '*fuck*' all the time. Every other word out of their mouth is '*coño* this' and '*coño* that.'"

"Funny," I said, still not sure where I stood with Heath.

"Yeah, it doesn't make a lot of sense to call them all Dominican . . . since some of them aren't."

"That's true," I said. "I'm sure they're much happier being called 'the Fucks.'"

"Whatever," Heath said, starting to make another phone call.

I later learned from one of my Dominican patients that the word had a much broader meaning. Depending how it was used, *coño* could mean "hey," "damn," "ouch," "vagina," or "fuck."

We were supposed to play Ogden at home tonight, but since it was

Sunday, we had to drive up to their place. Before we boarded the bus, I got a call from Breslow.

"Sorry we haven't been able to talk more," I said. "It's weird seeing you playing for the enemy."

"Yeah. Same here."

I told him about my terrible outing against Casper and how I'd been bounced back and forth between the starting rotation and the bullpen.

"Yeah, they're making me a full-time reliever," he said. "I'm cool with it."

"I know I'll end up being a relief pitcher, too. My problem is I can't put together two good outings in a row. How 'bout you? How you throwing?"

"I haven't given up a run yet."

My heart sank.

"Really?"

"Yeah. Something like nine straight scoreless innings."

"Jesus. That's amazing."

"Yeah, I'm pretty happy with it."

"Well, I'll see you in a few hours. We're heading up now."

I shook my head. How had Breslow been able to make such a seamless transition to professional baseball? Clearly, we were no longer clones.

It was an excruciatingly hot day—just under 100 degrees—and for some reason, the air-conditioning on the bus wasn't turned on.

"Hey," yelled Kotchman from his perch on the front seat, loud enough so even the Coños in the back could hear, "bus driver . . . turn on the air . . . bitch!"

Everyone laughed and Kotchman turned around to acknowledge his adoring audience. The driver was an obese middle-aged man with glasses who hadn't driven for us before.

"Seriously," he continued, speaking more to us than to the driver, "turn on the AC. It's hot as hell, bitch!"

The bus driver kept his eyes on the road and didn't acknowledge Kotchman.

"Hello?" said Kotchman, still trying to get some reaction.

The driver shook his head and pulled the bus over to the side of the road. We were just outside of Provo, far enough away that the mountains behind our field were barely visible in the distance.

The driver stood up, his shirt drenched in sweat, and said, "The air-conditioning unit on this bus is not functioning properly. I apologize for the inconvenience."

A few players groaned.

"Additionally," he continued, "profanity will not be tolerated on the bus. Thank you."

He tucked in his sweaty shirt and got back behind the wheel. As soon as we were back on the road, Kotchman stuck his middle finger in the air and pointed it at the driver. We all cheered. The driver clearly had a lot to learn.

It was another ho-hum day at the ballpark as we jumped out to an early lead against the Raptors. One of the strangest things about the season was how the games and series started to bleed into one another. For every close game or game that I pitched in, there were a half dozen that trudged by unremarkably.

Breslow was brought in to pitch in the eighth inning and I was summoned to give a scouting report to our hitters. It was an awkward situation to be in.

"He throws strikes," I said to the group of ten hitters. "Breslow's got a fastball in the high eighties, a slow curve, and a changeup. Be ready to hit because he'll probably throw you a first-pitch fastball for a strike."

We beat the Raptors, 5–0, despite Breslow throwing another scoreless inning. His seemingly effortless success was infuriating and made me feel all the more inadequate. We were now 14-7 and still in first place. If it hadn't been for my abominable outing, we'd be in the midst of a ten-game winning streak.

"TWENTY-FIVE BUCKS," Clayton said to me the next day in the clubhouse. "I want it in my hands by this time tomorrow."

"For what?" I asked innocently.

"Didn't do your Jobes," he said with a big grin. "Looks like I'll have a little more spending money for the strip clubs in Canada."

In addition to lifting weights twice per week, we were all expected to participate in an injury prevention program that included a series of shoulder exercises with five-pound weights three times per week. Named after orthopedic surgeon Frank Jobe—who pioneered the so-called Tommy John Surgery—these "Jobe exercises" were intended to protect each player's rotator cuff and the Angels organization took them very seriously. Failure to do them meant you weren't taking your career seriously—that you were cavalier about your health—and it also meant an extra lap dance for Clayton.

I looked at the chart and saw that he was right—I'd logged only two Jobe workouts last week.

"Sorry about that," I said.

"Hey, don't say sorry, just more fun for me in Canada."

He was our team's strength and conditioning coach, but it wasn't hard to tell where his priorities were.

Weight-lifting infractions were not the only way we'd lose money from our meager paychecks. In fact it seemed like just about any lapse in judgment or effort could cost us. Failure to run hard to first base, failure to slide at the appropriate time, missing a sign, or being late to any team function resulted in a twenty-five-dollar fine. And the fine increased by ten dollars with each subsequent offense. Fines not related to weight lifting were paid directly to Kotchman, who would use the money to buy movies for the bus. I had the tardy players before me to thank for *"Comedy Central Presents"* Gilbert Gottfried and the entire *WrestleMania* catalog.

Tonight was the third and final game of the series against Ogden and it was our twenty-second game in twenty-two days. It was another exciting game to watch as Joe Saunders was matched up against the Raptors' left-handed flamethrower, Manny Parra.

Parra was what scouts call a "draft-and-follow," which is a rule that allows clubs to maintain exclusive signing rights to a drafted player until a week before the following draft if that player attends junior college. Parra had been selected in the twenty-sixth round of the 2001 draft out of American River Junior College in Sacramento. The Brewers didn't offer him a contract right away, instead opting to watch him develop over the course of the year, and when he added 8 miles per hour to his fastball, they offered him a $1.55 million signing bonus just weeks before the 2002 draft. I'd enjoyed mentioning Parra's signing bonus to Breslow, who'd also been a twenty-sixth-round left-handed draft pick by the Brewers, but had signed for slightly less.

Saunders was hardly intimidated—with every passing day he seemed to become more brash.

"Parra can't touch me," Saunders said, pacing around the dugout in Ogden just before game time. "Just a chump from some no-name school."

He wasn't talking to anyone in particular. It seemed that this was his way of psyching himself up for the game.

"Twenty-sixth-round draft pick . . . give me a break."

Glances were exchanged with every comment. Patience with Saunders was wearing thin.

Neither pitcher disappointed, as Saunders once again delivered an excellent performance. I'd never seen two pitchers throw so well before—hitters looked silly as they tried to make contact. The score was tied going into the eighth inning, when we strung a few hits together and scored a run. We held on to win the game, improving to 15-7 on the year. Like Saunders, Parra would eventually make the big leagues, but he would undergo major reconstructive rotator cuff surgery and spend five years toiling in the Brewers' minor league system before getting his big break. The Brewers, it seemed, were not in the habit of forcing players to do Jobe exercises.

Tomorrow would be our first off day and I couldn't wait for the chance to do something not related to baseball. But Kotchman killed those plans shortly after the game ended.

"We leave for Canada in two hours," he said. "We should be on the road by midnight. Some of you may have noticed that tomorrow is our first off day. Maybe you've got some big plans. I don't know. I advise you to take a look at a fuckin' map. We're driving from Provo to Alberta-fucking-Canada. It's a seventeen-hour drive if we're lucky. Hopefully we'll be there by dinnertime tomorrow."

I swear I saw him smile as he walked away.

A moment later I felt a tap on the shoulder. It was Matt Brown, the baby-faced third baseman who was just one year removed from Coeur D'Alene High School in Idaho.

"Want to get some beer for the trip?" he asked as I undressed. It was one of the first times he'd spoken to me.

"Uh, yeah, sure."

"It's gonna be a long ride. I figure we can use it."

"We can't take it on the bus, you know."

"I know," he said, wiping his nose with his jersey, "but we can pound a few beers in the parking lot."

"Sure. Hey, how are your nuts doing? I saw Larry King's kid got you pretty good."

"I'm fine. I coulda killed that little shit. He hit me hard! He's gonna grow up to be a boxer . . . just like his dad."

Brown was younger than the youngest students I'd tutored in organic chemistry at Yale, and I never would've purchased beer for them. But in this case, it just felt nice to be wanted and I couldn't say no.

Only as we were walking to my Jeep did I realize that he'd approached me because, of the handful of drinking-age players on the team, I was the only one with a car at his disposal. We drove to the neighboring town of Orem and I bought a twelve-pack of Miller Lite.

"Ambitious," he said as I climbed back into the car.

We drove back to the parking lot across from our stadium and began furiously drinking the beers. Sure, I was breaking the law—but what the hell, it was gonna be a long ride to Canada.

"So you went to Yale," he said in between huge sips.

"Yeah," I said, trying to keep up.

"So are you, like, a genius?"

"Honestly?"

"Yeah, honestly," he said, crushing the empty can between his hands.

I couldn't resist. "I am."

"For real?"

"Yeah."

"So what's that mean? Can you, like, read a book and remember every word of it?"

"Of course."

"Jesus."

"Yeah, it freaks me out sometimes."

"Sometimes I think I shoulda gone to college," he said, staring straight ahead. Brown had been the Angels' tenth-round pick in 2001 and had received $48,500 to turn down a scholarship to Oregon State.

"Oh, yeah?" I said, somewhat surprised. Most of my teammates were fond of saying they hated school.

"Yeah, everybody says it's the best time of your life."

"It is pretty great," I said, as a thousand memories of college breezed through my mind. "But not many people get to do this."

"Yeah, but I visit my buddies in the off-season. I see what college is like . . . all the girls . . . all the parties. And I'm stuck here drinking beers in some empty parking lot."

"Thanks, man."

"No, no, no offense . . . but this ain't college."

"No, it's not."

"But it'll all be worth it if I make the big leagues, I guess."

"Definitely."

We sat for another half hour, talking about Idaho and Yale, Kotchman and the Coños, and came close to finishing all the beers.

THE NEXT FEW HOURS were excruciating.

Brown and I stumbled across the empty parking lot and waded into a row of shrubs and relieved ourselves as cars raced by. Matt was able to spell out his name and briefly urinate on my ankle, which I chose to interpret as a sign of endearment. A few more unsteady steps and we were back on the sidewalk heading toward our stadium.

On the concourse just outside the clubhouse, we ran into Blake. He was holding a duffel bag with his left hand and placing some tobacco in his cheek with his right.

"That's it," he said as we approached him.

"What?" I asked.

I stopped to talk while Brown kept walking straight into the clubhouse.

"I'm done," Blake said, before letting out a sigh and offering me a pinch.

I shook my head.

"What?" I asked, still feeling a bit woozy from the beer.

"You heard me . . . I'm done. I just retired."

Hearing the last word immediately sobered me up.

"You did?"

"Yeah. Just now."

"No."

"Yeah. You know I've been wrestlin' with it for a while."

"I know, but shit," I said, putting my arm on his shoulder. "Shit, man." I hadn't yet acquired a bedside manner.

"You know I've been leanin' toward this . . . getting closer and closer . . ."

"Why now?"

"Why now? Well . . . you know, it was a lot of things. Family stuff, of course . . . but the straw that broke the camel's back? Two words: Leonardo D'Amico."

"D'Amico? My roommate? What the hell did . . . ?"

"He ain't your roommate no more. Clayton just assigned him to me. He said they switchin' up the rooms. . . . Kotch thinks it'll help us gel or somethin'. But I just . . . I just can't do it."

"Jesus . . . Blake, I lived with D'Amico. He's fine. I really don't think you should go and . . ."

"Like I said, it was a lot of things, but havin' to room with him put me over the edge. You know I've been thinkin' about this a long time. My arm ain't gonna get any better. And the idea of having to get on that bus. To ride seventeen hours to go to fuckin' Canada . . . to go to Medicine Hat . . . is that even a real place? To be even farther away from my family . . . I couldn't do it."

"Are you sure you want . . ."

"And then the idea of gettin' off that bus and havin' to share a room with one of those fuckin' immigrants . . . shit . . . that was it."

"So this is really it? You said yourself you were gonna regret it as soon as you retired."

"This is it," he said, spitting a rather large amount of tobacco onto the pavement. "And I don't regret it."

"Well . . ."

"Not one bit. Fuck this place."

"I guess when you know . . . you know. I'm gonna miss you, man."

"Yep, I just told Kotch and he wished me luck. Now I'm just waitin' for my cab. Flyin' out first thing tomorrow."

"Jesus. It happens fast. Well, I'll wait with you."

We stood for a few more minutes, mostly in silence, until his cab came. He shook my hand and sauntered down the concourse to the taxi. It was the last time I ever saw him.

I walked back into the clubhouse to grab my equipment and found the place deserted. Everyone had already headed out to the bus. Panic ensued as I furiously stuffed my hat, glove, and a few Red Bulls into my bag and sprinted out the door, chanting, "Oh shit, oh shit, oh shit." I'd lost track of time and didn't want to begin to think about what Kotch would do to me if I missed the bus. And how on earth would I get to Medicine Hat, Canada? I sprinted to the parking lot and found the last player putting his equipment under the bus.

"That was a close one, bitch," Kotchman said as I calmly boarded the bus, trying to catch my breath. The lights were off but I found an empty seat next to Brown.

"Jesus," I said, looking at him, "the bus almost left without me."

He didn't respond. He was playing a handheld video game and listening to his CD player. It was nearing midnight and the bus felt warm. Either the air conditioner was still broken or I was just worked up from my panic attack.

Kotchman turned around in his seat but did not stand up.

"We've got a long ride ahead of us . . . a real long ride. And yes, the AC is still broken."

Quan and a few others moaned.

"As long as you play this game, you will never have a road trip longer than this one. Seventeen goddamn hours on this piece-of-shit bus. But if you can go out and play hard after crap like this, you'll be proving something—to me and to yourselves. I like the way we're playing right now. Keep it up. I'm proud of you bitches."

I nudged Brown and motioned for him to take his headphones off.

"We've got a long ride," Kotchman continued, "so I got some new movies for the bus. We got three options: *The Natural, Eddie Murphy Raw,* and *Pootie Tang.*"

There was a brief moment of silence before Callaspo yelled from the back of the bus, *"Pootie Tang!"*

"What'd you say, bitch?" asked Kotchman as he raised a hand to his ear.

"Pootie! Pootie! Pootie!" Callaspo sang as he stood up and simulated doggie-style intercourse with his headrest.

Kotchman tried to fight it, but he was quickly laughing along with the rest of us. Then he reached for the movie and said, *"Pootie Tang* it is."

For some reason, Kotchman decided to play all the movies at a decibel level approaching that of a pneumatic drill, so I was forced to watch this movie—one of the worst of 2001—as we glided past Great Salt Lake along Interstate 84. It was a satire of old blaxploitation films, starring Lance Crouther as a ghetto folk hero who speaks in unintelligible phrases, though this was lost on Matt Brown.

"What's a 'pone tony'?" he asked me a few minutes into the film.

"He's speaking gibberish," I replied.

"No, he's not. . . . It's Hindu or something."

"It's definitely gibberish. That's the joke."

"No . . . it's not. I swear I've heard people say 'pone tony.' And I know I've heard 'sa da tey' before. I'm serious. This is gonna drive me nuts."

"It sounds familiar because he's switching the first letters of the words. You're thinking of a tone pony."

"No . . . I'm not," he whispered. "I want to know what he's saying."

Perhaps all the talk in the parking lot about college had gotten Brown in the mood to learn something. And since he'd just pissed on my leg, I decided to have some fun with him.

"Oh, did you hear that?" I said a few minutes later, "He just said 'panny sty.'"

"What's that mean?" Brown replied quickly, trying not to miss the dialogue.

"You were right. . . . It *is* Hindu. It means 'hello.'"

"Yeah?"

"Yeah—I took a bit of Hindu at Yale."

"No shit?"

"Seriously. I just had to hear it for a few minutes before it all came together. '*Sa da tey*' means 'thank you.' And '*pone tony*' means 'goodbye' or 'as you wish.'"

"See," he said triumphantly, "I'm not just some redneck retard from Idaho."

I started to speak but he raised his finger to his mouth so I would keep quiet. He was quietly repeating every sentence out of Pootie's mouth. Eventually I broke in.

"I have to call a spade a spade—you were right and I was wrong."

"Don't be so shocked, Mr. Yale. I can teach you something every once in a while, too."

"Brownie," I said, putting my hand on his shoulder, "I think you're a smart guy. I mean that."

"Seriously?"

"Yeah."

From the light of the television, I could see a puckish grin appear on his face. He nodded his head to acknowledge the compliment. Then he extended his hand and said, "*Sa da tey.*"

Maybe I was being a little harsh, but the following year in spring training Matt Brown and I were paired together as roommates and we'd often speak fondly of our brief, drunken night in the empty parking lot. I continued to follow Brown as he spent one year after another bouncing around the minor leagues—from Cedar Rapids to Little Rock, California, to Salt Lake—and I thought he was destined to be just another minor league washout like me. I often thought of our conversation in the Jeep and I believed he'd come to regret his decision to skip college. I was certain he'd made the wrong decision as I watched Oregon State win the College World Series in 2006 while Matt was still wasting away in the minors. But then, in May 2007, still a few months shy of his twenty-fifth birthday, Matt Brown got the call he'd been waiting for, and made his major league debut at third base for the Anaheim Angels.

We watched the movie for another hour and I continued to make up phrases every time he asked me what something meant. The movie ended a little before two A.M. and Kotchman called for lights-out. Without the distraction of Brown and Pootie, I immediately felt the urge to urinate. I was sitting near the front of the bus and the journey to the bathroom in the back looked insurmountable. Everyone was trying to sleep and several players were lying in the aisles. I'd have to climb over a half dozen large men whom I'd said less than a dozen words to all year before dealing with the Coños if I wished to urinate. It seemed I had only two options—infuriate half of my team by trying to use the toilet or let it go and fester in my own urine on a hot bus for fifteen hours. I tapped Brown on the shoulder.

"I have to piss," I whispered. "Do you?"

"No."

"I really have to go, man. I shouldn't have had all those beers. What should I do?"

"Didn't you go before we left?"

"Yes. No. I don't know. . . . I was talking with Blake."

"Not such a smart guy after all," he said, again smiling. He shrugged his shoulders and went back to sleep.

I fidgeted back and forth in my seat, thinking of all that beer trying to get out of me. I was about to burst.

And then, something happened.

Somewhere near Pocatello, Idaho, the driver thought he saw a deer in the road and slammed on the brakes. It caused players to go cascading down the aisles, bouncing awkwardly into the seat backs in front of them.

The bus screeched to a halt and Kotchman yelled, "Is everyone okay?"

No one responded.

"I'm not fuckin' around," he continued. "Is everybody okay?"

We all answered in the affirmative and the journey continued. The moment of terror briefly took my mind off my bladder, but the agony soon returned. A few seconds later I looked between my legs and noticed a Gatorade bottle was resting against my left leg. It was mostly empty, save for about 20 milliliters of brown liquid—undoubtedly tobacco spit—and it was the answer to my prayers.

"Sorry, Brownie," I said as I unzipped my pants. He had already fallen back asleep.

I quickly relieved myself and sealed the top. No one had noticed. I leaned back in my chair and let out a deep breath. Thank God for chewing tobacco, I said as I shut my eyes and faded to sleep.

But before I knew it, I was being summoned. Someone was shaking my shoulder from behind.

"Hey," the voice said. It was dark and I couldn't tell who it was behind me. "Hey, Matt, did you see my spitter?"

"What?"

"Did you or Brown see my spitter?" My eyes adjusted to the dim light and I realized it was Heath in search of his bottle. "It must have rolled up here when we hit the brakes. I'm asking everybody. I gotta get it back."

"Oh," I said, as I glanced at the Gatorade bottle between my legs. "No, sorry."

"All right, thanks."

He continued to walk up the aisle, asking Quan and Gray if they'd seen it. Now he was standing next to me.

I gingerly picked up the bottle and started to put it on the floor. When my task was half-complete, I felt a shove.

"What the hell is that?" Heath asked.

"What?"

"That bottle. Is that my spitter?"

"I don't know. I don't think so."

"Let me see it."

He picked up the warm bottle and gave it a long look. It was dark brown with the black residue of tobacco at the bottom. He gave it a swirl.

"What the fuck? What the fuck is this?"

"I don't know."

"You pissed in my spitter?"

"No. It was just sitting up here. I woke up and had to go and I . . ."

"Fuck you!" he said and punched me in the arm. Luckily it wasn't my throwing arm.

"Dude, I'm sorry. I woke up and it was sitting next to me. How was I supposed to know it was your spitter?"

"Because it had tobacco juice in it. What the fuck did you think it was?"

He was growing increasingly angry and woke more than a few people up.

"I had to go, man. I'm sorry. I don't know what else to say." I was trying to keep my voice down, but his was growing louder with every word.

"Fuck you, you arrogant prick!" he said and again punched me in the arm.

"Chill the fuck out!" I replied. He was starting to punch harder.

"No, I will not chill the fuck out. I have to ride the next fifteen hours without my spitter because you had to piss in it like a little fucking bitch."

"Dude, I'm sorry. We'll stop for breakfast in a few hours and I'll buy you two spitters."

He was seething. He leaned his small, freckled face close to mine. He was either going to tell me something very important or punch me in the face.

"Don't try to buy me," he whispered, "you fucking asshole."

Our noses were just a few inches apart. I'd had enough of his comments about my supposed money and arrogance. I needed to end this before things got out of hand.

"Consider it a gift," I said, nodding at the bottle that he was still holding. "I'm sure you can use some clean urine for your next drug test."

His eyes grew wide.

"You shut your fucking mouth!" he whispered.

He stuck his finger in my face and quietly returned to his seat. Sure, it was below the belt, but fuck him—we were competing for the same roster spot and one of us was a cheater.

WE WERE SOMEWHERE NEAR Dillon, Montana, when the sun came up. Brown was asleep on my shoulder and my left calf was quivering, on the verge of an all-out cramp. I pushed Brown's head off my shoulder and stood up to stretch. To the west stood the Pioneer Mountains, to the east a pine forest, and below me lay a cadre of slumbering giants.

We stopped a few hours later to get breakfast and I bought Heath a Gatorade and a tin of tobacco as a peace offering. He took the bottle but refused the tin, saying he hated the brand Copenhagen.

The next few hours proceeded very slowly. We baked as the sun rose and the smell of body odor gradually suffused the bus. We watched *The Natural* and *Eddie Murphy Raw* as we continued down Interstate 15, passing through Butte and Helena, slowly inching toward Alberta. Brown slept the whole way and my leg cramped off and on during the movies, but I didn't stand to stretch for fear of blocking someone's view of the television.

"We're almost there, bitches," Kotchman said as we crossed the border into Canada. "Four more hours to the Hat."

Around six P.M. we mercifully pulled into the parking lot of the Medicine Hat Comfort Inn. Named for the headdress worn by the medicine men of the Blackfoot Indian tribe, Medicine Hat was now a retirement community best known for the Kipling line "All hell for a basement," in reference to the ample natural gas reserves several miles below.

We limped off the bus and began stretching.

"New room assignments," Clayton said as we gathered in the parking lot. "Deal with it."

He read out the names and I learned that I'd been paired with Randy Burden, one of the undrafted free agents who'd recently joined the team. Randy had been with the team for nearly two weeks but I hadn't yet spoken to him. And to be honest, I knew only two things about him—he was a right-handed reliever and he was the only player on the team with a mustache.

We introduced ourselves and parted ways. Randy went to the room while I went out with a group of players in search of food and an ATM. When I returned two hours later, I found Randy on his knees. He was at the foot of the bed and his hands were clasped together.

"Whoa, what's up?" I said as I entered the room, sipping my soda.

He raised a finger and indicated he was almost finished. I put down the drink and lay on my bed.

"I pray every night," he said as he stood up. "I hope it doesn't bother you." He was six feet three with short brown hair, a soft midsection, a softer voice, and a mesmerizing pencil-thin mustache that I couldn't take my eyes off.

"No, no, that's fine," I said.

"Cool."

"Actually, I should be the one praying. . . . Have you seen how I've thrown lately?"

"I've been praying a little extra the past few days. Just, you know, to say thanks to the man upstairs for getting me into pro ball."

"I'm sure he appreciates it."

"I think it's more than a coincidence that I ended up with the Angels."

I had to make a conscious effort not to be condescending. Yale had been a place where overt piety was generally taken as a sign of backwardness.

"That's great," I replied.

He stretched out on his bed and looked at the low ceiling.

"Looks like they put the smartest guy on the team with the dumb-est, huh?"

"You're the smartest guy on the team?" I said with a smile.

"Yeah, right. . . . I bet you've never even heard of Chowan College."

He was right.

"Of course I have," I said, trying to think of something safe to say. "I know it's a long way from here."

"You can say that again."

"Don't even try to tell me you're dumbest," I said, looking over at him. "Brownie thought Pootie was speaking Hindi."

"No!"

"Yes!"

"Wow."

"I think I'm gonna call it a night," I said. "I know it's early, but I'm beat."

"Be my guest," he said, reaching into his bag. "I hope you don't mind if I read for a while."

"Of course not. Whatcha got?"

"The Bible."

I WOKE UP as fresh as a Canadian daisy the next morning. Randy was still asleep so I walked down to the lobby to begin my customary tour of the new town. Of the numerous brochures in the lobby, one jumped out at me. It read "Where Is the World's Largest Teepee? The Answer Is Here!"

The Saamis Teepee had been built for the 1988 Winter Olympics in Calgary and was moved to Medicine Hat in 1991. It sounded pretty random, but I decided to go for it. I flagged down a taxi and headed out on the Trans-Canada Highway. The man let me out on the side of a quiet road next to an empty parking lot. In the distance stood the enormous teepee.

"Give me two minutes," I said to the driver. I could tell this was going to be short.

I jogged over to the teepee and gave it a good look. It was a teepee, all right, but not what I'd expected. The 215-foot construction before me was really just nine white concrete poles leaning together to form a half-teepee—and there wasn't any birch bark or animal skins. I stood in the open plain, looking toward the sun, and wondered, What the fuck am I doing here?

When I got back to the room, Randy was once again reading the Bible.

"Do you ever read the Good Book?" he asked innocently as I turned on the television.

"Honestly, no."

"I'm not trying to be pushy or anything, but I wouldn't have a problem if you ever wanted to read mine. Take it anytime you want."

I wasn't interested.

"I know you're not very religious . . . or whatever . . . but I have to tell you this," he said, standing by the door to our room. "Two years ago a friend of mine saw a homeless man sitting outside of a convenience store. When he walked out of the store he looked at the man and saw the face of Jesus. My friend . . ."

"Your friend is an idiot," I said curtly and immediately regretted it. "We should probably head down to the bus."

Randy put his head down and sat in silence until we left the room.

The Medicine Hat ballpark was distinctly Canadian—behind the baseball field stood a large hockey rink and a curling center. It was a nice stadium, and they managed to fill it most nights with the retirees of the community. We had a three-game series with the Blue Jays and most of us couldn't wait to get the hell out of Canada.

During the team stretch, I overheard several of my teammates talking about the previous night.

"I can't believe he drank three pitchers . . . himself!"

"How about Clayton getting us kicked out of the strip club!"

"Unbelievable!"

"You can't throw coins at the strippers."

"Heath was puking all morning."

"Bilke was doing shots in the Champagne Room!"

"Yeah, but he didn't drink as much as Williams!"

The name Williams caught my attention. After Saunders, Brian Williams was our best pitcher and he was starting tonight's game.

"I had to walk his ass home," Heath said. "Williams couldn't even put one foot in front of the other."

Williams was in the top ten in every pitching category in the Pioneer League. He was third in the league in strikeouts and ERA and had walked only two batters in twenty-six innings of work. I saw Williams's flushed face in the dugout a few minutes before game time. His eyes were bloodshot and he was feverishly drinking one cup of water after another. It wasn't hard to predict what would happen next.

Williams looked worse on the mound than he did in the dugout. He lasted only three innings—his shortest outing of the season—and allowed three runs and four walks, tripling his season total. He had the bases loaded every inning and was lucky the damage wasn't far worse. The rest of my teammates didn't fare much better. We made several errors and had trouble hitting every pitch they threw at us. It was clear which team had just endured a seventeen-hour bus ride.

We lost badly, and after the game, Kotchman was livid.

"Well," he said as he paced down the aisle of the bus, "it was an embarrassment to be your manager tonight. Fuck! I had to stand in the third-base coaches' box for nine goddamn innings listening to the opposing team talk about how bad you guys were. They can't *believe* you're in first place. It makes me sick. You guys came out flat and never showed any energy. I don't give a damn about the bus ride. Be professionals!"

He walked back to the front of the bus.

"And Williams, son, I don't know what the hell was wrong with you tonight. But you were just plain terrible. Terrible!"

WE LOST THE NEXT NIGHT in extra innings and Kotchman resumed the silent treatment. The following day was David Wells BobbleHead Doll Night and the stadium was packed.

I was brought in to pitch the seventh inning of a high-scoring, sloppy game. Once again my stomach turned when I realized Junior Guzman would be catching instead of Dvorsky. He was standing at the pitcher's mound when I took the ball from Kotchman.

"Outs plus one with a runner on second," I said to Junior, indicating which set of signs I wanted to use with a runner on base. We typically used one set of signs if there were no runners on base, and a second, more cryptic set of signs if there was a runner on second base. "Outs plus one" meant we would use the first sign if there were no outs, the second sign if there was one out, and the third if there were two outs.

"No," he said.

"What?"

"We use third sign with runner on second."

"Fine."

I quickly gave up a hit and a walk and with it came the panic I was unfortunately getting accustomed to. I threw a curve to the next batter but Junior was expecting a fastball. He lunged awkwardly at the ball and missed it. The batters advanced a base and Kotchman was irate.

"Get it together out there," he yelled from the dugout. "Jesus Christ!"

I had to call Junior to the mound to get things straight.

"My bad," I said. "I was thinking outs plus one."

"Is okay," he said, patting me on the back and returning to the plate.

I looked around the stadium and saw thousands of plastic David Wells heads bobbing in unison. The next pitch was a single to left and two runs scored.

The next inning was a carbon copy of the first one. Guzman and I once again had our signals crossed and Kotchman continued to scream.

"If you can't pitch . . . I'll get someone who can!"

It was an awful thing to hear while standing on the mound.

My second bad outing in a row lasted two innings and I allowed four runs. When I came into the dugout, I was treated like a leper. Players averted their eyes and no one would speak to me. We'd always give someone space after a poor performance, but this time I just wanted someone to talk to. There was no Breslow to tell me that the umpire was squeezing me and that my infielders weren't making the plays. We lost the game, 14–11, and for the first time all year, we were swept in a three-game series. We were in for a miserable ride to Great Falls, Montana.

An hour into the trip, Kernan called for me.

"Take a seat," he said as I stood in the aisle.

"What's up, Kernan?"

"Talk to me, Mac."

"I pitched like shit tonight."

"Yes. Yes, you did."

"For the second time in a row."

"Yep."

"I don't really have an answer . . ."

"I was looking at the gun readings," he said, producing a spread-sheet from his bag, "and your velocity has been down the last two times you've pitched."

"Really?"

"Yeah, it's down around eighty-five. When we drafted you we had you closer to ninety."

"I don't know . . ."

"Are you hurt?"

"No, I wish I could say that was it, but I feel fine."

He took a deep breath.

"Get some rest and let's talk about this tomorrow. We need to work some things out."

I was unable to sleep for the rest of the ride. What did Kernan mean, we needed to work some things out? We pulled into the parking lot of the Great Falls Midtown Motel at 4:45 A.M. and I immediately crawled into bed.

"Mind if I read for a bit?" Randy said.

"Whatever."

THE NEXT MORNING, I could think only of my impending meeting with Kernan and my lagging velocity. I skipped my morning walk and stayed in bed, staring at the ceiling.

"What's up, Matt?" Randy said as he emerged from the shower. "You've been just layin' there all morning."

"I've been pitching like shit and I don't know what's wrong," I said without looking at him.

"Well, are you trying as hard as you can?"

"What?"

"Are you giving it all you got?" he continued.

I was in no mood for his Christian pep-talk bullshit.

"Yeah."

"Well, that's all you can do. Just do your best. The rest will work itself out."

"That's idiotic."

"Suit yourself. Just keep working hard, it'll work out. Have faith."

CENTENE STADIUM IN GREAT FALLS was a quaint park. The outfield walls were painted Dodger blue, as were the dugouts, concession stands, bleachers, and awnings lest anyone forget the team was an affiliate of the Los Angeles Dodgers.

Kernan found me during batting practice.

"Walk with me," he said as we headed toward the center field warning track.

"Let's talk about goals, Mac."

"Okay."

His stopped near the blue fence and folded his arms.

"What are your goals in baseball?"

"To make the big leagues." There was no other answer.

"Good. Now I'm gonna be frank with you, Mac. Okay?"

"Sure." He put his hand on my shoulder and looked deeply into my eyes.

"You're not going to make the big leagues if you continue throwing like this."

"I agree."

"Something's got to change. I've been talking with Kotchman and we think you should change your arm angle."

This was not a good sign. Kernan usually gave advice like "Keep the ball down," "Get ahead on the first pitch," and "Don't be afraid to pitch inside." Suggesting that I change my delivery meant he thought something was very wrong, and the fact that he'd brought it up with Kotchman was even worse.

"Change my arm angle?"

"Yes. You're not going to make the big leagues by overpowering guys. You know that. You're going to make it based on deception."

"Right."

"We think you can be more deceptive. Dropping your arm angle will make you tougher to hit."

"Like throwing sidearm?"

That would be the kiss of death.

"No, not sidearm. Just drop it down a little."

"Okay."

"Now, Mac, you don't have to take my advice. Ultimately this is your career. If you don't want to do this, you don't have to."

Kernan always provided that disclaimer after giving his opinion.

"I understand. We both know I've been pitching like crap. I'm willing to try anything."

"Good," he said, putting his hand on my shoulder. "Let's spend the next few days working on it in the bullpen and we'll put you back in a game when you're ready."

"How long are we talking?" I asked.

"Oh . . . I don't know . . . a few days."

It would be nine days before I'd pitch again. In the interim, a few things happened.

THE FOLLOWING DAY I signed my first baseball card contract. A representative from Topps baseball card company met with us in the small maroon conference room of our hotel in Great Falls. Topps agreed to pay me five dollars up front for the right to use my picture and an additional two thousand dollars for the right to mass-produce my baseball card if I ever made the big leagues. The representative handed out the five-dollar checks and concluded the meeting by saying, "And guys, just so you know . . . nobody actually cashes these checks. It's supposed to be a souvenir." From there, Sunshine, Matt Brown, and I walked out the door and down the street to the nearest bank to get our five dollars.

The next day I arrived at the park to find a white sheet of paper taped to every locker. Before I could read it, Brett Cimorelli pulled me aside.

"Can you believe this?" he said out of the left side of his mouth.

"What is it?"

"You know that Web site . . . futureangels.com or something. Remember in spring training when they came around . . . asking for volunteers to keep a journal of the season?"

"No, I wasn't here in spring training."

"Oh, yeah. Well, they did. But nobody took 'em up on it . . . until now."

I, of course, was keeping a journal of my own and wanted to know more about this Web site.

"Is that what's attached to our locker? Somebody's diary?"

Brett leaned in close as more players filed in and discovered the paper.

"Jamie Steward posted something . . . and it's ridiculous. It's a full page of him bitching about how he's been jerked around by the organization, how he's been lied to by nearly everyone, how he never shoulda been sent down to Provo, and how he's considering retirement because of the way he's been treated."

"Wow. He wrote all that?"

"Yeah."

"What an idiot."

"Yep."

"Who made the copies?"

"Don't know. I bet we'll never know. The funny thing is . . . I don't think anyone would care if he *did* retire."

"Yeah, he's pretty bad."

Steward walked into the clubhouse a few minutes later. His usual self-satisfied grin quickly gave way to a look of terror as he read his own words and looked around the room. He buttoned his pants and started to walk out of the room when Kotchman entered.

Kotchman made a beeline for Steward.

"Listen," he said, sticking his finger in Steward's face, "I don't know who made the damn copies, but if you've got problems with this organization, you bring it up with someone within the organization. Do you understand me?"

"Yes, sir."

I had expected Kotchman to be indignant, but he wasn't yelling and he seemed rather calm.

"Doing this kind of shit will get you nowhere. I know you're upset you got sent back to Provo, but you've got to talk to someone like a man. You don't go and broadcast it on the goddamn Internet. Is that clear?"

"Yes. It will never happen again."

"Good. Live and learn, Jamie. Now it's time to move on, bitch."

Jamie Steward was promoted back to Cedar Rapids the following day. He was out of baseball within a year.

We lost two of three to the Dodgers and headed back to Provo with only one win from our six-game road trip. The thirteen-hour trip was once again done in silence and we were back in Provo by one P.M. the following day.

WHEN I WALKED THROUGH the door, my host family was seated at the kitchen table. I'd had my twenty-second birthday during the road trip and they were waiting to celebrate it with me. But all I wanted to do was sleep.

"Happy birthday!" they all said.

The two eldest children sprinted toward me and hugged my legs. It was nice to be home—and there was a cake and four cards waiting for me at the table. The children had all finger-painted their cards, but Michael's had a message:

> Dear Matt,
>   Thanks for staying at our house. Thanks for being awesome. And thanks for being fabuless!
>   —Michael

After dinner, we all piled into the Expedition and drove up the road to Sundance, the ski resort just outside of Provo owned by Robert Redford. We had dinner, my first real dinner in six weeks, at the foot of the mountain.

"So what's it like playing for Kotchman?" Jeff asked as he picked at his salad.

"Well," I said, trying to buy time to deliver a suitable answer, "he's a character, but he's a great guy to play for. Really cares about his players."

"A character, huh? Do you have any stories?"

His face lit up at the thought of getting a juicy tidbit.

A dozen thoughts raced through my head, none of which was appropriate for the dinner table.

"Oh, I don't know, he likes to do impressions. He's pretty funny."

"Impressions of who?" asked Sarah.

It was a safe bet that Jeff and Sarah had never heard of Andrew Dice Clay, and if they had, they weren't fans.

"Oh, well, uh, a lot of politicians. Mostly Clinton and Bush."

"Ugh," said Sarah, "I do not like Bill Clinton. Not one bit."

After dinner, Jeff showed me the bench next to the frog pond where he had proposed to Sarah twelve years earlier. We didn't have a game that night, so when we went home, Jeff and I stayed up late drinking milk and watching the Angels game. They beat the A's and Jeff was thrilled.

The next morning I came down for breakfast and found Sarah sitting in the living room with a dozen teenage girls. She was reading from the Book of Mormon and they were all taking notes. I made a U-turn as soon as I saw them, but Sarah called out for me.

"Matt," she said, "come back. I want to introduce you!"

I slowly walked back to the living room and Sarah stood up.

"Ladies," she said, "this is Matt. He's living with us this summer. He's an Angel."

"It's nice to meet you all," I said and a few girls giggled.

"Would you like to join us?" Sarah asked. "No pressure, but you can if you want."

I looked at the girls, who were all smiling up at me, and I thought of my teammates.

As the season had progressed, my teammates had grown fond of ridiculing Mormonism, turning it into a game of one-upmanship in the bullpen or the clubhouse. It invariably started with Heath, who would issue the first salvo by saying, "They have their own underwear!" which would lead someone to say, "They think the Garden of Eden is in Missouri!" or, "They baptize dead people!" or, "Their God lives on a planet called Kolob!"

I had been pondering the idea of tactfully asking my host family about these beliefs, but clearly this was not the time.

"You know," I said to Sarah as I stuck my hands in my pockets, "I think I have to go out to the field pretty soon. Otherwise I would. Really."

I stood before them for a few seconds, wondering about the Mormon underwear, before heading back to the kitchen and making a sandwich.

Chapter 7

||||||||||||||||||||||||||||||||||||||||||||

A FTER THIRTY GAMES, our record was 17-13. We were in sole possession of first place, but Ogden and Casper were just two games back. If we could win the first half, we would be assured a spot in the playoffs against the winner of the second half. But with eight games to go, we knew it was going to come down to the wire.

Our next game was at home against the Billings Mustangs, an affiliate of the Cincinnati Reds. We played an uninspired game against them, committing several errors and mustering only four hits in the loss. But the clubhouse was strangely upbeat after the game. Reggae music was being played and players were chatting like it was a victory. When Dvorsky came in, dirty from head to toe, he was furious. He was the closest thing we had to a captain and was probably the only one who actually cared if we won or lost.

"What the fuck is going on in here?" he said as he lumbered in, still wearing his catching equipment.

The room went silent except for Aybar and Callaspo, who continued to laugh. Dvorsky slowly advanced across the locker room and dropped his glove. Then he walked over to Aybar and grabbed him by the neck. He slammed him into the concrete wall, and began yelling.

"What the fuck is your problem, asshole?"

Aybar was frail and terrified. Dvorsky squeezed harder. No one moved.

"No!" yelled Callaspo, trying to defend his friend. But he was easily swatted away by Dvorsky, who had four inches and forty pounds on him.

"So help me God I'm going to kill you," Dvorsky continued. "I've had enough of this shit!"

Aybar's eyes were bulging and he was looking for help.

I thought about intervening but decided to let it play out. This was the first time a player had laid a hand on a teammate and the fact that one was American and the other Dominican was not insignificant. It would be treasonous for me to take the side of a Dominican, and besides, Dvorsky looked like a man possessed. You could tell this outburst was about a lot more than tonight's loss. Watching the scene transpire, there seemed to be a chance he would actually kill Aybar, and in the very manner he suggested we do away with Larry King.

I looked at Astacio and wondered what he was thinking. He was leaning back in his chair, watching along with everyone else. It appeared Aybar was on his own.

But then Junior intervened.

He lunged at Dvorsky and tackled him. Aybar fell to the ground and gasped for breath. The two catchers rolled around for a minute while we all watched from our seats. Junior had Dvorsky pinned when Kotchman entered.

"Well, well, well," Kotchman said as he surveyed the scene, "I'll be damned. You guys finally got a little life in ya."

Junior released Dvorsky and the two returned to their seats. Kotchman was grinning proudly.

"That's the kinda shit I like to see," he said.

He went over and shook hands with both players.

"Shows me you guys care. Well done."

He walked around the room, making eye contact with each player.

"Somebody actually cares that we fuckin' lost. I don't believe it.

Nice work, fellas. Go get 'em tomorrow," he said, and walked out of the room, seeming to have completely forgotten that we'd just lost a crucial game.

A FEW DAYS LATER we played a doubleheader and I pitched two innings, my first since changing my arm angle, and found immediate success. I allowed no hits or runs and had two strikeouts. But the real fireworks came in the second game.

Brian Williams gave up a long home run. It was initially called a foul ball, but the home plate umpire overruled the third-base umpire and awarded the batter a three-run home run. When he did this, Kotchman flipped.

He sprinted out to home plate like George Brett during the infamous pine-tar incident nineteen years earlier, yelling, "How can you miss that call? How! How can you miss that?"

He was nose-to-nose with the umpire screaming obscenities the likes of which Provo had never seen. After thirty seconds of jawing, it was clear that Kotchman was trying to get ejected from the game. It's a tactic that managers occasionally employ to fire up their team. But there was one problem—the umpire simply wouldn't toss him. Kotchman cursed at him, stuck his finger in his face, bumped his chest, and even kicked dirt on the man, but he just wouldn't eject him.

After two minutes of these antics, it appeared that Kotchman had given up. He put his hands on his hips and walked back toward the dugout a defeated man. He'd almost reached the top step when he returned to home plate to continue berating the guy. Perhaps the umpire realized he'd made the wrong call, or maybe he knew that Kotchman was a highly respected coach. For whatever reason, he took all that Kotchman gave him.

Eventually, Kotchman made his way back to the dugout. He poured himself a cup of Gatorade, put it on the top step of the dugout, and kicked it at the umpire. Unfortunately he missed his target and the batboy got soaked. To the eight-year-old's credit, he didn't complain.

The tirade seemed to sap Kotchman of his strength. He sat quietly for the rest of the game and his postgame speech was short.

"You've got five games left in the first half, fellas, and we're in first place by a thread. If we can hold on, we'll guarantee ourselves a spot in the playoffs. I want one of those rings so bad. And I want *you* to want one of those rings as bad as I do. And I think some of you do. Let's finish out the first half strong and we'll be one step closer to the championship." He stuck his fist in the air and added, "You guys can do it!"

Kernan pulled me aside as Kotchman walked out.

"The new arm angle looks great," he said as I put on a shirt.

"Thanks, Kernan, it felt good."

In truth, it felt awful—like I was slinging a shot put at home plate—but the quality outing served as an excellent opiate.

"Great. I really liked what I saw tonight. Keep it up."

We won three of the next five games and narrowly edged Ogden for the first-half crown, assuring ourselves a spot in the Pioneer League playoff in September.

"I KNEW IT WAS GOOD, but I didn't know it was *that* good," Kotchman said as he entered the clubhouse in Idaho Falls a few days later. I'd pitched dreadfully the night before but I felt better when my eyes met Kotchman's, who was sauntering into the clubhouse with a twenty-four-inch black dildo wrapped around his neck like a scarf. We'd just had a big ninth-inning rally to beat the Padres and he was on top of the world.

"I call it the Rally Penis," he said, taking the large object into his hands. Two baseballs were glued to its base, apparently serving as testicles. "It's been with me as long as I've been a manager, and I only bring it out for special occasions."

We all started to giggle as he stroked the thing.

"Three years ago, when we were down three games to one against Ogden and we came back to win . . . who do you think was at my side?"

He looked around the room before pointing to the dildo. "This guy was. The motherfucking Rally Penis. And two years ago, when we got lost on the way to Medicine Hat, what did I do? I smacked that bus driver with the Rally Penis and next thing you know . . . we're back on track."

He tried to fend off a smile but it was no use.

"And tell me, McCarthy," he said, looking at me, "when we needed to beat Billings to clinch the first half, what do you think I pulled out in the eighth inning?"

"The Rally Penis," I said firmly.

"This thing is amazing," he continued, pacing back and forth like one of my manic patients in the psych ward. He placed it over his groin and swung it around.

"Now I look like one of you guys," he said, looking at several of the Dominicans. They all laughed, except Astacio.

"Me and this penis have been through a lot together," he went on, looking at the dildo. "Twenty-four years as a coach and it has never let me down. And tonight was no exception. . . . Four walks in the ninth inning . . . are you kidding me? God, I love this thing!"

He leaned in awkwardly and gave it a kiss on the shaft.

The room erupted in laughter.

Callaspo grabbed Aybar and began humping him. Even Kotchman chuckled.

"Line up and get some," he said and we formed a line. I was mildly frightened.

One by one, Kotchman smacked the dildo back and forth in our faces, saying, "Get some, get some Rally Penis. Yeah."

When he finished christening us, he smiled proudly.

"You guys are my boys," he said, and walked out of the room with the limp dildo dangling by his side.

The next day I threw a scoreless inning and attributed my success, of course, to the Rally Penis.

"That's what I'm talking about," Kotchman said to me as I came off the field. "You just needed a little dick in your face."

I searched for a response, but settled on "Thanks."

The penis was not so kind to Randy. He gave up three runs in one inning of work and was distraught in the dugout.

"Gawwwlee, that was awful," he said as I walked by. He was looking for someone to talk to.

"It wasn't so bad," I said. "You're still getting your feet wet. It takes a while to adjust to all this."

They were hardly the words of a seasoned veteran.

"Thanks, but they hit everything I threw out there."

It was true and I struggled to find reassuring words. What he needed now was Breslow, who always knew what to say after a rough outing.

"Well, they didn't hit your curveball," I offered.

"Yeah. They were too busy hitting the fastball."

We pulled off the victory in spite of Randy's shaky outing and I eagerly awaited another entertaining postgame speech from Kotchman, and perhaps a cameo by the Rally Penis.

"Sit down and shut up," Kotchman said as we entered the clubhouse. He was standing in the same spot where he had dildo-whipped us a night earlier, but last night's levity was gone. He looked around the room to make sure all players and coaches were present.

"It has come to my attention that there is a player on this team who's too hurt to play but healthy enough to go out to fucking dance clubs."

We all looked at Felix Nuñez, the only player on the disabled list. He'd been the team's leading hitter until two weeks ago when he strained his back during a swing. He'd been on the disabled list ever since.

Nuñez didn't speak English, at least I didn't think so, but he dropped his head when he heard Kotchman say his name.

"Mr. Nuñez apparently feels good enough to dance but he's too hurt to play ball. Something doesn't add up, gentlemen."

Kotchman glared at Nuñez. I'd never been part of a public shaming and I wondered how much Nuñez understood. "If you can swing your hips on the dance floor, fellas, you sure as hell better be able to swing a bat during a game.

"You think you've seen me angry," he said, pounding his fist onto a table, "but you have no fuckin' idea. You haven't seen me angry."

He stood up and punched the ice cooler next to him, knocking it to the ground. Ice flew across the room.

"As far as I'm concerned, Felix Nuñez, you are finished playing for me. You have betrayed me, the coaches, and, most importantly, your teammates."

Felix sat motionless with a smirk on his face.

"I've informed the front office of the situation and your future is in their hands. I don't know what's going to happen, but if it was up to me, your ass would be on the street. I don't put up with this kind of crap."

He walked closer to Nuñez. "So you can take off your uniform, pack it in your bag, and watch the game from the stands from now on. You are suspended indefinitely."

He looked around the room to make sure he still had everyone's attention before adding, "And another thing . . . this has nothing to do with the fact that he's Dominican. Nothing."

First Steward's diary and now this? There was a mole on our team, and he'd covered his tracks well, taking down an American and a Dominican. I wondered who would be next.

JOE SAUNDERS WAS PROMOTED to Cedar Rapids the next day and that meant there was an open spot in the starting rotation. I'd thrown well the previous night and was hoping to get a chance to return to it. I was the first person Kernan came over to speak with during our pregame stretch.

"Mac," he said, "walk with me."

We took a walk down the left-field line but he didn't say a word until we were thirty yards from the other players.

"Nice job last night," he said.

"Thanks. I felt really good."

"I'm going to be frank with you, okay, Mac?" he said, putting his hand on my shoulder.

"Of course."

I was worried—it didn't sound like he was about to deliver good news.

"I can't remember the last time you had back-to-back good games."

"It's been a while."

"You'll go out there and look great one day . . . and then look like total dog shit the next."

"You're right. I know you think it's a concentration issue, but it's not. I'm focused every time I go out there."

"I'm sure you are. But Mac, you're never gonna make it if you can't pitch well in back-to-back games. You gotta be good *at least* two out of every three games. At the very least."

"You're right."

"I wanna see you go out there and have another great game. Whatever you did last night . . . just keep doing that. Okay?"

"You got it."

"All right, go finish stretching."

"Thanks, Kernan. By the way, who's taking Joe's spot in the rotation?"

"We brought up Raffy from Mesa."

Raffy was Rafael Rodriguez, a seventeen-year-old right-hander from Cotuí, Dominican Republic. I'd seen him pitch in Mesa and had been thoroughly impressed—he could throw 95 miles per hour consistently, with an effortless delivery. Word around camp was that he'd signed for close to $1 million but no one knew for sure. Like Joe Saunders, Raffy was considered the next big thing in the Angels' organization. Physically he'd been ready for Provo a year ago, but questions about his maturity had kept him in Mesa.

Rafael arrived in the clubhouse the next day surrounded by an entourage of five people. Two were carrying his bags, one was holding a boom microphone, and another was carrying a large video camera that was focused on a man in a suit speaking to Rafael in Spanish. Raffy was wearing gray jeans and a black T-shirt featuring a tiger made out of sequins and he had three large gold chains around his neck. He immediately walked over to the Dominican side of the room and said hello, with the camera following his every move. Like Steward, he didn't bother introducing himself to those on the other side.

Kotchman walked in a few minutes later and was not pleased.

"What the fuck is this?" he said to the cameraman.

"We're here to . . ."

"I don't care why you're here. . . . Get the hell out of my club-house!"

"But we have permission . . ."

"I don't give a damn," Kotchman said, putting his hand over the camera. "Get the hell out!"

Sunshine and I chuckled as the men left with their tails between their legs.

"This ain't Hollywood," Kotchman said as he walked by us. "Right, Sunshine?"

"You can say that again," he replied.

I had some free time, so I decided to walk outside and see what they were doing. I ran into the cameraman—a slim man of about thirty with a long black ponytail and a beard—and he told me they were making a documentary about Rafael.

"We're following him from the Dominican to the U.S. . . . Charting his every move . . . all the way to the big leagues. We want to show what it's like for these guys to come over here."

"Sounds interesting," I said.

"Raffy's perfect, isn't he?"

"I guess."

"He's the next big thing, right? When we're finished we're hoping to sell it to ESPN," he said before flipping open his cell phone to call Raffy.

"WHATCHA WRITING ABOUT in that notebook of yours?" Randy asked me.

We were in a small, dimly lit hotel room in Missoula, Montana, and I was scribbling down a description of the Rally Penis as he watched *SportsCenter*.

"Oh, you know, just keeping track of my pitching stats and stuff."

We had played forty-four games and my stats weren't pretty—my ERA was close to six and I had more walks (fourteen) than strikeouts (thirteen).

"You write in that thing every day, don't you?"

"Yeah, pretty much."

"But you only pitch like once or twice a week. What else you writin' about?"

"Lots of stuff," I said, trying to end the conversation. After the Jamie Steward incident I was even more determined to keep my journal to myself. "I like to keep track of all the running and lifting and stretching we do."

"So you'll know what to do in the off-season?"

"Exactly."

We were wrapping up our series in Missoula and I was genuinely sad to leave the place. We'd been frequenting the Missoula Ale House after every game—playing pool, drinking beers, and watching Aybar and Callaspo chase one slump buster after another.

It was our last night in Missoula, and the topic of conversation in the bullpen was Josh Gray, our hulking first baseman who'd been mired in a thirty-game slump.

"See what McCarthy has to say," said Heath.

"What's up?" I asked as I took a seat on the bench.

"I can already tell you what he's gonna say," said Reed.

"Try me," I said, looking at the two of them.

"Gray slept with a girl in Idaho Falls," said Bilke.

"Good for him," I said. "He needs something. He's been hitting like shit."

"He slept with a black girl," added Reed.

"Nice," I said, smiling. "Wait . . . Gray did? Isn't he from Oklahoma?"

It was an odd response, I know, but that's what I said.

"Who gives a shit?" said Sunshine.

"Who gives a shit?" asked Heath incredulously. "He's taking slump busting to a whole new level."

"Are we really having this conversation?" I asked. "Is this turn-back-the-clock night?"

"Yes, we are having this conversation," said Reed.

"Okay."

"You know . . . you're just what I expected—another East Coast self-serving liberal. This is the real world, Mac. This ain't Yale."

"Thanks for enlightening me."

"It's disgusting is what it is," said Reed.

"And that's exactly what I expected to hear from an inbred racist fuck like you," said Sunshine, glaring at Reed.

"Whoa," said Reed, putting his hands up. "I am *not* a racist."

We continued on like this for the better part of the game, and in the sixth inning, Kernan shot an arrow in my direction.

It happened. I threw a scoreless seventh inning and, for what seemed like the first time all year, recorded back-to-back quality outings. I couldn't wait to discuss my performance with Kernan; unfortunately we lost the game, 12–10. It was our third straight loss to the Missoula Ospreys and all I got from my pitching coach was a nod of the head.

The dog days of August were starting to set in, and with it came more than a few lackadaisical performances. With forty-nine games under our belts and twenty-seven left before the playoffs, many were starting to daydream about the off-season. Others were so fixated on the minutiae of the daily experience in Provo that nearly all of us failed to notice that the big-league club was surging, putting together a ten-game winning streak in August that would propel them into the playoffs.

Anaheim may have had the Rally Monkey, but we had the Rally Penis.

After the game, a group of about fifty mentally handicapped fans came over to our dugout seeking autographs. I cringed when I saw them, anticipating the way my teammates were likely to respond, but to a man they handled themselves with class. It wasn't until we were on the bus that Brown and Saunders began their imitations. And as I looked out the window, I saw two players still signing autographs. Heath and Reed had stayed behind to make sure each fan received one.

"Trust," Kotchman said a few minutes later as the bus left for Provo. "There is nothing more precious on this earth than trust."

He took a deep breath and put his hands on his hips.

"Something woke me and Black Magic up last night," he said, smirking at Coach Rowson. "It was three in the morning, and there was a helluva lot of noise on our floor." He gave a dramatic pause before continuing. "I wandered down to Guzman's room and what did I find? Seven of our players making all kinds of noise with seven girls."

He stared at the back of the bus for twenty seconds before continuing.

"When I say curfew is at one-thirty, damn it, I mean it! It's gonna cost each of you fifty bucks for breaking curfew and another fifty bucks because the girls were butt-ugly. I don't know where you fuckers find these girls. Every goddamn town you've got 'em. If you spent as much time working on the fundamentals of baseball as you do chasing fat girls, you'd be in the big leagues."

It was hard to tell how upset he was. But then his voice started to waver.

"You only get to play the game for so long, so you better make the most of it. Who knows . . . someday you may end up sitting at a desk working for some jerk. Be thankful that you're out here. Be thankful that you get to put on the uniform every goddamn day, and give it all you got while you still can."

It sounded like a cliché, but his words rang true. We couldn't make a living playing minor league baseball; we could barely subsist. But playing professional baseball was better than not playing professional baseball, and for many of us this was about seeing how long we could play the game and not do anything else.

"And another thing," he said. "If you've got a good woman at home, for God's sake don't cheat on her with some slut that you meet on the road. It all comes down to trust."

"BIG NEWS," AUSTIN BILKE announced in the Provo bullpen several days later. "My host family is out of town."

Bilke's journey to Provo had been an unconventional one. He'd been a prized recruit coming out of Beaver Dam High School in Wisconsin and had secured a scholarship to pitch at Purdue. He played one year for the Boilermakers before an arm injury sidelined his career and cost him his scholarship. He left the school and moved to Florida, and it was there that Kotchman saw him lighting up the radar gun in a men's league and signed him on the spot for forty thousand dollars. He had short blond hair and shaved only a few times each month. He was the heaviest drinker on the team, but he had a softness to him that you wouldn't expect from a six-foot-three-inch, 250-pound flamethrower.

"Brett's leaving for football in a couple of days," he continued, "so I'm having everyone over for a little going-away party tonight."

By everyone, he meant just the Americans.

"You know I'll be there, Bockey," said Williams, who was drawing a baseball in the dirt with his finger. He was Austin's closest friend on the team and referred to him only as Bockey, the name of a childhood neighbor with cerebral palsy. "Does the host family know about it?"

"Nah," he said, waving his hand, "I don't think they'll mind," and we all shared a laugh.

Austin lived with a Mormon family just a few streets down from me in a house that was even larger than my posh estate. His family had also made their offer via the radio station, telling Becwar that they'd like to house a player—but he had to be American, and preferably attended college. Since moving in two weeks ago Austin had, coincidentally, discontinued his daily rant against the Mormon Church.

"And I've got a surprise," he said, with his blue eyes growing wide as he looked down the bench. "A big surprise. You guys are gonna love it."

We were playing the opening game of a three-game set with the Medicine Hat Blue Jays that night, and I was hoping to see some action. Over the fifty-four games we'd played, I'd gradually been phased out of Kotchman's pitching rotation. I'd gone from a starting pitcher to a reliever to a seldom-used reliever, and with every demotion my professional aspirations deteriorated a bit more. The only guys who were struggling more than I was were Heath and Randy, who pitched only when we were losing by at least a half dozen runs. I was averaging about an inning a week and was starting to worry about my long-term prospects in baseball.

"Something's gotta change," Kernan had said to me in the locker room after my most recent outing. I'd given up two runs against the Rockies and walked several batters. "I thought the new arm angle was the answer, but maybe it's not."

"I don't know. I feel good, I'm just missing the zone," I said, trying to put a positive spin on my poor performance.

"Your velocity is down and you're not throwing strikes. I don't know, Mac, but you need to start getting people out. The status quo ain't gonna cut it."

"I know."

"This is rookie ball, for God's sake," he said before walking away.

I felt like I'd tried everything—more Red Bull, less Red Bull, more sleep, more running, more lifting, less lifting. I'd even taken Randy's advice and started praying before bed. But nothing seemed to work. I considered hitting up Sunshine for some greenies, the amphetamines he freely dispensed from his locker, but decided against it. The thought had gradually started to enter my mind that perhaps I just wasn't good enough to play professional baseball. But every time I became aware of it, I immediately tried to put it out of my head.

Kernan shot the bow my way in the seventh inning, and after thirty warm-up tosses I tipped my cap to indicate that I was ready. I hadn't pitched in six days and was eager for the chance to be back on the mound. But in the middle of the eighth, Kernan looked at me from the dugout and ran his finger across his neck, indicating that I would not be going into the game. The mime act continued as he pretended to turn the pages of a book, and Anthony Reed quickly took my place on the bullpen mound.

"Goddamn it!" I said as I slammed my glove into the dirt by the bench. "I haven't pitched in a fucking week!"

"Another AGI," said Heath, referring to a mythical statistic that we kept in the bullpen. It stood for "Almost Got In."

"I think I'm leading the damn team in AGIs. That's three in a row," I said, looking at Reed.

"Somebody's always getting screwed," said Brett. And it was true. At least half of my teammates at any one time felt they were being screwed by Kotchman. Whether it was at-bats or innings pitched, everyone had a story to tell about how they'd been wronged. Brett thought the Angels resented him for playing two sports. Heath said he got no respect because he was short. Williams thought he was drafted too low (twenty-seventh round) to be considered a prospect, and Bilke thought he was getting shafted because he was signed as an undrafted free agent. I'd pitched poorly in my last two outings, allowing several runs in both games, so I understood why Kotchman wasn't using me, but frustration was starting to get the better of me. We lost the game that night, and when I arrived at Bilke's place for the party, I was ready to blow off some steam.

"Welcome to my lovely home," Austin said as he greeted me at the front door. Brett, Williams, and Sunshine were already inside along with two young ladies.

"What's up, Matty?" Sunshine said as he handed me a beer. They were all standing in the middle of the large living room next to a fifty-two-inch television. Flanking the television was a grandfather clock on the right and a grand piano on the left, and behind the television hung a large family portrait taken in front of a horse stable. All eight members of the family were decked out in matching denim outfits for the painting and their ear-to-ear smiles seemed genuine.

"I'm hoping they put me in the next family photo," Austin said with a smile when he saw me checking out the portrait. "I think I've adjusted quite well to the Mormon way of life."

"God bless the Mormons," Williams said before chugging the rest of his beer.

The two girls were standing in the kitchen talking to each other when Austin brought them over to introduce me. This was his big surprise.

"Make sure you take your shoes off," Bilke said as he walked toward me.

"Oh, sorry," I said, reaching for my shoes.

"Just kidding," he replied, slapping me on the back. "I don't give a shit."

We formed a circle in the large living room and Austin began the introductions.

"So, Matt, this is Jessica and this is Karen," he said, pointing to the two young blond women before me. They were both wearing white jean shorts and tank tops. Karen had green eyes and didn't look a day over sixteen. Jessica looked slightly older and was proudly exposing her hefty cleavage.

"Nice to meet you," I said, extending my hand.

"They go to Provo High School," added Sunshine, who then winked at me.

"Where did you two meet Austin?" I said, looking askance at my host.

"At Applebee's," said Karen happily.

"That is great," I said as my teammates all smiled proudly. "Really great. I love Applebee's."

Sunshine was standing across from me and mouthed, "Jack Mormon."

"They want to party," said Austin as he handed both girls a beer. "Let's play a drinking game."

For the next hour we watched the movie *Summer Catch* and played Never Have I Ever—a game where players go around in a circle making statements like "Never have I ever had sex" and everyone who has had sex takes a drink. The game quickly turned raunchy and the girls were drinking more frequently than Austin, Brett, or I, but they were well behind Sunshine.

That these girls were several years younger than my sister was not lost on me. I could imagine her shaking her head in disapproval.

"Two words," Austin said just before midnight. "Hot tub."

The girls didn't bring bathing suits but wanted to take a dip in the hot tub, so Austin brought them to his host sister's bedroom and sifted through her belongings until he found two bikinis. How he later explained this to the family, I'll never know.

It took all of twenty minutes in the water before Sunshine was making out with Karen. Every few minutes he'd take a break from swapping spit to give me another wink.

"That's just criminal," Austin said as we all looked on. "I love it!"

"He's not a pedophile . . ." Williams said as he splashed water at the new couple.

". . . he's just an adult with boundary issues," said Austin, completing a favorite refrain among my teammates.

As the night progressed, I thought more and more about my own troubled relationship with Cara—we were talking on the phone with decreasing frequency—and continued to drink as I watched Sunshine attempt to defile the young Mormon girl. At four A.M. Austin cut me off and Sunshine took me home. I was completely bombed and needed his help just to get into my house. In doing so he turned down a night with one of his precious Jack Mormons just to make sure I got home safely.

The next day was not pretty. I woke up with a pounding headache and threw up in my mouth during "The Star-Spangled Banner." Unfortunately for me, we were playing a Canadian team, so I had to hold the bile in my cheeks for the Canadian national anthem as well.

"You look like shit, Mac," Kernan said after he saw me returning from the restroom.

"Food poisoning," I mumbled.

"Christ. What did you eat?"

"Sushi," I said, remembering his aversion to seafood.

"Well," he said, putting his hands on his hips, "there you go. Playing with fire. Take the night off, all right?"

I didn't like the idea of missing a chance to pitch, but I was in no condition to take the mound.

"I don't know, I'm feeling okay."

"Well, you let me know."

"Sure."

My reception in the bullpen wasn't much better. I sat quietly at the end of the bullpen bench for all of five minutes before Heath opened his mouth.

"Awfully quiet down there, Yale," he said from the other side of the bench.

"Just watching the game," I said, not looking at him.

"Oh, come on . . . I think it's more than that," he continued with a bit of excitement in his voice. "Austin said you boys had a big night."

"It was all right."

"All right? It must've been more than all right," he said and a few players smiled.

"We had a few drinks, Heath," I said casually while turning toward him.

"You're pale as shit, Mac. And you look like you're about to puke. Now, that's not very professional, is it?"

He was looking up and down the bench trying to identify team-mates who were enjoying his line of questioning.

"I feel fine," I said firmly.

"It's just that . . . it's just that I'd expect a bit more professionalism from an Ivy League cocksucker like you."

"Easy, Heath," Austin interjected. "We all had quite a few drinks."

"So he's the only one who can't hold his liquor?"

"Honestly, I don't remember," Austin said before putting his arm around me, "but he does have a little bit of Boot in him."

Boot was Chris Bootcheck, the Angels' first-round draft pick in 2000 and Austin's personal hero. Boot stood six feet five inches with long arms and tan skin, and he had pitched for three years at Auburn before signing a seven-figure contract to play for the Angels. Boot was known for his animated way of telling stories and was widely regarded as the heaviest drinker in the organization, aside from Bobby Jenks, of course.

Quan had explained to me that Boot was the reason we no longer had a day off during spring training. In his first month in Mesa, Bootcheck crashed his rental car into a ditch after a night of heavy drinking on the one off day of spring training. Realizing that he could be charged with driving under the influence, he stumbled home to his apartment without notifying anyone. The next morning he informed Tony Reagins of the incident and the Angels quietly took care of the rest.

"But don't tell anyone," Quan had said to me before raising his finger to his lips. "It's the Angels' little secret."

Eventually, Heath left me alone and the topic turned to Sunshine's new love interest.

We lost a close game that night and Kernan never came close to using me.

Kotchman was his typical cheery self after the loss.

"You guys disgust me," he said. He was pacing again, trying to decide exactly how he wanted to disparage us.

"The worst thing that ever happened to you guys was winning the first half. You locked up a spot in the playoffs and you've played like shit ever since. And some of you don't even realize it. You only get one chance, fellas. It's about making the right decisions . . . and you are all failing miserably."

Chapter 8

||||||||||||||||||||||||||||||||||||||||||||||||

TWO DAYS LATER, my girlfriend came to Provo. Jeff and Sarah offered to find her a place to stay with a neighbor, but I sprung for a hotel room because I knew that if there was one thing that could save our troubled relationship, it was a conjugal visit. I picked her up at the Salt Lake City airport at noon and drove straight to the Marriott. I was thrilled to see her, and as we drove I pointed out the various mountains and spoke at length about the baseball season while she told me a bit about the sports camp she had been working at.

"We've got two hours till I have to be at the field," I said hurriedly as I dropped her bags next to the bed. "That's plenty of time."

I gave her a big hug and we fell on the bed.

"Wait, wait, wait," she said playfully.

"What?" I asked.

What could she possibly need to say?

"I want to tell you something."

"I love you," I said preemptively.

"I love you, too. But that's not it. A lot has happened since you left. I've been doing a lot of thinking . . ."

I pulled back and looked into her big blue eyes.

"Are you about to break up with me?" I asked.

"Of course not!" she said and slapped me on the stomach. "Don't be ridiculous. But I want to tell you something."

"Okay."

"I've been working at this lacrosse camp all summer . . ."

"Right."

"And the little girls are so cute. Every week we get a new group of kids and we teach them the game and make them all promise to live their lives the way Jesus would have wanted."

"That's great," I said halfheartedly.

"We make this pledge . . ."

"I'm really happy for you," I said as I kissed her neck.

"Let me finish," she said, pushing me away. "I've decided . . ."

"Yes," I said, returning to her neck.

"I've decided to become a born-again."

I stopped what I was doing.

"A born-again?" I asked as I looked at her wet neck.

"A born-again virgin."

I pulled away and again looked into her eyes. She wasn't kidding.

"What?"

"I knew you were going to be upset."

"I'm not upset," I said, taking a deep breath. "I'm not upset. Does this mean . . ."

She bit her lip and softly said, "We can't have sex anymore."

"Even once in a while?"

"No."

"Cara," I said, trying to choose my words carefully, "I think it's great that you've made a pledge to these girls. But they're a bunch of god-damn eight-year-olds. They don't have to know."

"I'm sorry," she said and got up off the bed.

"Am I that bad in bed?" I asked emphatically.

"It's not that," she said. "I've made a promise and I intend to keep it."

We watched television in silence for the next hour and fifty-eight minutes before we headed to the ballpark. She walked me to the field and then she took the car back to the hotel. Life seemed to be getting away from me. I was nearly incapable of pitching well in back-to-back games, the new arm angle was killing my shoulder, and it now appeared that my personal life—what little of one I had—was in similar miserable shape.

"Hey, Mac," Kotchman said a few minutes later in the clubhouse. "Did you find yourself a slump buster?"

Heath was walking by us and announced, "Mac's got himself a slump buster!"

"No," I said firmly.

"Well, who was the broad outside?" Kotchman asked. "She looks like . . ."

I had no intention of letting him finish his thought.

"Not a slump buster," I said. "That's my girlfriend."

"Oh," Kotchman said, taking a step back. "Well, did you get your dick wet?"

"What?"

"Laid, Mac, did you get laid?"

"Oh, of course," I said dismissively.

"Nice work," he said, giving me a high five.

He took a few steps back to the center of the clubhouse and whistled loudly.

"Listen up!" he announced as he picked up a baseball bat by his foot and started to swing it. "You guys are going to meet someone very special today."

I prayed that I wasn't about to be the butt of some joke.

"My best friend," he continued. "You guys are going to meet my best friend in the whole fucking world."

I tried to imagine what type of person would be friends with Kotchman and drew a blank.

"Howie Gershberg coached with me for a long time. He was the pitching coach when I used to manage up in Boise and we've been through a lot together. He's one hell of a man and you guys are fortu-nate to have the chance to meet him."

Kotchman put the bat down and took a deep breath. "Howie's got cancer . . . and it's bad. His days on this earth are numbered, so do yourself a favor and listen to what he has to say."

Howie walked into the room a moment after Kotchman stepped out. He was a gaunt sixty-six-year-old with short black hair, a large nose, and bigger ears. He was well under six feet tall, and spoke with a thick Brooklyn accent. He'd been a pitching coach in the Angels' or-ganization for eighteen years and made a name for himself in 1990 when he turned a backup minor league catcher named Troy Percival into the future All-Star closer for the Angels. He'd also written the highly acclaimed book *Championship Baseball: Techniques, Fundamentals and Drills.*

"How's everybody doing?" Howie said softly as he leaned on the same bat Kotch had been swinging. "I'll make this brief. I'm here be-cause I love two things: baseball and working with young people. I'm sure Kotch gave you some sob story about me . . . but I don't want to hear it. Kotch is a softy underneath that asshole exterior . . . but I want you to know I'm here to do one thing and that's talk baseball. I'll be around for a couple of days and I'll try to meet with all of you."

He took his hat off and ran his fingers through his thin hair.

"Some of you will be playing in the big leagues someday, and some of you won't. But the lessons you learn out here will carry you the rest of your life. I keep in touch with a lot of my former players and to a man they say the same thing—that the principles you learn on a base-ball field will help you the rest of your life. This game is a metaphor. Remember that."

We all sat quietly as he examined the bat.

"You've all got talent. That's why you're here. Our job as coaches is to help you harness your ability. Your job as players is to bust your ass and respect the game. I know Kotch can be tough on you," he said with a smile, "but remember that you're supposed to be having fun out there. If you work hard and have fun, everything will fall into place."

I tried to remember the last time one of my outings had approached something I might call "fun."

Howie came down to the bullpen in the third inning to get acquainted with the relief pitchers. After introductions, he asked each pitcher to describe his strengths and weaknesses.

"I throw hard but my mechanics are pretty bad," said Austin. "I know it's going to catch up with me eventually. My shoulder's hanging together by a thread."

"I'm pitching great, but my slider could be better," said Reed.

"I throw strikes, but I don't throw hard," said Heath when it was his turn, "so I have to fool people."

"I have faith in my ability, but I don't throw strikes," said Randy.

"Randy's also a Bible-thumping inbred homosexual," Sunshine interjected, "but I'm sure Howie already knows that."

"I didn't know that," Howie said graciously, "but thank you."

"I pitch well one game," I said, "but I throw like shit the next."

Howie nodded after each pitcher made his statement and said he would try to help in any way he could.

In the sixth inning I recorded another AGI and as I sat down on the bench, Howie approached me.

"Let's talk," he said. "Follow me."

We walked about twenty yards away from the other pitchers and stopped by the left-field fence.

"You're the kid from Yale, right?"

"I am."

"In eighteen years with this organization, you're the first Ivy Leaguer I've come across."

"Is that right?"

"Which can only mean one thing," he said with a wide grin. "Either you signed for a lot of money or you graduated in the bottom half of your class."

"No on both counts."

He put his hands on his hips.

"What'd they sign you for?"

"It's embarrassing to say."

"A couple thousand?"

"One thousand."

His only response was to whistle.

A foul ball rolled near Howie, who picked it up and threw it to the left fielder. He still had a good arm.

"I've got a connection with Yale, you know."

"Really . . . what's that?" I said, assuming my alma mater was about to be the butt of another joke.

"I coached in the greatest college game ever played. It was at Yale Field."

"It certainly wasn't during the four years I was there."

"No, no, it was back in 1981—the Northeast Regional between Yale and St. John's. Ron Darling against Frank Viola. I was the pitching coach for St. John's."

"I can't say it rings a bell."

"You're an Ivy Leaguer . . . you ever read *The New Yorker*?"

"From time to time."

"Roger Angell wrote a story about that game . . . and it made it into *The New Yorker*!"

"Must have been one helluva game."

"Darling had a no-hitter through eleven innings."

"Jesus."

"But we beat 'em in the twelfth!" he said, giving me a high five.

"We beat those fancy Yale boys. But enough about the past," he said, wiping away the saliva that had built up in the corners of his mouth. "Let's talk about you. When I hear that a pitcher is inconsistent on the mound, it usually means one thing . . ."

"Concentration," I said, resigned to the fact that this was my reputation.

"Exactly."

I nodded.

"But I don't think that's the case with you."

"You don't?"

"No, I don't. I just watched you a few minutes ago in the bullpen and I'll tell you what the problem is. . . . It's your damn windup. Your mechanics are all off. And don't get me started about your arm angle. You can't repeat the same delivery two times in a row."

"Really?"

"It's no wonder you're inconsistent. Get me a ball and I'll show you."

He spent the next fifteen minutes putting me through various drills to show me that my balance point was off and that my arm angle was creating an undesirable torque on my midsection.

"Try going back to your old arm angle," he said as he stood with his hands on my waist. "At this point it really couldn't hurt."

"I think you're right," I said, trying to balance on one foot while simulating my windup.

"But then again," he said, stepping away to assess my delivery, "it's your career and you're going to get a lot of advice. You have to be able to make sense of it all, not just bend whichever way the wind blows."

After the game, I found Cara in the parking lot and she gave me a hug and kissed me on the cheek. Two sexless days later she changed her plane ticket and flew back to Wisconsin. Our relationship was finished.

"GATHER ROUND," KOTCHMAN SAID two days later. It was a few minutes before game time and we were about to line up for "The Star-
Spangled Banner."

"We've got another guest in our midst," he said, "and this one is a
VIP."

"I hope it's better than Larry King," Sunshine whispered to me.

"Bill Stoneman is here tonight," Kotchman continued as he looked
down the bench. "You may be asking yourself, 'Who is Bill Stoneman?'
Well, if that's the case . . . then you are a fucking idiot. He's the Angels' general manager and he's responsible for all Angels personnel.
Ultimately he will decide if you fit in the Angels' plans or if you are
expendable."

He adjusted the bill of his cap before adding, "Most GMs don't
bother to scout rookie ball games, but Stoneman is the best in the
business. He personally evaluates every player in the system. Believe it
or not, he knows something about each and every one of you."

I had no doubt that he knew me as the inconsistent Yale kid who
needed to learn how to concentrate.

We played the Great Falls Dodgers at home that night and faced
Greg Miller, the Dodgers' seventeen-year-old left-handed phenom. He
stood six feet six and threw an easy 94-mile-per-hour fastball, and
watching him throw made the big leagues feel that much farther away.
From the first pitch we all knew it was going to be a long night. He
overmatched every hitter in our lineup and we lost badly in front of
Mr. Stoneman. It dropped our second half record to 9-14.

We waited for twenty minutes in silence before Kotchman entered
the clubhouse.

"I've got nuthin' to say," he said as he walked through the door.
"You guys faced the best pitcher in our league tonight. He was just better than you."

A few heads shook, but most acknowledged the truth of his statement.

"Mr. Stoneman wants to say a few words."

With that, Bill Stoneman entered the room. He was five feet ten
and slender, with a round face, thin dark eyebrows, and male pattern
baldness. He looked more like an accountant than a former major
league All-Star who'd thrown two no-hitters.

"David Eckstein and Darin Erstad . . ." Mr. Stoneman began. It
seemed that everyone who took center stage in our clubhouse spoke
softly, if for no other reason than that they were inevitably following
Kotchman. "They are two of the smartest players in the game and
they are the heart and soul of the Anaheim Angels. They know exactly what they want to do whenever they step into the batter's box or
when a ball is hit to them in the field. And you know what . . . you
guys have just as much talent as they do or you wouldn't be here. The
difference between you guys and big leaguers is entirely mental. To
make it in this game you've got to be both physically and mentally
tough."

He spoke for a few more minutes about professionalism and work
ethic but I zoned out for most of it. I was still fixated on the idea that it
was the mental aspect of the game that was holding me back.

"And you guys are lucky," Stoneman said. "You're playing for one of
the best damn coaches in the game. Take advantage of all that Kotchman has to offer. He's been around a long time and he knows what he's
doing."

STONEMAN WAS WAITING for us in the clubhouse the following day.

"Pitchers," he said, "come with me."

It was just after two P.M. and we had five hours until game time. I usually spent those hours playing cards and chasing down fly balls in the outfield, but today that time would be spent with Stoneman.

"I used to pitch in the big leagues," he said as we all stood around him on the pitcher's mound. "I played for the Cubs, Expos, and Angels, and I used to throw two hundred innings every year. How many guys do you see doing that today?"

"Zero," said Bilke.

"Well, no, there are some, but not many. And would you like to know why? Any guesses?"

"Specialization," said Heath. "Big-league clubs are paying relievers to eat up innings late in the ball game."

"Well, that may be true," Stoneman conceded.

"There's no incentive to pitch two hundred innings when they'll pay you just as much to throw a hundred fifty innings," said Williams.

"Well . . ."

"And we throw harder today," said Reed.

"I don't know about that," replied Stoneman, appearing somewhat flustered. "The answer is arm injuries. More and more guys are having shoulder and elbow surgery. As an organization we are very concerned about this and we want to do everything we can to prevent those injuries. That's why we have you do those Jobe exercises."

Stoneman kicked some dirt on the mound with his patent-leather shoe before adding, "If you look at pitchers in the olden days, they all had the same windup. They went over their head before they delivered the ball to the plate. But if you look around the game today, nobody does it anymore. The only guy who still does it is Paul Byrd. Do you guys know him?"

"No," said Sunshine. "At least I haven't heard of him."

"Nope," said Reed.

"He's a pitcher for the Royals," Stoneman said as he folded his arms. "Guys call him 'Frasier.' He looks just like Kelsey Grammer and he's got one of the most durable arms in the game. Is it a coincidence that guys in the past could throw until the cows came home? I don't know. But it's something to consider. If you're still tinkering around with your delivery, try going over your head before you start your windup."

Just what I needed—another person suggesting I change my delivery.

"All I'm saying is that guys fifty years ago weren't going under the knife as much as they are today. And maybe, just maybe, it has something to do with the windup."

Less than a year later I found myself chuckling at another player's misfortune. I opened the sports pages in July 2003 to find that Paul Byrd, despite his injury-proof delivery, had just suffered a traumatic elbow injury while pitching and would require season-ending reconstructive surgery. But it was no surprise that in 2005, after a year and a half of grueling rehabilitation, Byrd was aggressively courted by Bill Stoneman and ended up signing a major league contract with the Angels.

We lost another game that night to the Dodgers and were again overmatched by a pitching sensation. This time it was Jonathan Broxton, a six-foot-three-inch, 288-pound goliath from Waynesboro, Georgia, who went by the nickname "The Ox." Broxton hit 98 miles per hour consistently against us as one batter after another failed to put the ball in play. He had a slow Southern drawl and a swagger on the mound that made his success all the more infuriating. And he bore a striking resemblance to Bobby Jenks.

Two days later I found myself warming up in the Idaho Falls bullpen to go into a tied ball game. It was the seventh inning and the score was 1–1. I was prepared for another AGI, but Kernan tipped his cap between innings to indicate that I'd be pitching the eighth. I was thinking about my new windup, which was actually my old windup, when Heath called out to me.

"Hey, Mac," he said as I finished my warm-up tosses in the bullpen. "If you don't give up any runs tonight . . . throw in a dip."

I didn't respond initially. My teammates had been trying to get me to try chewing tobacco all season but I hadn't given in. But from the way Heath said it, it seemed like he was making a peace offering. I looked back at him, sweat dripping off my forehead, and tried to decide if I wanted to meet him halfway.

"Do it!" said Randy.

"Yeah, do it!" said Bilke.

"He won't. I know he won't," said Reed, and that pushed me over the edge.

"All right," I said and my teammates cheered. A minute later I was jogging onto the field. I felt great on the mound and threw a scoreless inning, retiring the first three batters I faced.

"You looked awesome!" said Kernan as I came off the mound. "The velocity is back!"

Howie was also in the dugout, standing by himself sipping a cup of water when I made eye contact with him.

He walked over and put his arm around me.

"Really nice job out there," he said softly. "I think you've got it figured out."

Anthony Reed came in after me and hit the first batter he saw in the head, knocking the man unconscious. It was unintentional, but the player was carried off on a stretcher and Reed felt terrible about it afterward. He was the only one not celebrating after our 7–2 victory.

"It's always better when you win," Kotchman bellowed from the top of a chair he was standing on in the clubhouse. "Your food tastes better, your wife looks better, it's all good."

He threw his arms in the air and added, "God, I love to win!"

He stepped off the chair and tried to fight back a smile.

"If my wife tries to talk to me after a victory," he said, reverting back to the Diceman persona, "I just say, 'Baby, quit your grinnin' and drop your linen.' Oh!"

After the game, Randy and I picked up a twelve-pack of beer and a box of Pop-Tarts and watched *Back to the Future*. Around eleven P.M., there was a violent banging on our window. As Randy opened the door, Heath stormed in, followed by Reed, Bilke, Williams, and Sunshine.

"Don't think I forgot about the deal," Heath said as he muted the television.

Bilke placed a case of beer on the television and distributed a bottle to each of us.

"There comes a time in every young man's life," Heath said as he reached for his tin, "when he has to stop being a little bitch and grow a pair."

It was hardly the olive branch I'd imagined.

"Aww, be nice," said Sunshine, which made me feel even smaller.

Randy kept a small boom box next to his bed, and in all the time I roomed with him he played only one CD: *Chicago's Greatest Hits*. He queued up "Saturday in the Park."

Heath smacked the tin against his index finger and handed out a pinch to each of us.

"And, last but not least," he said, handing me what looked like a handful of mulch, "the future stockbroker gets to slum it with the rest of us."

"Thank you," I said. "It's an honor to take part in this with two of the Klan's most respected members."

"You better not spit it out," Reed said sternly. "No point in wasting it if you're just gonna spit it out."

"Don't worry," I said, putting the tobacco in my cheek as I'd seen dozens of my teammates do it.

Heath and Randy sat on the beds and the rest of us sat on the floor. I leaned against the door and started to sing along to Chicago while Sunshine told Heath about the Jack Mormon he'd recently kissed.

Within sixty seconds I could feel the nicotine surging through my blood. The feeling wasn't much different than being drunk, except that it burned my gums.

"How you doing?" asked Bilke after a few minutes.

"Fine."

After five minutes I was starting to get dizzy.

"I can definitely feel it," I said.

"Just don't spit it out," said Reed.

After ten minutes I felt like I was going to vomit. I could taste bile, like the day I puked during the national anthem, and I didn't want to duplicate that performance. I needed an exit strategy.

"Oh, man," I said a moment later, "I have to take a shit."

"You better not be going in there to spit it out," said Heath. "I'm serious."

"You know how I get," I said to the group. "When I'm nervous my stomach starts acting up. All this attention made me nervous, I guess."

I slipped into the bathroom and took the tobacco out of my mouth. It looked like a rotted wood chip.

"You better not be spittin' it out," Reed yelled from the other side of the door.

I was getting dizzier by the moment and decided to take decisive action. I stuck my right index finger down my throat and flushed the toilet. As the water surged I vomited into the porcelain bowl. Then I turned on the faucet and vomited some more, all the while holding the disgusting tobacco chunk in my left hand.

I placed the lump back in my mouth and returned to the party.

"Show me," said Heath, and I pulled down my bottom lip to expose the tobacco.

"Nice," said Sunshine, who put his arm around me and said, "I knew you wouldn't spit it out, Matty."

We hung out for another hour, drinking beers and watching television, and one by one the guys filtered out.

As soon as the last one left, I spit the tobacco into the trash can.

"Ugh," I said to Randy, who was shaving. "That was awful!"

"You're funny," he said into the mirror.

"Well, I didn't spit it out," I said proudly.

"Yeah," he said, turning toward me, "but we all heard you vomit like a son of a gun."

"RAFFY BETTER PITCH GOOD tonight," Kotchman said to me as I passed by him thirty minutes before game time. "A little birdie told me he missed curfew last night."

The mole strikes again, I thought, as I reached for a cup of water. It was a sweltering day and Raffy was in the midst of his warm-up routine. His documentary camera crew was filming him from a hill behind center field since Kotchman had banned them from the premises.

When Raffy took the mound, he seemed out of it. He couldn't throw strikes and he looked nervous. His night ended very much the way mine had six weeks earlier in Casper. He lasted only 1⅔ innings and allowed six earned runs. Kotchman screamed at Raffy for a solid minute on the mound as he relieved him of his pitching duties.

"No one speak to him," Kotchman said when he returned to the dugout. "Do not shake his hand and do not talk to him."

We lost the game to the Padres, 11–3. Afterward we showered quickly and boarded the bus around eleven o'clock. We were playing

Ogden the next day and assumed Kotchman would do his yelling as we drove there.

"Get off the bus," he said quietly. "And go to the bleachers in right field."

For the next forty minutes, we watched as Raffy ran back and forth from one foul pole to another. Kotchman presided over the punishment with his arms folded, saying nothing except an occasional "Fuck!"

During this time, Howie came over to say his good-byes. He was headed to Rancho Cucamonga and then on to Little Rock. "There's a lot of pitchers to see," he said as he shook my hand, "and I've gotta make the most of it."

Kotchman spoke firmly when we were back on the bus.

"Mr. Rodriguez made a grave error in judgment last night," he said as we cruised down Interstate 15. "By missing curfew, he screwed not only himself but the entire team because he could not pitch worth a damn today. And for that . . . I'm fining his ass one hundred dollars."

He let out a deep sigh.

"And I've said it before but I'll say it again. . . . This has nothing to do with the fact that he's Dominican. Nothing. I'd fine any one of you for missing curfew. I don't give a damn if you're black, white, or yellow. It's all the same to me."

A smile slowly developed on Kotchman's face.

"As long as you're not a queer. That's when we have a problem. I don't want you guys having to worry when you drop the soap in the shower."

The bus erupted in laughter. No matter the situation, there's always time for a gay joke among baseball players. Though I couldn't help but think back to Aybar and Callaspo on Weenie Wednesday. With that, Kotchman sat down and we spent the rest of the trip in silence.

After working with the teams in California and Arkansas, Howie returned to his home in New York to help prepare a scouting report on the New York Yankees. The Angels used his report when they faced the Bronx Bombers that fall in the playoffs, and they surprised everyone by beating the heavily favored Yankees. When the Angels won the World Series a few weeks later, they awarded Howie his one and only World Series ring. He died a year later.

"I COULD WRITE A BOOK about all of the games you guys have blown this year," Kotchman said as he entered the clubhouse two days later. We'd just lost to Ogden and Breslow had once again pitched brilliantly. I, on the other hand, had allowed two runs in the eighth inning and walked the leadoff batter in the ninth before being taken out.

"And McCarthy," he said, glaring at me with arms folded, "you can't walk the leadoff batter in the ninth. It's like Dr. Jekyll and Mr. Fucking Hyde with you. If I can't rely on you I will not put you out there. Walking the leadoff batter . . . Jesus Christ!"

He kicked a bucket of baseballs and they scattered across the room. He wasn't finished with me yet.

"He's terrible! You have to make him swing the damn bat. You're giving him a free pass by walking him. You have got to throw more strikes, damn it!"

I looked at him and nodded.

"I have to wonder if we drafted the wrong Yalie," he said as he shook his head. "Breslow shuts us down night after night and you . . . you just . . . you're just not getting it done out there."

It was difficult to swallow, but Kotchman was right. I had trouble locating my fastball and my off-speed pitches were more likely to bounce than cross the strike zone. Although I didn't want to admit it, my daily struggle had changed. It was no longer about making the big leagues; it was simply about surviving in the minors. With the loss we dropped to 12-17 in the second half.

The next day there was a diaper and a tampon in each player's locker. There were also dozens of diapers scattered across the floor. Kotchman was obviously sending us a message, but it was lost on most of my teammates.

"Hilarious," said Matt Brown as he entered the clubhouse. "What a great prank!"

"Who do you think did it?" asked Sunshine.

Aybar and Callaspo were giddy as they surveyed the room. They quickly undressed and each put on a diaper. Then Aybar started sucking his thumb while Callaspo briefly pretended to hump him from behind. I wanted to look away but couldn't. It consistently amazed me how far they were willing to go for a joke.

We were all in stitches except, of course, for Hector Astacio.

An hour later we were in the midst of a heated dispute about the greatest athlete of all time when Heath walked into the clubhouse. He had changed out of his uniform and was folding the clothes in his locker.

"Taking the night off?" Reed said from across the room.

"You could say that," Heath responded somberly.

"Game starts pretty soon," Bilke said.

Heath put down his clothes and walked toward our table.

"I'm done," he said softly. "I just got the pink slip."

The room fell silent. Heath had been pitching quite well over the past two weeks and had moved up the ranks to become one of the most frequently used relievers. His release came as a shock to us all.

We formed a line and said our good-byes. I was the last one to speak to him.

"I can't believe it," I said, trying to end on a good note. "You don't deserve to be released."

"I know," he said plaintively. "I have better stats than you."

"Is that . . ."

"They're releasing the wrong lefty," he said and walked out of the room.

SMARTING FROM KOTCHMAN'S TONGUE LASHING, I decided to call Steitz, who was still playing for the Brewers' Single-A affiliate in Beloit, Wisconsin.

"Jon-Jon," I said as I watched Sunshine and Bilke sword-fight with their tampons, "how's life in the Midwest?"

"Brutal," he said flatly.

"Can't be worse than Provo," I said. "I'm a mess out here. Kotchman ripped me in front of everyone last night. Called me Dr. Jekyll and Mr. Fucking Hyde."

"Excuse me if I don't sound more sympathetic," he said, "but I'm having a rough time myself."

"And Kotchman put diapers and tampons in our lockers," I continued.

"I bet the Dominicans had a field day with that," he said with a laugh.

"You have no idea."

"I can imagine."

"So how's the Fresh Prince of Beloit?"

"Well . . . I've been better."

"What's up?"

"Let's see," he said. "How do I say this?"

"What?"

"Statistically I am the worst pitcher in the country."

"You are?"

"I've pitched in eleven games and lost all of them," he said quickly. "It's August and I haven't won a game yet. And my ERA is approaching my shoe size."

"Really?"

"And the fans in Beloit boo me every time I come in to pitch."

"Wow."

Like I said, Breslow was much better with the reassuring words.

"Yeah, they do. It's awful."

"I'm sorry."

"Listen, I gotta go," he said. "I'm late to go lose again."

Chapter 9

||||||||||||||||||||||||||||||||||||||||||||||

WE'VE BEEN LOSING way too much," Kernan said in a pitchers-only meeting the next day. "That's why we had to let Heath and Torres go. Had to toss the deadweight overboard. There's less than a week left before the playoffs," he said while wiping his glasses. "We've given all of you ample opportunity to show what you can do on the mound. Now it's time to give some others a shot."

He extended his arm and pointed to the three newest members of our team—Daniel Arias from Bani, Dominican Republic; Jeff Balser from Venice, Florida; and Ambroix Delgadillo from San Pedro de Macoris, Dominican Republic.

"Now, I want to meet with each of you before the game to reflect on the season. We'll talk about your strengths and weaknesses and what you can do to improve in the off-season."

I was the fifth pitcher to meet with Kernan and knew exactly what he was going to say.

"Mac, Mac, Mac," he said as I sat down on the bench next to him. "Talk to me."

"Well, I think this season was . . ."

"Let's be honest, it was an up-and-down season."

"It was."

"You showed flashes of brilliance."

"Thank—"

"And you showed flashes of dog shit."

"Yes."

"I don't know what to make of it, really. I've got to do a write-up of each pitcher on this team and yours is by far the hardest."

"Is that . . ."

"It's a tale of two pitchers with you. You heard Mr. Stoneman. . . . You've got to master the mental aspect of the game."

"I agree."

"Some of these crazy fucks from the Dominican have already mastered the mental part of the game. It has nothing to do with IQ or having some fancy Ivy League diploma."

I nodded.

"But that's just one thing we need to address. I think the big mistake I made with you," he said, putting his arm around me, "was the whole arm-angle thing."

"Yeah."

"The thing is . . . we didn't go far enough."

"How so?"

"I think you should be throwing sidearm."

There it was: the kiss of death. Every pitcher knows that's the last resort. The only thing worse would be to become a knuckleballer.

"Sidearm?"

"Yeah. Sidearm. There's a million kids out there who can do what you do. You need something."

"You mean a gimmick?"

"That's one way of putting it. You need something to be more deceptive."

"Okay."

"Let me show you."

"Before you do that," I said anxiously, "I need to use the restroom. I'll be right back."

My bowels were equally displeased with the idea of throwing sidearm.

When I returned, Kernan taught me the basics of throwing sidearm. We discussed the ideal release point and the new shoulder exercises I should do to protect my arm from the wear and tear of throwing from a new angle.

After the meeting there was one thing I was certain of: I had no plans to ever throw sidearm. It made my arm ache just thinking about it.

IT WAS LATE AUGUST and the season was drawing to a close. Minds were starting to wander and off-season plans became the hot topic in the clubhouse. Most were heading south for the fall and winter—to places like Florida, Georgia, Texas, and the Dominican Republic, of course. Sunshine said he was going to spend the off-season in Hollywood as a stuntman, and part of me believed him. Bilke and Williams were planning a road trip while Reed and Dvorsky were planning their weddings. And on his way out the door, Heath had said he was going home to propose to his girlfriend. I spent most days wondering if I would survive in professional baseball and didn't bother to mention that in the off-season I'd be heading back to New Haven to work on the kinetics of gene splicing.

We played the Casper Rockies the next night, and after seven innings we held a 7–4 lead. I looked into the dugout and saw Kotchman delicately pull out the Rally Penis and place it on his right shoulder. He sat on the bench motionless for the next two innings until the final out was recorded and our six-game losing streak was over.

"Finally!" was the only word he said as he boarded the bus back to the Casper Motel.

Randy and I ordered pizza and watched *SportsCenter* until we both fell asleep around midnight. At 1:45 A.M., the phone rang.

"It's Kotch," Randy whispered after I came to my senses. "He wants to see me."

"He wants to see you?" I asked. "It's almost two in the morning. What could he possibly . . ."

I trailed off because we both knew what this phone call was about.

"This is it," he said as he frantically put on a shirt. "I'm gettin' released. I know it. I'm gettin' released. Oh, my gosh."

"No you're not . . ." I said, trying to think of something, anything, to allay his fears. "He probably just wants . . ."

"Wants what?" he asked sternly. "What could he possibly want at two in the morning?" He rushed out of the room and I began to wonder who my new roommate was going to be.

Randy came back ten minutes later with tears in his eyes.

"Randy," I said, again searching for words. His head was down and he was running his hands through his hair.

"Somebody was fuckin' with me," he said softly.

"What?"

"I said . . . somebody was fuckin' with me."

He looked up at me with bloodshot eyes.

"It was a prank."

He wiped a tear away from his left eye and took off his shirt.

"No."

"I walked down to Kotchman's room, woke him up, and asked what he wanted to talk about. He looked at me like I was crazy. He said he never called me and that someone must be screwin' with me."

"Jesus."

"I just about dropped to my knees right then and there. I don't know what I woulda done if I'd been released. I don't know what I would tell all the folks back home."

He sat down on the edge of the bed, threw in a dip, said a prayer, and opened his Bible.

Kotchman was not amused by the joke. The next day he began his pregame speech by saying, "I don't want any of you coming over to my room in the middle of the night and waking my ass up again. At first I thought it was kinda funny, but you know what—you guys shouldn't mess with each other like that. We're a team. You shoulda seen Randy last night," he said, pointing to my roommate. "He looked like he had a date with an executioner."

A few people laughed.

"Hey!" he said. "It's not funny. I want to know who was responsible for this. You have until the end of the day to come forward. I want to know what coward did this to Randy."

We looked up and down the bench at one another. The prankster had to be one of the Americans, but who? It was a dirty trick, and cruel, considering how on edge many of us were. The year had not been kind to the nerves.

"WELL," KOTCHMAN SAID after the game, "I'm not happy."

We'd just defeated the Rockies but something else was on the man's mind.

"Alex Dvorsky," he said, "did you make that prank call to Randy last night?"

We all looked at our catcher—the one man whose uniform was dirty after every game and the one man who actually seemed to care if we won or lost.

"I, uh . . . I . . . yes, sir, I did," he replied.

"Well, why the fuck weren't you man enough to tell me that? Didn't I say I wanted to know who made that phone call? Why did I have to hear it from someone else?"

Dvorsky's roommate turned him in! The thought briefly flashed through my mind before I remembered he was rooming with one of the new Dominicans—Ambroix Delgadillo. The Dominicans all hated Dvorsky because of the incident with Aybar, but Delgadillo hadn't been around for that. Nonetheless, he remained a suspect.

"I was . . . going to tell you," Dvorsky muttered.

"Bullshit!" Kotchman yelled. "Do you think I care that you made the All-Star team? Do you?"

"No, sir."

"I don't give a shit who you are. You can be the best player on this team or the worst, but you have to remember one thing—we are a team. And of all people, I thought you understood that, Alex Dvorsky. Jesus Christ!"

"I'm sorry."

"Don't apologize to me," he said, waving his hand. "Apologize to Randy."

Dvorsky turned to Randy as we all looked on. You could hear a pin drop.

"Randy," he said quietly, "I apologize. What I did was wrong."

"Don't worry about it," Randy said, before putting his head down.

"You're suspended," Kotchman said. "Two games, Dvorsky. Maybe that'll get your attention."

Dvorsky, Aybar, and Callaspo were the only players from our squad to make the All-Star team that year, but while Aybar and Callaspo steadily climbed the minor league ladder, Dvorsky's career sputtered. Word spread quickly around the organization that he wasn't a team player, and within a year he was out of baseball.

I never found out if Dvorsky took steroids. But he never failed a drug test and we never spoke again of that dinner conversation with Heath and Sunshine where he seemed so conflicted about the decision before him.

THE LAST DAY of the regular season fell on a Wednesday. It was our seventy-sixth game in eighty days and we were all ready to go home. We still had the playoffs to look forward to as well as the end-of-the-season luncheon held at BYU's Riverside Park a few hours before the regular season finale.

There were two large tables and about a hundred people in attendance when we showed up for the picnic in our honor. We immediately segregated into an American table and a Dominican table, and the emcee, Mayor Billings, felt compelled to comment on it.

"I'm glad race relations are alive and well in Provo," he said with a chuckle. "What's the old saying about a house divided?"

There was an awkward silence before he moved on to introduce himself, the city council members, and a few sponsors of the Provo Angels. He thanked us for a wonderful season and wished us luck in the playoffs before asking Kotchman to come up and say a few words.

"I'll try to keep this PG," Kotchman said as he took the microphone and looked around at his large audience. He was clearly uncomfortable, probably because he knew he couldn't curse.

"One thing my team appreciates is good food," he said, pointing to the large trays of meat, potatoes, and vegetables. "So on behalf of my team . . . thank you."

There was brief applause before he continued. "I married the only Italian woman in the godda . . . in the entire world who can't cook. So this is a real treat for us. Provo has been very good to this team and we want to thank you. The playoffs start tomorrow and we're all excited as hell . . . heck . . . to get out there and win this town a championship!"

After lunch we posed for a photo with the mayor and headed to the ball field. We were 37-38 going into the game and Kotchman desperately wanted to end the season at .500. He hadn't coached a team that finished with a losing record since the 1980s.

An hour before game time, I got a call from Breslow.

"Looks like we're facing you guys in the first round of the playoffs," he said.

"Is that right?"

"Yeah, we just locked up the second-half title."

"Congrats, how you doing?"

"Okay," he said, not quite sounding his usual chipper self.

"What's up, Mr. Osteen? You sound down. Don't you get paid to motivate people?"

"It's just that I didn't make the All-Star team."

"That's what you're upset about?"

"I have better stats than most of the guys who made the team. But you know how it goes. . . . Nobody wants to put a twenty-sixth-round draft pick on the All-Star team."

"I wish I could be more sympathetic," I said, quickly tiring of the conversation. "I'm sure everyone knows you had a great season. I gotta run. Kotch is handing something out."

"I've given every player who's ever played for me one of these shirts," Kotchman said as he gave me one and shook my hand. It was a gray short-sleeved T-shirt with the Anaheim Angels' logo on the front. On the left sleeve it said "Every inning . . ." and on the right sleeve it said "Complacency Sucks."

"I've coached a lot of guys," he continued. "Roger Clemens, Garret Anderson, you name it. They all have this shirt. I know guys in the big leagues who still wear this thing under their uniform."

He picked up one of the shirts and examined it. He kissed the An-gels' logo and said, "Wear this baby with pride!"

We had a two-run lead when I came in to pitch the sixth inning. I breezed through that inning and the next, allowing no runs, one hit, and two strikeouts. My arm felt great, my velocity was back near 90 miles per hour, and Kernan was pleased.

"Great job," he said as I walked into the dugout. "You want to go back out there for another inning?"

I quickly weighed my options—end the regular season on a high note or go back out for another potentially disastrous inning. As I saw it, I had nothing to gain by pitching another inning.

"Nah," I said casually, "that's it for me."

"Suit yourself," he said. "I'll put Randy in."

My decision not to pitch another inning ran contrary to everything Kotchman had preached all summer and it stood in stark contrast to the beginning of the season, when I threw a tantrum after being taken out of a game. I simply wasn't the same person I had been at the sea-son's start. I wasn't playing to win; I was playing not to fail. It was the last game I would ever pitch in a Provo Angels uniform and I regret it to this day.

Randy came in and pitched two scoreless innings and we won the game to end the season 38-38. My statistics for the season weren't pretty: I pitched in 15 games and finished with a 6.92 ERA, 19 walks, 16 strikeouts, 6 wild pitches, and even managed to record a balk.

Everyone was celebrating after the game. We'd survived the regu-lar season and had just the playoffs to get through before the off-season. We all danced, or tried to dance, as reggae played in the clubhouse. But that all stopped when Kotchman walked in. I was expecting a grand oration that would sum up the season and motivate us for the playoffs.

"I just got a call from the Angels' scouting director," he said with tears in his eyes. "My son Casey just got the game-winning hit in the twelfth inning for Cedar Rapids."

He wiped the tears away with the sleeve of his jersey.

"You guys will never know anything," he sobbed, "until you have a kid of your own. You think about them day and night and you just want the best for them."

Many of my teammates looked confused. I made eye contact with Matt Brown, who was wrinkling his brow.

"You dedicate your whole life to your kids," he said, becoming progressively more choked up.

Now we were all averting our eyes.

"You just want 'em to be healthy, and you just want 'em to grow up right . . . and be good at sports."

I looked up quickly to see if the last comment was an attempt at humor, but it wasn't.

"That's all I got for you guys," he said softly. "Good job, and be ready to play tomorrow. The playoffs are finally here. It's what you've been waiting for all season."

As he walked out of the room, Reed tapped me on the shoulder.

"Hey," he whispered, "who the hell cares about his son?"

THE PLAYOFFS PASSED in the blink of an eye. Despite Breslow's best efforts, we defeated the Ogden Raptors in the best-of-three series to advance to the finals to face the Great Falls Dodgers. Kotchman did his best to motivate us, but the pitching of Greg Miller and Jonathan Broxton turned out to be simply too much to overcome. Kotchman didn't use me once in the playoffs, although I did collect a few AGIs.

When the final out was made and our season was laid to rest, my eyes turn turned to Kotchman. As my teammates walked off the field, he muttered something unintelligible and tore up his scorecard. Then he dropped the Rally Penis back in his gym bag and sat alone on the bench with his head in his hands. After more than two decades he still took it personally.

The mood in the clubhouse, however, was somewhat brighter. We all knew we were supposed to be disappointed, but there was a restrained excitement that the season was finally over. A few players were upset— Dvorsky slammed his catching equipment into his locker and Astacio, like Kotchman, sat quietly with his head in his hands by his locker—but the rest of us were fighting off smiles.

Callaspo was walking around the clubhouse shaking everyone's hand when Kotchman entered. One last time we stopped what we were doing to listen.

"It's over, gentlemen," he said softly from the center of the room. "It's been a long season and you guys survived. This championship really mattered to me and I'd like to think it mattered to all of you, too."

We all knew that it didn't.

"There's not much left to say at this point. You came close, but they were the better team. The season's over and we've booked flights outta here for all of you first thing tomorrow morning. Hopefully you know what you need to work on in the off-season. All I can say is you better work your asses off in the winter and be ready for spring training. It'll be here before you know it, gentlemen."

He walked around the locker room shaking hands and saying good-bye before exiting with his black gym bag by his side. It was the last time I saw Tom Kotchman.

The mood improved significantly after he left. Aybar turned on the reggae music as we continued to clean out our lockers and say our good-byes. Sunshine slapped me in the arm with his hat and gave me a big hug.

"It's over, Matty!" he said as he ran his fingers through his hair. "We're free."

"I can't believe it," I said.

"If you're out in California this winter . . . make sure you look me up."

"Of course."

"There's a guest bedroom in Beverly Hills with your name on it," he said.

"I'm sure there is," I said, patting him on the back. "I'm sure there is."

I folded up my clothes and started planning my off-season. I was returning to my research and looked forward to discussing my first season in the minors with Stuper. In a few hours I would gather my remaining belongings and say good-bye to Sarah, Jeff, and the kids.

I was shoving my clothes into my duffel bag when I felt a tap from Austin Bilke.

"Uh-oh," he whispered as I leaned over in my chair, "Grim Reaper is here."

I turned to my left and saw the black snakeskin leather boots. Reagins had several sheets of paper in his hand, but they didn't look pink.

"He wouldn't release somebody on the last day of the season, would he?" I asked Austin.

"I don't know," he said, shaking his head, "but I wouldn't put it past him."

Reagins walked over to Quan and handed him a sheet of paper. The music was too loud for me to hear the conversation, but I saw Quan nod solemnly. From there, he walked over to Callaspo and did the same thing. He slowly made his way to my side of the room, passing me on his way to Matt Brown. He handed Brown a sheet of paper, patted him on the back, and left the room.

Matt's face lost all color as he read the document. He collapsed in the chair in front of his locker and let out a deep sigh.

"What's up, Brownie," I said from my locker. "You okay?"

Brown had played well toward the end of the season and I was certain he hadn't just received his walking papers.

"No," he said firmly, "I'm not okay."

I walked over and sat down beside him.

"Talk to me," I said quietly.

"Unbelievable!" he said before emitting a brief fit of laughter. "I can't fucking believe this."

"What?" I asked.

"I can't escape these fuckers. This is gonna kill me."

I grabbed the sheet of paper from his hands and quickly read it. Matt Brown had just been assigned to the Anaheim Angels' Winter Baseball League in San Pedro de Macoris, Dominican Republic, effective immediately.

"I can't do it," he said, shaking his head. "I'll shoot myself."

"Well," I said, patting him on the back, "it'll give you a chance to brush up on your Spanish."

"Fuck you!" he said without looking at me. He crumpled up the sheet of paper and threw it at the trash can.

I CLEANED OUT MY LOCKER and shook a few more hands before I left the clubhouse and headed to the parking lot. I walked through the concourse and thought of my last moments with Blake before reaching my car. As I was opening the car door, I heard someone call my name. It was Randy Burden.

"Matt," he said, jogging over to me, "wait up. Matt!"

"Hey, Randy, what's up?"

"Were you going to leave without saying good-bye?" he asked innocently.

"Of course not," I lied. "I was just putting my bag in the car."

"Oh, okay. Well . . . I've got something for you."

"You do?"

He put his duffel bag on the ground and unzipped a side compartment.

"This is for you," he said, handing me a book. "Your very own copy."

It was a brand-new leather-bound King James Bible with gold embossing.

"Randy," I said, searching for the right words. "Wow. I don't know what to say . . ."

I shook my head as I flipped through the thin pages.

"Consider it a little off-season reading," he said proudly.

"Thank you. I'll try to read through it if I get the chance."

"That would mean a lot to me."

"Any recommendations?"

"Well," he said, scratching the corner of his mustache, "I'd have to recommend the Book of Matthew. Your namesake is as good a place as any to get started."

I gave him a hug and again thanked him for the gift.

"I wish . . . I wish I had something to give you," I said, somewhat embarrassed.

"Matt," he said, putting his large right hand on my shoulder, "if this book touches you in some way . . . that's more than I could ever ask for."

"Thank you," I said, shaking his hand. "Have a great off-season and I'll be in touch."

I thought about calling Randy twice that off-season—first, when I finished the Book of Matthew, and again two weeks later, when the Angels won the World Series. But I never picked up the phone.

A few weeks after the series, I received an e-mail from my host family's account with the subject "Randy Burden."

Dear Matt,

    So sad to hear about Randy. But for some reason I can't place him. Was he the bullpen catcher you called Sunshine?

      All the best,

      Jeff

I assumed Tony Reagins had mailed Randy his pink slip and released him from the organization. But just to be sure, I checked the waiver wires. After an exhaustive search, however, I could find no documentation that Randy had been released, so I entered his name into Google. The first article that popped up was from his hometown newspaper, the *Roanoke-Chowan News Herald*.

December 9, 2002

MURFREESBORO—Back on June 28th, tears of joy rolled out of 23 year old Randy Burden's eyes. The right handed pitcher had just fulfilled his dream of playing professional baseball, signing a one year deal with the Anaheim Angels organization.

Tragically, Friday afternoon tears of sadness flowed freely here in the small town of Murfreesboro as word quickly spread that the former Chowan pitcher had died in his sleep in the early hours of Friday morning.

An autopsy revealed that Burden, who had returned to his hometown of Suffolk back in September after his first season with the Provo Angels (rookie league farm club of Anaheim), died of an apparent heart attack.

Burden was living at home during the offseason working out and fine tuning his pitching in preparation for spring training in February.

During Burden's four year stay in Murfreesboro, he worked diligently on his game, especially in his final two years according to Chowan head coach Steve Flack. Flack reminisced about Burden saying, "Randy was truly a success story. His work ethic was unbelievable. He was kinda what it was all about."

Flack continued, "When Randy first arrived, he had never pitched. He played third base in high school (Nansemond River). I suggested pitching to him and he didn't really show a lot of interest. I finally convinced him to give it a try and after a semester of work, he accepted his new role and ultimately excelled at it. By his senior year he had become a leader of our team and a valuable asset to the Chowan baseball program. Randy stood for everything, as coaches, we try to preach."

Despite not being drafted in the Major League Draft in early June, Burden continued to pursue his dream of playing in the big leagues. His hard work and dedication finally paid off when Angels scout Chris McCallum offered Burden a one year contract. After signing his name, Burden became the first Chowan baseball player to sign professional in recent years.

Burden then packed his bags and journeyed out to Provo, Utah, where he joined the Provo Angels, a rookie league team. During his short stint as a professional pitcher, Provo manager Tom Kotchman commented that "Burden was the hardest working kid on the club."

Randy was laid to rest in Portsmouth, Virginia, on December 10th in his Chowan College baseball uniform. The service was overflowing with friends, family, former classmates, and teammates from high school and college, but there were no members of the Provo Angels in attendance.

Chapter 10

||||||||||||||||||||||||||||||||||||||||||||||||

I T TOOK A WHILE to sink in that I had survived my first season in the minors. Lab work helped the winter pass in New Haven, and before I knew it, I found myself back in Arizona, about to begin my first full spring training and my second go-round with the Angels.

Spring training itself was a grand production—close to two hundred players, coaches, and staff had been flown in from around the world and were now packed into the clubhouse at Gene Autry Park in Mesa, preparing to begin a new season representing the reigning world champions. World Series banners, flags, and pennants now hung all over the clubhouse, serving as a constant reminder that we, as minor leaguers, were affiliated with greatness, but also that the big-league Angels seemed to be doing just fine without us.

The clubhouse was buzzing with stories from the off-season when Coach Hines brought us together on the first day.

"Gather round and shut up," he bellowed from the center of the room. Conversations gradually tapered off as we turned our attention to Hines, who in his sixteenth year with the Angels had just been promoted to the position of minor league field coordinator.

"Welcome to spring training," he said with mock enthusiasm. "We've got over a hundred fifty guys in camp this year, fellas, so competition is going to be stiff. I hope you all put in a lot of hard work in the off-season, because you have just four short weeks to show us what you've got. A lot of guys who are used to being here . . . aren't going to be around at the end of spring training."

He paused to let the gravity of his words sink in.

"This is a new era, fellas. We're world champs, which means that everyone is gunning for us. Expectations have been raised . . . and you'll need to perform accordingly to keep your job. But before we get started, I have the pleasure of introducing someone to you. He's the heart and soul of this organization, the best manager in baseball, Mr. Mike Scioscia."

Muffled whispers overtook the clubhouse as Scioscia, the 2002 American League Manager of the Year, emerged from the back of the crowd and slowly took his place next to Hines.

"Welcome," he said softly as he gazed around the expansive room. "Welcome to spring training. I'm going to keep my remarks short. Last year was a great year for us. We achieved our goals and we played the game the right way. But last year is over."

He was softer now than in his playing days, but he still looked like a catcher—like he could still drop to his knees at a moment's notice and block a fastball.

"At the big-league level," he continued, "we've got a lot of guys back this year. But there are some areas where we could use some help . . . and that's where you come in. We have the best farm system in base-ball, gentlemen, and that's because of you."

He pointed around the room and we all followed his finger.

"I'm going to be keeping tabs on you guys all season," he said before he took a sip of his coffee, "and I don't just mean the big prospects or big-money guys or whatever. I mean all of you. Take a look at what we're doing at the major league level. Do you think anyone expected Eckstein to be doing the things he's doing?"

David Eckstein, the Angels' diminutive shortstop, was always being held up as the type of player that we, as minor leaguers, should strive to be. In every sense of the word, Eckstein was an average major leaguer. He was a solid hitter who didn't hit for power, didn't run well, and had a bum arm. But at five feet six he was so small, had so little natural talent, and played the game so hard that coaches couldn't resist telling their large, physically gifted minor leaguers to be more like him.

"Play every game like it's your last," Scioscia continued, "and you'll get noticed. I can promise you that."

I took a quick look around the room and figured there were at least two dozen left-handed relievers vying for a spot in the Angels' bullpen.

"And good luck, gentlemen," Scioscia added as he tipped his cap. "Hopefully I'll be seeing some of you real soon."

With that, he left the clubhouse and Coach Hines returned to center stage.

"Behind me is a bulletin board," Hines yelled. "You have all been assigned to one of our six minor league affiliates. Your tenure with that team may be temporary or it may be permanent. When you walk through those doors each day," he said, pointing to the double doors through which Scioscia was now exiting, "you should come right here, right to this bulletin board, to find out what your team is doing that day. It will have all of the instructions you need. As long as you can read, you'll be just fine. A lot is going to be expected of you this . . ."

Hines trailed off when he heard a voice in the crowd.

"Did somebody say something?" he asked.

We all remained silent.

"Is that some kinda joke?" the voice said firmly. It was Bobby Jenks.

"What's that?" Hines asked, still unsure of who was speaking or what was being said.

"I asked if that was some kinda joke," Bobby said loudly.

Hines glared at Jenks and put his hands on his hips.

"What?" he asked flatly. "What are you talkin' about?"

"You said we'll be fine as long as we can read," Bobby said, fighting back a smile, "but half the fuckers in this room don't speak English. How do you expect 'em to read it?"

Laughter broke out in the crowd but Hines was not amused. He walked over to Bobby and addressed him the way a drill sergeant would address a new recruit.

"I don't fuckin' know," he shouted as he stood a few inches from Bobby's nose, "but somehow they do it. Which is a helluva lot more than I can say for you."

He bit his lower lip before adding, "Patience with you is running real thin around here, Bobby."

Hines stepped away from Jenks and shook his head.

"Just read the damn bulletin board," he muttered before walking out of the clubhouse, still shaking his head.

I quickly learned that I had been assigned to the Rancho Cucamonga Quakes, the Angels' High Single-A affiliate in Southern California. Only a few of my Provo teammates had been promoted to the Quakes—Saunders, Aybar, and Callaspo—so at first I thought I had been placed there by mistake.

"Man, I wish I was a left-handed pitcher," Dvorsky said to me when he saw the list. "What was your ERA last year, Mac? Five? Six?"

"Six-something," I said quietly. "But, you know, it's a new year. I changed some things in the off-season . . ."

"Sure, Mac," he said, patting me on the shoulder. "New year."

Although I tried to fight it, a newfound fatalism had seeped in over the winter and replaced the sanguine disposition that marked my first trip to Mesa. I had been disabused of any naïveté I might have had about the process. But Dvorsky didn't need to know that.

I jogged over to Field 2 to formally meet my new teammates. In addition to Aybar, Callaspo, and Saunders, the Quakes' roster included more than a half dozen future major leaguers. Catching duties were to be split between Jeff Mathis and Mike Napoli, Casey Kotchman was at first base, Howie Kendrick was at second, Tommy Murphy was at short, and Dallas McPherson was at third base. Needless to say, it was the only team I had ever played on where the entire infield would go on to play in the big leagues.

"Your manager's not here yet," Coach Hines announced as we assembled around him. "So I'll be coaching you boys until Roadie gets here," he said, referring to our new manager, Steve Roadcap, whose Dickensian appellation seemed to provide little amusement for my teammates.

"We've got some new faces around here . . . and even a few new names," he said as he nodded at Ervin Santana, a tall, thin twenty-year-old Dominican with a chinstrap beard who had changed his name from Johan in the off-season to avoid being confused with the Twins ace of the same name. Ervin was known to have one of the best fastballs in the organization, but there had been quiet rumblings about his commitment to the game since the Angels had signed him as a seventeen-year-old phenom out of San Cristobal, Dominican Republic.

"We've got a full day today," Hines said as he surveyed our group and pointed at Casey Kotchman with his bat. "How ya doin', Casey? How's your father?"

"He's doing well, sir," Casey responded. "Thank you for asking."

"Like I said," Hines went on, "big day. We're going to stretch, throw, run, lift, take infield and outfield, work on bunt plays, first-and-thirds, take batting practice, and finish up with pickoffs and rundowns. Should have you outta here by dinnertime."

The feeling of being out on the baseball field again was incomparable. There were no aches and no pains. The sun was shining, the birds were singing, and hope, as they say, sprung eternal. I had spent the off-season in New Haven investigating the mechanisms by which neurons in the hippocampus were able to communicate with one another and was more than ready to be out of the laboratory and back on the field. Normally dreary tasks like chasing down fly balls were fun again. And the dry Arizona air was a much-needed reprieve from the oppressive winter weather of New England.

After lunch we took four hours of batting practice before gathering in the infield to work on pickoffs. As a left-handed pitcher, I was supposed to have a good pickoff move, but I didn't. My move to first was so bad that most of the runners in the drill were able to reach second base before I had delivered the ball to Casey over at first.

"Not gonna cut it," Hines said curtly as the third consecutive runner stole on me. "Somebody else get up there."

Ervin Santana took my place and proceeded to throw four balls over the first baseman's head, leaving Hines apoplectic.

"Jesus fucking Christ!" he screamed.

I actually felt a tremendous sense of relief as I heard those words—it meant I wasn't the day's only screwup.

"That's it," he muttered. "We're done here. Go home. Everybody, go home. We'll get after it tomorrow."

I looked over at Ervin, who was drawing an X on the pitcher's mound with his shoe.

"Go home," Hines repeated, and we all walked off the field.

"Eighty-nine," Casey Kotchman said as we headed toward the clubhouse. "Eighty-nine," he said again.

It took a moment before I realized that he was trying to get my attention. I had been given the number 89, which was like wearing a jersey that said, "No Chance."

"What's your name?" he asked as he jogged over to me.

"McCarthy. Matt McCarthy. Mac."

"Listen, Mac," he said as he took off his hat, "you're telegraphing your move to first. That's why runners are getting such a big jump."

"Is that right?"

"Yeah. Your glove is giving it away. When you go to the plate you drop your glove and when you come to first you keep it up. I'll show you."

He was right, and in a matter of seconds he had corrected a major flaw in my delivery.

"Need a ride home, Mac?"

"Sure."

A few minutes later I was sitting in the passenger's seat of his Volkswagen Beetle as we cruised down the freeway in silence. The radio was turned off and Casey made sure to drive 5 miles per hour below the speed limit and signal each time he changed lanes.

"I played for your father last year," I finally offered.

"Is that right?" he said as he turned to me with a smile. "And you lived to tell about it?"

"He's a helluva manager."

"Baseball's his life."

"I've never played for anyone like him."

A few minutes passed before Casey spoke again.

"Did you like it?"

"Like it?"

"Did you like playing for my dad?"

"Oh, yeah. It was great. He cares more about his players than anyone I've ever met. He knows the game inside and out. And he sure made those bus rides go by a lot faster."

"Hickory . . . dickory . . . dock," Casey said playfully before we both broke out in laughter.

THE FIRST FEW DAYS of spring training turned out to be almost completely stress-free. Pitchers were asked to throw at just 50 to 75 percent of maximal effort and we weren't expected to face hitters until the second week of camp. On the fifth day of spring training, Kernan rounded up all the left-handed pitchers.

"We've got some visitors today," he said with a hint of a smile. "Scioscia and Bud Black are here and want to take a look at our southpaws."

All twenty-two of us smiled in unison. News that the Angels' manager and pitching coach were coming to evaluate us immediately got my mind racing. A strong performance in front of Scioscia might be enough to erase my mediocre season in Provo.

"Now, this is going to be hard for some of you," Kernan continued, "but I want you all to stick to the program and throw seventy-five percent today. It's still the first week . . . and we don't need anyone getting hurt."

Thirty minutes later I was toeing the bullpen rubber as Scioscia, Black, and Kernan stood a few feet behind me with their arms folded.

I took a deep breath, started my windup, and threw the first pitch to Mathis with every ounce of effort that my body could muster. I could see Mathis smile as the ball hit his target on the outside corner.

"Who is this?" Black asked and my head reflexively jerked toward him.

"McCarthy," Kernan said. "Played for me in Provo last year. College kid. Average fastball. Average off-speed stuff. Nothing special."

My heart sank as I heard those last words.

I wound up and delivered another fastball with even more effort that hit Mathis's target on the inside corner. I followed that with two sliders for strikes before bouncing two changeups.

"That's enough, Mac," Kernan said after my seventh pitch. "Give me eight laps and join the rest of the pitchers on field three for bunt defenses."

I nodded at the three coaches and jogged off the mound, quietly hoping that Kernan would choke on his own saliva and die a long, agonizing death.

I joined the rest of the pitchers to work on bunt plays with former Minnesota Twins catcher Brian Harper, whom I remembered for being on the receiving end of a violent collision at home plate with Lonnie Smith during the 1991 World Series. Standing before me, he didn't look like he had aged a bit in the dozen years that had elapsed since I'd last seen him on television.

"We've got a lot to accomplish today," he said as we formed a horseshoe around him, "so let's get going. You should be able to do these drills in your sleep."

Harper ran us through a series of exercises—fielding bunts, backing up third base, covering first base—and we all performed them without incident, except Ervin Santana. For some reason, Ervin couldn't remember to cover first base when a ground ball was hit to the first baseman. And when he did cover the correct base, he did it at half-speed. Harper let it slide three times, but the fourth transgression sent him over the edge.

"Fuck!" he screamed from home plate as he slammed his bat on the ground.

He jogged to the base of the mound, a few feet from Ervin.

"What the fuck is that?"

Ervin grimaced, but did not say anything.

We all looked on in silence, and again I felt some relief that I wasn't the one doing something wrong.

"I'm serious, what the hell are you doing?"

Santana shook his head and frowned. It was unclear how well he spoke English.

Harper gestured toward first base.

"Cover the damn base," he said. "And hustle. Is it too much to ask for a little hustle?

"I've never seen anything like it," Harper said as he turned to address the rest of us. "How does a pitcher forget to cover first? I've never seen a guy with his head so far up his ass that he can't remember to cover first base."

A few players chuckled, but it was not the response Harper was looking for.

"This isn't funny," he said, before spitting on the mound. "You guys are in this together."

Harper started to walk back toward home plate but stopped halfway there.

"This is a team game! Some of you are so fixated on your damn stats that you forget to do the little things. Well . . . if you're going to succeed in this game, it's going to be as a team. And if you're going to fail . . . it's as a team."

We were all aware that this statement wasn't exactly true.

"Some of you guys don't give a damn about this game, this organization, or your teammates. You only care about yourself and your stats. And I'm sick of it. This is the first week and I'm already sick of it. When I played we were all friends. On the field and off. Today, you guys don't even know each other's names."

I looked around and figured I could name about half of the players around me.

"This is a team game!" he shouted again.

Ervin cleared his throat but did not say anything.

"Who . . . who is that?" Harper asked.

He was looking at Ervin and pointing at me with the barrel of the bat.

"Who is he?" he repeated.

Ervin looked clueless as he stared me up and down. This was not going to end well.

"Who is he?"

Ervin cleared his throat again and said, "Mmm."

"'Mmm'? Who is 'Mmm'?"

Ervin scanned our group, possibly looking for help, while Harper glanced at his watch and ran his hands through his dark, wavy hair.

"Who the fuck is he?"

Harper was not going to let this one go.

"Mmmaaa . . ."

"What? What are you saying?"

"McCorksky!"

A large smile emerged on Ervin's face and the few players who knew me started to laugh.

Harper looked at me blankly and I realized that he had no idea who I was.

"Is that right?" he asked quietly. "Is that your name?"

"Um, yeah," I said.

"Well, is it?"

"Basically. Yeah. It's McCorksky."

With that, Harper turned around and walked to home plate and we finished the drill.

I'd like to say I did it to save Ervin further embarrassment, but in reality I was just hungry. I knew that the sooner we finished the drill, the sooner I could get in line for lunch.

From that day on I was known as McCorksky.

IN THE SECOND WEEK of spring training I appeared in two games and, as usual, had mixed results. My first appearance was in an intrasquad game in which I walked two batters before giving up an inside-the-ballpark home run to Howie Kendrick, a soft-spoken second baseman from Jacksonville, Florida. The Angels had drafted Kendrick eleven

rounds ahead of me on the insistence of Tom Kotchman, who had quietly scouted Kendrick at St. Johns River Community College in Palatka,
Florida, for the better part of two years. Kotchman had lobbied hard for
Kendrick, a relative unknown going into the 2002 draft, and when the
Angels selected him in the tenth round, Kotchman proudly told the
local newspaper that St. Johns River was a place "where nobody's ever
been drafted out of, except for the military."

But there were some who thought drafting Howie Kendrick that
high had been a mistake. The Angels were stocked with talented
young middle infielders, and at first glance there wasn't anything about
Howie that made you think he was destined for greatness. He wasn't
particularly big or strong, he didn't have great range at second base,
and he had been cut from two junior college teams before walking on
at St. Johns River. So instead of having him join Tom Kotchman and
the other new draftees in the Pioneer League after he signed his contract, Tony Reagins elected to hold Kendrick back in Mesa and awarded
the starting job in Provo to Alberto Callaspo.

After the intrasquad game, Kendrick pulled me aside in the dugout.

"Corky," he said as I sat doubled over, unlacing my cleats.

"It's McCorksky," I replied without looking up.

"Yeah, McCorky, I gotta tell you something. You're tipping your
pitches."

"I am?"

I spun my head up and found Kendrick putting on my glove.

"Look," he said as he mimed by windup. "When you grip a fastball,
your arm does this. But when you grip a changeup . . . you do *this*."

He gently twisted his elbow and proceeded to go through my pitching motion.

"You see what I'm saying?"

He handed me my glove and I scratched my head.

"Shit."

"Guys can see the off-speed stuff coming a mile away."

"How long . . . have I been doing that?"

"I don't know, man. Today was the first time I've seen you pitch. But I just sat on that changeup you threw me. I knew it was coming, man."

"Jesus."

"But it shouldn't be hard to fix," he said as he picked up a ball by his feet. "Just start every pitch with a changeup grip."

Two days later I threw two scoreless innings against the Oakland A's minor league affiliate, the Stockton Ports, and Kendrick came over to congratulate me like a proud father.

"Better, McCurdy, much better."

"Thanks, Howie."

He put his arm around me and smiled.

"Just lookin' out for ya, kid."

Brian Harper would have been pleased. But it was strange that other players were giving me these tips. I wondered if the coaches had simply given up on me.

Strolling out of the dugout, I ran into Joe Saunders, who had been manning the radar gun during the game.

"How was my velocity?" I asked as we walked toward the clubhouse.

"Same."

"What was it?"

"Eighty-five."

He put a large wad of chewing tobacco in his left cheek and spit on the ground.

"That's it?"

"Maybe eighty-six a few times."

The big-league club was expected to trim its roster any day now—sending about ten players back to the minor leagues—and I was more than a little concerned that the trickle-down effect coupled with my sagging velocity might cost me my job.

That night, Casey Kotchman, Kendrick, and I had dinner at T.G.I. Friday's and they both ordered the same thing—a large glass of water and chicken fingers.

"I'm dying to know . . ." Howie said as he wiped honey mustard off his mustache. "What's Provo like?"

"A lot of Mormons," I said as a thousand thoughts whirled through my head.

"I hear that. Did you like it?"

"Yeah, man, it was a lot of fun. Beautiful town . . . good fans . . . great ballpark . . ."

"I'm hoping they send me there this year."

"Well, I should warn you . . . the coach in Provo is insane."

Casey smiled without looking up from his food.

"How was Mesa?" I asked.

"Good, man. I liked the place. It's like home."

Howie was the only person I ever met who said he had enjoyed the experience of playing minor league baseball in Mesa, Arizona.

"Excuse me, fellas," Howie said as he took a cell phone out of his pocket, "but I gotta make a quick call. Told my grandmother I'd call her tonight."

Kendrick had been raised by his grandmother, Ruth, in the small town of Callahan, Florida—population 962—and he was fond of saying that she was the one who first put a bat in his hands.

A few minutes later he returned and apologized for stepping away.

"So you survived a summer in Mesa with the Dominicans?" I asked.

"Aw, man," Howie said, "those guys get a bad rap. They're good kids."

Casey nodded.

"Plus, they liven things up around here," he added. "Keeps everyone from being so uptight."

A few minutes later the waitress brought us our bill and Casey insisted on paying. As we got up to leave, an attractive blonde in a low-cut dress walked by our table.

"I love Mesa, man," Howie said as he pounded his fist on the table. "I love it!"

Casey smiled and shook his head.

"But I think I'm ready for some greener pastures," he added.

Kendrick was reunited with Tom Kotchman that summer and hit .368 for the Provo Angels. The following year he was promoted to Cedar Rapids and from there he moved quickly through the Angels' minor league system. He was named to minor league all-star teams in 2004 and 2005 before making his major league debut with Anaheim in April 2006, just a few months before his grandmother died of lung cancer.

"My whole career is dedicated to her," Kendrick said in an interview shortly after her death. "She got to see me play major league baseball and I got her a jersey before she passed away. She knows what she meant to me. I would send her pictures with writing around the edges about how much I respect her and love her and that the game is truly what she has given me."

I first learned of Kendrick's rise to the majors from one of my patients at Massachusetts General Hospital. The woman had been complaining of explosive diarrhea throughout the night, and when I walked in to check on her, she shoved *People* magazine in my face.

"Would ya look at that," she said, showing me a picture of Kendrick diving into the stands at Fenway Park. An overzealous Red Sox fan appeared to be fighting with Howie to catch a foul ball, and that fan happened to be Ben Affleck.

I smiled at the picture and reached into the cabinet for a pair of gloves.

"Affleck needs to get a life," the woman said as I bent down to examine her rectum.

WHEN ANAHEIM DID MAKE their first round of cuts, I was demoted to the Angels' Low Single-A affiliate, the Cedar Rapids Kernels, where I was reunited with many of my former Provo teammates. I was disappointed with the assignment, but it certainly beat getting released. We had reached the point in spring training where we were playing games against other organizations every day and most pitchers were throwing in every other game. But for the six days I spent with the Kernels, I didn't pitch once. On the seventh day, Kernan pulled me aside in the weight room.

"We're bumping you up," he said.

I was still angry about his lackluster appraisal of my pitching, but it sounded like he was about to deliver some good news.

"Triple-A needs a lefty and I suggested you. They're playing the Giants tomorrow and you're gonna throw at least an inning."

"Great!"

"This is a big opportunity, but that doesn't mean you should do anything differently. Just stick with what works."

The next morning I reported to my new team, the Salt Lake Stingers, where I learned from the manager, Mike Brumley, that we would be playing the Giants' Triple-A affiliate, the Fresno Grizzlies, that afternoon. He also mentioned that both the Angels and the Giants would be sending over a pitcher from their big-league starting rotation to get in some extra innings of work. Jarrod Washburn, who won eighteen games for the Angels the previous year, would start for our team, while Livan Hernandez, who as a twenty-two-year-old was the 1997 World Series MVP, would start for the Giants. Brumley told me I would follow Washburn, who had faced Hernandez five months earlier in the 2002 World Series.

I was sitting at the far end of the dugout when Washburn came in from the bullpen with his glove balanced on top of his head. A fellow southpaw, he was my height (six-foot-one), my weight (195), and we were wearing the same pair of cleats. I had been told by a dozen coaches that I looked like Washburn and that my pitching style mirrored his, but this was the first time I'd seen him in person. The only real difference between us, as far as I could tell, was that I had spent last October dissecting rat brains in a dimly lit laboratory basement while he had spent it leading the Angels to the World Series.

Washburn took the mound a few minutes later and threw a scoreless first inning—three up, three down. I gave him a high five as he entered the dugout with his catcher, Bengie Molina, and sidled up to the two of them to hear what a big-league pitcher said to his catcher between innings.

"Look good out there," Molina said as he took off his catcher's equipment.

"Yep," said Washburn.

"Stay there all day."

"Yeah."

They stood next to each other in silence, both sipping cups of water as they watched Livan throw the last of his warm-up tosses.

As Hernandez toed the rubber to face his first batter, Washburn took a big sip, threw his cup on the ground, and blurted out, "Jesus Christ, he's fat."

Hernandez was listed at 250 pounds, but he looked closer to 280. His ample belly was largely obscured by his baggy uniform, which was so loose it looked like he was wearing pajamas.

"How much you think he weighs?" Washburn said to no one in particular.

A moment passed before I said, "Two-sixty."

"No way!" he said incredulously. "He's pushing three bills."

Hernandez struck out our leadoff hitter, Nick Gorneault, on three pitches and untucked the back of his jersey.

"Yeah, he could be."

Weight had been an issue for Hernandez since he defected from Cuba as a twenty-year-old. In 1997, Buster Olney had written a piece about Livan for the *New York Times*:

> Tall and skinny when he defected, Hernandez immediately began adding weight, often eating at fast-food restaurants. His weight reportedly neared 250 pounds, about 30 pounds heavier than his listed weight. Hernandez was 2-4 with a 5.14 earned-run average for Class AAA Charlotte before being demoted to Class AA, in Portland, Me.
>
> "Last year, I ate quite a bit at McDonald's," he said. "Last year, I went by a Burger King and I had to stop. But now I am eating different foods."

"I just can't get over it," Washburn continued. "He's as big as a house. The guy's gotta try a salad once in a while. I mean . . . how does he even throw with that gut?"

"He's a fat motherfucker," Molina said.

Hernandez retired the next two batters in short order and casually strolled off the field. Washburn took his glove off his head and walked back out to the mound while I headed to the bullpen to stretch. For the next two innings, Washburn and Hernandez made pitching look easy, effortlessly retiring all nine batters they faced.

At the end of the third inning, Brumley signaled down to the bullpen that the next inning was mine. I walked over to Bengie Mo-lina and took a seat.

"I'm pitching next inning," I said.

"Good luck, kid."

"Do you want to go over signs?"

"Hey, I'm just here 'cause of him," he said, pointing at Washburn, who was now busy trying to balance a cup on his head. "We're going home."

I looked down the dugout and saw Mike Napoli putting on his equipment.

"I got the next inning," I said to him. "Want to go over signs?"

"Sure," he said while buckling the hooks on his shin guards. "What do ya throw?"

"Fastball, slider, change."

"One, two, wiggle?"

"Sure."

"Outs plus one with a runner on second?"

"Sure."

"Take third-base side on a bunt, back up the bases, keep the ball down."

"Got it."

The first batter I faced that inning was Lance Niekro, nephew of Hall of Famer Phil Niekro, whom I had played against a few times in high school. He always hit my fastball well, so I planned to start him off with a slider.

Napoli put down a single finger and I shook him off. He put the finger down again and I shook him off again. He called time-out and jogged out to the mound.

"Throw a fucking fastball," he said without taking off his mask, and returned to home plate.

I delivered Niekro a fastball and he creamed it 415 feet to dead center field. The ball was hit so high, it gave our center fielder plenty of time to track it down on the warning track, where it was caught for the first out of the inning.

"Atta boy," Napoli said from behind the plate.

I started the next batter off with a fastball that missed wildly for ball one. Napoli then put down two fingers and I threw a second pitch slider that was hit deep to left field, but again it was hit so high that our left fielder was able to track it down just a few feet short of the fence.

I took off my hat and wiped my brow. I don't belong out here, I thought to myself.

"You look good, kid," said the third baseman, Keith Johnson, who at thirty-one had logged 1,146 career minor league games with just four big-league at-bats. "Keep doin' what you're doin'."

I wondered if those four at-bats were worth a thousand games in the minors.

I decided to mix things up and threw the next batter a first-pitch changeup. He ripped a line drive to Keith, who caught the ball and rolled it back to the pitcher's mound and jogged off the field. It took me a minute to realize I had just retired the side in order on four pitches.

"That's it for today," Brumley said to me in the dugout. "Lift, run, and shower."

I let out a deep breath and untied my shoes. I had survived a day in Triple-A. My arm felt good and my spirits had been raised. I headed over to the clubhouse to change out of my baseball pants, when I ran into Dvorsky.

"McCorksky!" he said.

"What's up?"

"Was that you I saw over there playing with the big boys?"

"Yeah. I just gave up three of the hardest-hit balls of my career."

"Ouch."

"All for outs," I said confidently. "Three up, three down."

"Oh. Nice. You really . . . you've . . . you've been bouncing around quite a bit the past few weeks, huh?"

"Yeah, it's been . . ."

"You know what they say. It's never a good sign to get moved down and then up in the same week. . . ."

"I haven't heard that."

"Yeah, but I'm just sayin' . . ."

"Sayin' what?"

"Nothing. Nothing. Nice job today."

A FEW DAYS LATER, on a cool Thursday morning in late March, as Casey and I were walking to the clubhouse, Alex Dvorsky grabbed me by the shoulder and stopped me dead in my tracks.

"I am sorry," he said, before shaking my hand and walking away.

With those three words I knew that my baseball career was over. I walked like a zombie to my locker and found the pink slip taped to a clothes hanger.

"See Tony Reagins immediately," it read.

I experienced a strange tingling sensation around my lips and in my fingertips as I read and reread those four words. I was hyperventilating and had to sit down.

A few moments later, Kernan came over.

"Mac," he said plaintively, "I'm sorry."

He put his hand on my shoulder, like he had done so many times in Provo, and looked into my eyes.

"It's okay," I said, putting my head down.

"If you want me to make any phone calls for you, Mac, I will. I know a guy with the Giants and I could probably get you signed right now. On my recommendation alone I could get you back with another team."

Several seconds passed as I considered his offer.

"It's okay, Kernan," I said, looking back up at him. "I'm done. You don't have to make any phone calls."

"Suit yourself," he said, extending his hand. "It's been a pleasure."

"Certainly has," I replied.

I gathered up my belongings and put them into a navy Angels duffel bag and walked down the long corridor to Tony Reagins's office, where I found eight players in the hallway crying, talking on the phone, or both.

The thought occurred to me that I should call my parents, but I decided to wait until after I had spoken with Reagins. As I stood there, I was struck by the melancholy. I wasn't used to seeing guys my age openly weeping.

I wondered if I should be crying. I didn't feel like crying. I was trying to think about things rationally, and rationally I knew that my average fastball and average off-speed pitches just weren't going to get me to the big leagues.

"McCarthy," a voice said from the doorway.

It was Grant—the strength and conditioning coach—waving me into Mr. Reagins's office. He patted me on the back and said, "Sorry, buddy," before closing the door behind me.

Tony Reagins was sitting behind his desk with his head in his hands when I walked in. I stood at the door for a moment before taking a seat across from him. Ten seconds passed before he looked up. It felt like an eternity.

When he raised his head I saw that his eyes were bloodshot and there were tears streaming down his face. He clasped his hands together and said, "I'm sorry," before bursting into tears.

"It's okay," I said softly.

"You have no idea how hard this is," he said as he stared at his desk. "I love all of you guys. Every single one of you."

I nodded. This was not the Grim Reaper I had expected.

"Days like today *kill* me. They just kill me. To know that I'm ending some kid's dream . . . a dream that he's spent his whole life working for . . ."

He trailed off and put his face back in his hands. I cracked my knuckles and crossed my legs.

"I was up until four A.M. last night," he said. "Poring over stats, reading and rereading scouting reports, watching video, talking to scouts . . ."

I waited for him to continue but he didn't.

"We appreciate all of the work you guys do," I said awkwardly.

The tears continued to dribble down his puffy face. I reached into my pocket for a Kleenex but found only an old ATM receipt. Comforting him somehow made this process easier.

He let out a deep breath and produced a file from his desk. It had my name on it.

"Matt McCarthy," he said gently. "You're a good pitcher, Matt. You've showed us some good things around here. Some real good things. But your velocity is not what it was when we drafted you."

"I know."

"And your command isn't where we need it to be. You're walking far too many guys."

Tears streamed down his cheeks as he spoke.

"I agree."

"You had a difficult time getting batters out in Provo last year. And that was rookie ball. There were times when . . ."

He choked up and took a sip of water.

"Mr. Reagins," I said as he held the cup to his face, "I want to let you know something. I'm going to be fine. I appreciate all that you and the Angels have done for me, but I'm going to be okay. I realize this is a numbers game and that this time, I'm the odd man out."

He nodded.

"That's exactly what it is, Matt. A numbers game. And I hate that."

I stood up and shook his hand and walked with my belongings out to the parking lot. Two hours later I was standing in a security line at the Phoenix airport. The chain of events happened so fast that I really didn't have time to take it all in until I was at the gate about to board my flight back to Orlando. It was then that I decided to call the one man I knew who could relate to what I was going through.

"Coach Stuper?"

"Mac! How in the world are you?"

"Well . . ."

"I was just thinking of you. I've got the team down here in Florida and it's absolutely gorgeous. Just beautiful, beautiful weather. We've got some big games coming up this week."

"That's great."

"And I gotta tell you, we have one hell of a ball club this year."

And it was true. Once Breslow, Steitz, and I left New Haven, the Yale nine started winning more games.

"Coach, I gotta tell you something."

"Talk to me. Anything. What is it?"

"I just got my pink slip. The Angels released me today."

I waited for a moment, but he said nothing.

"I don't know what happened," I went on. "I pitched a scoreless inning in Triple-A just the other . . ."

"Mac, I want you to know something—"

"I figured as a lefty I could hang around for a while."

"Mac, I'm proud of you."

"It's just that, I don't know, you can try to prepare yourself for this day but . . ."

"Mac, I know there are a lot of thoughts going through your head right now."

"Yeah."

"But I want you to remember one thing: I am proud of you."

"Thank you."

"And Mac, there's another thing."

"Yes?"

"She's still off-limits."

When I boarded the plane I learned that the Angels had just released another minor leaguer from central Florida, Kevin McClain, a right-handed pitcher with a shaved head and bright green eyes, and the two of us were seated next to each other on the flight home. Kevin was twenty-five and in the midst of his sixth season with the Angels when Tony Reagins had called him into his office earlier in the day. We sat in silence for the first hour of the flight. I stared at the seat in front of me while Kevin ran his fingers through his short brown hair over and over and over.

"I can't believe it," he said to his tray table.

"Me either."

"I put in five good years and then this happens. Comes out of nowhere."

His eyes were welled up with tears. I tried to imagine five years of toiling in minor league limbo.

"I know."

"I don't know what the hell I'm gonna do," he murmured.

"Try to get back in the game?"

"I don't know," he said. "I'm twenty-five."

For the life of me, I couldn't think of the right words to say.

"I suppose I better," he added, "because I got a wife and kid at home and we need the paychecks."

"Yeah."

"I got no work experience . . . no education to speak of . . . I guess
I could get a job at Target. But I just don't know."

"This is a crazy time," I said.

He lifted his head up and looked me in the eye.

"What about you?"

"I don't know," I said as a tear rolled down my cheek.

Epilogue

||||||||||||||||||||||||||||||||||||||||||||

Six months later I enrolled at Harvard Medical School and tried to forget about baseball. I did a pretty good job of it until the spring rolled around, when, instead of gearing up for another baseball season, I found myself daydreaming of curveballs over cadavers in the anatomy lab. I decided I needed to get as far away from baseball as possible and on a whim responded to a classified ad seeking a trained animal trapper to work in Africa.

I had no experience catching animals, of course, but I began taking weekend classes at Tufts Veterinary School, and before long I was proficient at trapping apes, gorillas, monkeys, orangutans, bats, and rats. And I knew how to use a blow dart gun. At the end of my first year at Harvard, I flew to Cameroon, where I met my new team, a group of Cameroonians and Australians who were trying to solve the mystery of the Ebola virus. Every decade or so, there had been an outbreak of Ebola in western Africa, but after taking a couple of hundred lives it would disappear and no one knew where it went. The leading theory was that it was carried in the blood and saliva of fruit bats between outbreaks, and my job was to travel out to the jungle to catch the bats and find out. My assignment was straightforward: travel sixteen to twenty hours in the back of a military truck to a rural village where I would present whiskey to the chief and humbly ask his permission to set up bat traps on his land. Those rides made the trips to Medicine Hat look like a leisurely Sunday drive.

One warm night in the capital city of Yaoundé, I received a call from Breslow.

"Mr. Osteen," I said, "how the hell are you?"

"Henderson the Rain King," he said, "how are you? Been bit by any tigers yet?"

"Nah, not yet."

"You know I think you're out of your goddamn mind."

"I do."

"Well," he said, "it finally happened."

"What?"

"The Brewers released me today."

"They did?"

"Yeah, I've been pitching well but . . ."

"It's a numbers game . . ."

"They told me it was a numbers game, Mac."

"Well . . . you sound in relatively good spirits. What's the plan now?"

"I'm going to New Jersey."

"Jersey?" I said. "Why?"

"Independent ball. The New Jersey Jackals offered me a contract."

Independent ball was one step above playing in a men's league and I hadn't even considered it after I received my pink slip.

"Independent ball? Are you sure you . . . ?"

"Yeah," he said, "I'm still throwing the ball well."

"You don't think this is a sign? Maybe it's time to move on."

"I'll leave the bat catching to you. I still got some baseball left in me."

Our conversation was cut short a few minutes later—probably by one of the periodic blackouts that Yaoundé was experiencing at the time—and I was left with the impression that Breslow was making the wrong decision. He said dozens of times that I'd made a colossal mistake by not taking Kernan up on his offer to get me signed by another team, but the idea of going to New Jersey to pitch with a bunch of washed-up ex–minor leaguers seemed like a waste of his time and talents.

But Breslow pitched well for the New Jersey Jackals, and at the end of the season the San Diego Padres purchased his contract from the Jackals for one dollar and offered him a minor league contract.

I was in Ipoh, Malaysia, the following July when I received another call from Breslow. He had been playing for the Padres' minor league affiliate in Mobile, Alabama.

"Mac," he said quickly, "big news."

"What's up?" I asked.

My hands reeked of halothane, the chemical we were using to sedate the Malaysian fruit bats, and I was holding the phone between my shoulder and ear.

"I got the call."

"What call?" I asked, screwing the top on a vial of bat blood.

"The Padres . . . They just called me up to the big leagues."

I gasped and dropped the phone.

"Holy shit!" I yelled at the phone, which was now lying on the wooden floor.

I picked it up and continued to yell, "Holy shit! Holy shit! Holy shit!"

"Yeah, holy shit!" he said. "They're playing the Phillies tomorrow and they told me to be ready to pitch."

Breslow made his major league debut the following day, throwing $1\frac{2}{3}$ scoreless innings against a strong Phillies lineup. He remained with the Padres for the rest of the season and in the off-season signed a more lucrative contract with the Boston Red Sox, and he periodically pitched out of their bullpen for the next two years before moving on to the Indians and then the Twins.

Fellow Brewers farmhand Jon Steitz eventually washed out of the minors and, after acing the LSAT, enrolled at Yale Law School. After graduation, he moved to Boston, working as a consultant for McKinsey & Company, and on those rare occasions when the stars would align, the two of us would walk down to Fenway Park to watch our old teammate take the mound for the Red Sox.

As the years have passed, I've seen many familiar faces pass through the friendly confines of Fenway Park. Keeping an eye on the schedule, I've been in the crowd as Bobby Jenks, Joe Saunders, Casey Kotchman, Erick Aybar, and many others have taken the field. I've never approached any of my old teammates as they've come through Boston, but one time I came close. After a Sox game in 2006 I thought I made eye contact with Ervin Santana as he walked off the field. Santana had become a regular in the Anaheim starting rotation, winning sixteen games in 2006, and I considered yelling, "McCorksky!" to him and waving my arms, but I decided against it.

As it turns out, the only person from the Angels' organization that I kept in touch with was Kernan, who, as the Angels' roving pitching coordinator, continues to send me dispatches from the road throughout the season. And I never found out who the mole was on our team, although I'll always have my suspicions.

As much as it is possible, I've tried to follow all of my old teammates—both the ones who made it and the ones who didn't. Quan Cosby became a starting wide receiver on the University of Texas football team, helping the team win the National Championship Game in 2006. Brian Williams left baseball to become a teacher in Florida; Kelly Sisko got engaged and returned home to Oklahoma. Austin Bilke was promoted to Double-A in 2004 but retired the following year. Brett Cimorelli lasted one more summer in pro ball while Hector Astacio played two more years, advancing as far as Triple-A, before the Angels released him.

In the fall of 2007, I opened the newspaper and found a glowing story about Tony Reagins, the self-made man who worked his way up the ladder from intern all the way to his new position as general manager of the Anaheim Angels, replacing Bill Stoneman. Reagins became only the third minority general manager in baseball, and immediately made a splash by signing several star players to long-term deals with the Angels.

Tom Kotchman still coaches for the Angels in Utah, but the team has switched towns and names. In 2004 the Provo Angels became the Orem Owlz and moved to the stadium down the street from where we used to hold our Sunday practices. In a recent interview, Kotchman said he's planning to retire from coaching in the near future to focus all of his energy on scouting for the Angels.

I sincerely hope that he reconsiders.

With every passing year the faces of old friends become a little bit blurrier. And I have no doubt that many of my former minor league teammates would have trouble remembering me today. I'm sure Heath does, as well as Matt Brown and Brett, Austin and Williams, but for the others I'm probably just another name in a long list of ex-teammates. As for Sunshine, I never heard from him again after I left Provo.

When I walk into a patient's room at the hospital and see Bobby Jenks on the television screen, I think back to a time when he was just a screwed-up baby-faced kid with a few terrible tattoos. And when I put my stethoscope to the chest of one of my Dominican patients, I can't help but think of Astacio, sitting with his head in his hands after refusing to throw at a batter, or Aybar and Callaspo wearing diapers, or hot dog buns, and always about to hump each other.

But what I think of most frequently at the hospital, particularly late at night when the flurry of midday activity has died down and nothing can be heard but the incessant beeping of blood pressure monitors, is Randy Burden. As I respond to the pages about my octogenarian patients who are slowly losing their grip on life, I think about the young man from Virginia who just wanted to be close with God and play baseball. I think of him being buried in his baseball uniform and I imagine him in heaven, having his own conversation with God, undoubtedly trying to find out the best way to throw a fastball.